Marketing Financial Services

A Strategic Vision

Marketing Financial Services

A Strategic Vision

James H. Donnelly, Jr.
Leonard L. Berry
Thomas W. Thompson

DOW JONES-IRWIN
Homewood, Illinois 60430

ISBN 0-87094-517-3

Library of Congress Catalog Card No. 84–72996

Printed in the United States of America

6 7 8 9 0 D 2 1 0 9 8

To
Connie Vick
Abe and Mae Berry
Amy Thompson

PREFACE

More than 20 years ago, Peter Drucker entitled a chapter in *Managing for Results* "The Customer Is the Business." The statement rings as true and as important today. Customers provide the revenue that provides the profit potential that provides the incentive for investing in a business. The customer *is* the business. Without the customer, there is nothing.

Never before have financial institutions had to hustle for, struggle for, and fight tooth and nail for customers as they do today. Everyone— or so it seems—is after everyone else's *best* customers. Today it is harder to win new customers and keep old ones.

If ever there was a time for a financial services company to truly know the customer and to translate this knowledge into genuine *value* for the customer, that time is now. Value, not gimmicks, not story-telling, is the surest path to attracting and keeping financial services customers and to making them better customers. This book focuses on the challenge of shaping a financial institution to deliver value to customers. *Delivering value to customers is the marketing imperative.* Today financial services customers can go elsewhere. And they will if their present institutions offer insufficient value in service and services.

This is a book of ideas and concepts. It is our vision of what today and tomorrow in the financial services business are all about, and the strategic responses that these realities require. It is *not* a textbook that systematically touches every conceivable topic in financial services marketing. Nor is it a "how-to" book. The reader will look in vain for tips on running a chinaware premium campaign or managing a branch office opening. Nor is this a book about state-of-the-art technological innovation. We discuss the critical impact of technology on financial services marketing in broad brush strokes. Detailed treatment is left for other authors who are better versed than we are in the technical aspects of this subject and who are writing different types of books than the one we have written.

The book is designed to stimulate the creative energies of its readers.

The finest compliment a reader could pay us is: "It challenged me to rethink some of my assumptions about my craft and my company's future." The three of us have observed, studied, researched, lectured on, and written about financial services marketing for years. We are fascinated by the sweeping change impacting the financial services business and by the marketing implications associated with this onrush of change. We are teeming with ideas and thoughts about this "watershed" period for financial services marketing, and we want to share them. That is why we wrote the book. The mid-80s are clearly a critical time for financial institutions. Banks and thrifts are becoming much more than "banks and thrifts." Today's marketplace is a "financial services" marketplace, not a banking, or savings and loan, or credit union marketplace. Competing in this new marketplace requires *strategic* marketing, not just tactical marketing. It requires a marketing point of view in senior management and throughout the organization, not just in the marketing department. It requires a feisty, competitive corporate culture, a culture in which people "go for it." It requires viewing the business as a "people business" and recognizing that in 1988 or 1992 or whenever, people service will still make the difference between one institution and another.

Marketing Financial Services: A Strategic Vision intentionally plays down the distinctions between commercial banks and other depository and financial institutions. We accept and build on the proposition that in a deregulated environment traditional distinctions among types of institutions will continue to blur. This is a matter, not of advocacy, but of reality. We use phrases such as "financial institution" and "financial services organization" to convey the relevance of our message to many traditionally different institutions that are becoming more and more alike. Although we wrote the book from the point of view of commercial banking and thrift institutions, we believe that it contains material useful to executives from other financial services sectors.

Marketing Financial Services was written in late 1983 and in 1984. The change dynamics characterizing the financial services business today make writing a book about it a hazardous proposition. We hope that our focus on concepts rather than events will give the book an enduring quality. In any case, it has been a challenge to write a book in 1983–84 about the financial services industry in America for consumption in 1985–86 and beyond.

Dr. James Gibson, Professor of Business Administration at the University of Kentucky, wrote Chapter 4 on organizational structure. Gibson is an expert in this subject area, as will be evident in reading his work. We are indebted to him for his contribution.

As for the three of us, we take great pleasure in bringing to you, our reader, the product of our most recent collaboration. We three have enjoyed friendship and intellectual partnership with one another for many years. It has been especially satisfying to produce a book under these circumstances. We shared equally in the manuscript's preparation.

Welcome to our book! You are our consumer. We hope you find value.

James H. Donnelly, Jr.
Leonard L. Berry
Thomas W. Thompson

CONTENTS

PART ONE
The Marketing Imperative   1

1. **Revolution: The Era of Deregulation**   **3**
    Introduction: The Customer Is the Business. The Reality of De-
    regulation: *The Consequences of Deregulation. Deregulation:
    Strategic Responses.* The Marketing Imperative: *Strategic Plan-
    ning: The First Step. Strategic Marketing. Implementing Market-
    ing. Lessons.*

PART TWO
The Planning Imperative   **19**

2. **Strategic Planning: The Changing Managerial Focus**   **21**
    The Environment and Managerial Planning: *Stable Technology
    and Stable Markets. Changing Technology and Changing Mar-
    kets.* Dimensions of Organizational Performance: *Organizational
    Effectiveness. Organizational Efficiency. Shifting the Planning
    Focus. The Efficiency/Effectiveness Relationship.* Some Key
    Concepts of Strategic Planning: *Assessing the Institution's
    Strengths and Weaknesses. Identifying the Driving Force. Select-
    ing a Corporate Strategy.*

3. **Concepts and Issues in Marketing Planning**   **41**
    More Products, Less Time, Less Money. Product Portfolio Analy-
    sis: *Defining the Scope of the Analysis. Classifying Products.
    Establishing Priorities. Establishing Product Objectives. Devel-
    oping Marketing Strategies.* Making Product Portfolio Analysis
    Work. Confronting Intangibility with Elements of Marketing
    Strategy. The Concept of Intangibility: *Confronting Intangibility
    with Marketing Strategy.*

4. Organizational Structure and Performance   **57**
Purposes of Organizational Structures: *Dividing Work. Coordinating Work.* Characteristics of Organizational Structures. Organizational Structure and Performance. Function-Oriented and Market-Oriented Structures: *Function-Oriented Structures. Market-Oriented Structures.* Managers Must Manage Organizational Structure: *Top-Management Commitment Is Imperative. Organizational Strategy Must Precede Structure. Persistence Pays Off. Reward and Reinforcement. Change Takes Time.*

PART THREE
Strategic Marketing   **75**

5. Market Segmentation   **77**
The Process of Market Segmentation: *Evaluate the Institution's Current Situation. Determine Customer Needs and Wants. Divide Markets on Relevant Dimensions. Relevance of Segmentation Dimensions. Develop Product Positioning. Decide Segmentation Strategy. Design Marketing Mix Strategy.*

6. Market Positioning   **93**
A Place in the Sun. Positioning Choices. The Elements of Positioning. Institutional Positioning: *Structural Decisions and Options. Functional Decisions and Options. Managerial Decisions and Options.* Marketing Mix Positioning: *Delivery Systems Decisions and Options. Human Resources Decisions and Options. Product Line Decisions and Options. Pricing Decisions and Options.* Customer Markets Positioning: *Locational Considerations. Line-of-Business Considerations. Customer Need Evaluation Criteria. Institutional Profitability Evaluation Criteria. Putting It Together.*

7. Relationship Banking   **111**
What Is Relationship Banking? Benefits to the Institution. Does the Customer Want Relationship Banking? The Elements of Relationship Banking: *Market Segmentation. Core Service. The Account Representative. Relationship Pricing. Communications Management.*

PART FOUR
Implementing Marketing   **133**

8. Developing New Financial Services   **135**
Types of New Services. The Nature of Services: *Intangibility. Inseparability of Production and Consumption. Potential for*

Variability. Nurturing Innovation: *Creating a Climate of Trying. Organizing for Innovation.* Developing New Services Systematically: *Strategic Guidelines. Exploration. Screening. Comprehensive Analysis. Development and Testing. Marketing Introduction.* Maximizing New Service Success—12 Big Ideas.

9. Delivering Financial Services   157
Fitting It Together. First Southeast: A Model, circa 1990. Necessary Assumptions. First Southeast Financial—1990 or Thereabouts. Commerce and Trade. The Retail Network. Personal Banker Work Centers. Local Office Network.

10. Promoting Financial Services   183
Promoting Financial Services—Personal Selling: *Why Selling Is So Hard. Why Selling Is So Important. Improving Selling Effectiveness. Time to Bite the Bullet.* Financial Services Promotion—Advertising: *Paving the Way. Eight Guidelines for Better Financial Advertising. Summing Up.*

11. The New PR: Communications   203
Introduction: *A Business in Transition.* Communications Principles: *At the Edge of Change. We Have Met the Enemy. The Age of the People. Beyond Informing.* Communications Management: *Identify Communications Publics. Segment and Prioritize. The Media as Market.*

12. Internal Marketing   229
People Make the Difference. Internal Marketing. The Internal Customer. The Internal Product. Thinking Like a Marketer: *Marketing Research. Market Segmentation. First Impressions Marketing. Remarketing.*

PART FIVE
Lessons   **247**

13. It's Still a People Business   249
A New Culture. Teach Marketing. Making a Difference. Quality People—the Quality Difference. It Starts at the Top. The Planning Imperative.

Index   **257**

PART ONE

The Marketing Imperative

"I am talking about a marketing war with very high stakes: the provision of the full range of financial services to individuals, corporations, and other entities in the future. The winners will thrive and grow; the losers will wither and ultimately disappear. This war is in the United States, and it is just beginning, but the implications should be obvious to the providers of financial services in other nations."

Robert I. Lipp, *President, Chemical Bank, N.Y., from an address to the European Financial Marketing Association, Monte Carlo, March 22, 1982*

Revolution: The Era of Deregulation

"The revolution that is occurring in how we will do
business is one of those things on which you
can't turn back the clock."

Senator Jake Garn *of Utah, chairman,*
Senate Banking Committee[1]

INTRODUCTION: THE CUSTOMER IS THE BUSINESS

This is a book about marketing financial services in a deregulated environment. It is about *marketing*, about what is really involved in creating a satisfied customer and, if you perform that task effectively, turning that customer into a *client*. It is a book about customer satisfaction and client creation in an environment *where we all are banks*: commercial banks, savings and loans, credit unions, brokerage and insurance firms, retailers, mortgage banks, finance companies, and so many others today and even more tomorrow.

For this reason, *Marketing Financial Services* is necessarily a book about change and transition, which fundamentally is what *deregulation* is all about. *Change*. Perceive it as an equal dose of challenge and opportunity: challenge as financial institutions compete without marketplace protection and product line exclusives; opportunity as technology ever widens customer service possibilities. *Transition*. Perceive it as a passage from the narrow, clearly demarcated world of commercial banking or insurance to the less certain and still evolving financial services business. Perceive transition as a passage from an order-taking environment to a selling culture, an outreach culture. And perceive it as a passage to a market-driven financial environment.

THE REALITY OF DEREGULATION

Deregulation is not something new. It didn't just happen. It has been taking place and building up steam over the past two decades. The causes are numerous, and they are varied. Let's consider a few of them.

Deregulation happened because technology shattered historic time and space barriers, and thereby made yesterday's often bitter struggle over branch expansion redundant.

Deregulation happened because household and individual savers finally figured out that 12 percent annual inflation in the cost of living and a 5 percent return on their bank or thrift savings accounts—less the tax bite—no longer made much sense, no matter how many wigs, pots and pans, stemware, or other premiums depository institutions chipped in.

Deregulation happened because of a maturing customer base that had become now-oriented and me-oriented; that was better educated; that was more discriminating; and that no longer accepted the sacrifices inherent in the work-hard-and-save ethic. It happened because of a new customer who believed in maximizing short-term yields, who had developed an *investment* orientation. It happened because a time-conscious customer demanded more in the way of financial services, under one roof, in a more customized manner, and on his or her terms, at his or her convenience.

Deregulation happened because that $1.3 *trillion* pot-of-gold in household deposits became so terribly attractive to "national" banks and thrifts such as Citicorp and First Nationwide Savings *and* to "national" retailers, brokers, finance companies, insurance firms, and the travel card business, not to mention a growing legion of foreign players on America's retail banking turf. It happened because the race was on to get your share and then some in an environment where marketplace protection laws were crumbling.[2]

Deregulation happened because the federal and state regulatory perspective shifted from a protectionist to an expansionist philosophy, from the idea of restraining competition to the idea of force-feeding it. In this sense, it happened for the same reasons that prompted deregulation in the trucking and airlines industries. Deregulation also happened because each of the federal supervisory agencies was battling long and hard to convince the regulated institutions that this agency was the leader, that it was their champion, that it was the watchdog of progress, and that it was the leading advocate of long-needed change. And deregulation happened because individual states joined this leadership race, determined both to foster a more reasonable competitive environment and to retain necessary supervisory "rights."

Deregulation happened because of a major national policy shift—the decision to stop subsidizing borrowers, particularly home mortgage borrowers, at the expense of savers. It happened because this critical policy change led in turn to a pullback from administered or controlled rate structures (Regulation Q) and toward a greater reliance on market rate structures.

And finally deregulation happened because

- A Depression-influenced industry leadership gave way to younger executives who had matured in the era of postwar prosperity and who were conditioned to encourage banking, for example, to look well beyond the narrow business of taking money in and lending it out.
- There was a growing interface with the European financial system, or, to be more precise, with the European concept of "the universal bank."
- Deregulation fed on itself, step-after-step forcing thinner spreads and shorter asset-liability management time frames, not to mention covetous concern for fee-income opportunities. The "easy days" of buying money at 3 percent . . . lending it out at 6 percent . . . and making it to the golf course for a round with a corporate client by three o'clock gave way to longer days spent in figuring out better methods for maintaining a satisfactory yield spread.
- The credit card brought plastic branching and easy credit nationwide.
- And even because commercial banks propelled nonbank entry into their business by facilitating, for example, the Merrill Lynch Cash Management Account.

Deregulation happened for all of these reasons and for many others as well. As a case in point, it can be argued in a plausible manner that continued and ever more extensive deregulation grew out of the bank holding company stock issues of the late 1960s. Many of these issues quickly became the "darlings" of the equity market and its fierce pressure for earnings maximization *now*—this year, this quarter; year after year, quarter after quarter. In turn, the drive for ever-improved performance to acquire growth capital demanded the kind of operating environment characterized by earnings opportunities rather than earnings constraints, innovation rather than tradition, and a willingness to risk rather than a commitment to preserve.[3]

And certainly there would be many who would insist, and quite reasonably so, that deregulation happened all too late, all too slowly, and with too little concrete direction.

The Consequences of Deregulation

Marketing Financial Services is not a history of deregulation. It is concerned chiefly with the customer satisfaction response—the objective of marketing—in a deregulated environment, in a more competitive environment, in a high-technology environment that must be matched with desired levels of high-touch service. Still, there is no escaping a discussion of the major consequences of deregulation or, perhaps better said, its new operating *truisms*. Marketers must live with these parameters in devising workable strategies and tactics.

The first major "truth" about deregulation is that it led depository institutions into a new business. Yesterday banks and thrifts competed primarily against each other for a customer's business, and friend and foe alike enjoyed some form of marketplace and product line protection. Yesterday, in fact, commercial banking was in a preeminent position because of its checking account monopoly, its trust business monopoly, and its dominant role in the credit card arena, not to mention the fact that banks alone among depository institutions could engage in commercial lending. Yesterday banks were truly the only full-service game in town. *But this was yesterday.*

Today, and far more so tomorrow, banks and other depository institutions are competing in the financial services business with a growing number of so-called nonbanks. The critical consequence of deregulation is that today's listing of nonbank competitors will lengthen, as will their customer service capacity.

The second and clearly linked truth about deregulation is that commercial banking is no longer the preeminent force in this new business. An equal? Perhaps. Struggling uphill from the muddy marshlands against the likes of Sears and Merrill Lynch? Perhaps. With certain clear-cut advantages in what appears likely to be a long and bitter contest for supremacy? Again, perhaps. But preeminent as in the past? Not at all; no longer; no longer in the foreseeable future.

This is only one part of the competitive equality equation, however.

For many of today's 15,000 commercial banks, 3,500 savings and loans, 24,000 credit unions, even countless numbers of mom and pop finance companies, the fundamental truth-seeking prompted by deregulation is *survival*.

- How many will make it to 1990 or thereabouts? Most? Half as many? Less?
- And in what form will they make it? Will numerous smaller independent banks and thrifts become franchise units of nationwide financial organizations? Or will they become just branch offices or interstate holding company affiliates? Will savings and loans opt to become banks, mortgage banks, strictly funds brokers, or remain virtually unchanged as deposit gatherers and mortgage lenders? Will smaller community banks react to deregulation and the coming of interstate banking by forming local or regional confederations or at least shared servicing centers?

The reality of deregulation is a necessary focus on institutional survival. The issue becomes can we make it, should we try, and how do we go about making it happen? Or do we look early on for the best premium over book?

One community banker—it is not important who or where he is located—outlined his plan for a "few years down the road." We don't believe that his thinking is either radical or far out of line with clearly discernible trends:

> Tell you what deregulation means to me. My best strategy might be a quiet drink after a Saturday round of golf with the president of our local savings and loan, his counterpart at the locally owned finance company, and our community's major broker. Later we can chat with the insurance guy, . . . the mortgage banker in our area, and the people who run the computer-sales franchise. Maybe we can put something together that will hold up. None of us are likely to make it on our own.

We suspect that this conversation, this game plan, differs only in detail and dimension from current discussions among regional bank holding company executives plotting their response to the coming of interstate banking.

The third basic truth about deregulation is that we all are banks: operationally, in terms of product offerings, in terms of customer convenience, and in the minds of customers of financial institutions. Commercial banks, thrifts, retailers, brokers—today one and all are pretty much alike with respect to

- *Product lines.* Checking, savings, investment instruments, consumer credit, plastic. How significant are the *real* differences now? How significant will they be tomorrow?
- *Pricing.* Increasingly common to one and all are market-driven rather than administered rate structures—interest rates as well as fees for services performed.
- *Distribution.* The norm is becoming 24-hour-a-day, seven-day-a-week customer convenience, technology-based delivery systems

that differ little in character or capacity. And it is becoming better-skilled people-based structures anchored in similar commitments to high-touch customization.

- *Promotion.* Just think of all of those IRA ads that fill the media in February, March, and April. Same claims. Same promises. And a good deal of visual "sameness."

So how does a particular bank or thrift or finance company or brokerage firm stand apart? How does it successfully differentiate in an era when *we all are banks?*

The answer that must be given to this key question in a deregulated financial services industry environment appears to be fourfold:

- *First,* effective institu ional planning that moves the organization from what business it is now engaged in to what business it should be engaged in as the future unfolds. Who are we? What is our mission? How do we accomplish it?
- *Second,* carefully designed, well-researched market segmentation analysis. Who is our customer? Our best customer? Our preferred customer? Who is that critical mass, that 20 percent or so of any organization's retail customer base that presumably provides 80 percent of all retail profits? And then, what specifically are the characteristics of our desired segments?
- *Third,* thoughtful, reasonably constructed positioning strategies. How do we customize our operations and our marketing mix to optimize customer satisfaction? In an environment where very few institutions can any longer attempt to be all things to all people, how do we become very special to very special groups of clients?
- *Fourth,* effective as well as efficient differentiation through the quality of our organizat'on's performance, through what we do day by day at the firing line.

This, we believe, is the answer to deregulation's mandate: *we all are banks.*

It is also the framework of *Marketing Financial Services.*

The fourth truth about deregulation is that it has devastated customary thinking about the structure of the financial services marketplace. The institutional mind-set has been radicalized.

Yesterday most commercial bank or thrift industry markets were protected—to varying degrees, from state to state, but nonetheless protected—by law and custom. Law and custom carefully distinguished between the powers of banks, thrifts, brokers, and others. Each had its ordained orbit in the financial services universe. Such order was the rationale of McFadden and Douglas, Glass-Steagall, and Regulation Q.

Each in its proper place. No longer, however. The consequences of deregulation in specific terms has become:

- Interstate banking and regional reciprocity arrangements among the respective states.
- Intraindustry mergers.
- Franchising.
- Regional and national ATM networking, even the creation of a national mortgage financing network.
- Discount brokerage.
- And the battle over insurance offerings.

Said somewhat differently, deregulation coupled with proliferating service delivery technologies has radicalized the concept of "market" in the commercial, trust, and retail banking areas. For most institutions, the unsheltered customer market has become limitless. *It is wherever you want it to be and wherever you can serve it efficiently.* In the 1960s, Citicorp was struggling to break out of its retail banking straitjacket in the Greater New York area; a decade later it would be altering law and custom to crystallize its mission as a national and worldwide retailer of financial services.

The fifth and final truth about the consequences of deregulation is that it forced depository institutions to take off their deposit blinders. They are no longer in the deposit-gathering business but in the funds-trapping business. They are trapping any and all kinds of liabilities that can be pursued with market-sensitive rates and, once again, wherever they care to define their marketplace. Not just liabilities, but capital as well. Equity capital. Debt capital. Any kind of growth and expansion funds. Banks and the nonbank competitors are in the funds-trapping business.

The side-by-side development is that depository institutions have been required to look beyond the balance sheet and spread management techniques—*interest income*—to fee-earning business, to service income. Not just fees for traditional underpriced services such as safe-deposit box rentals, credit cards, and overdrafts, but fee structures for new categories of desired customer satisfaction necessities: cash management, tax preparation, budget counseling, vacation property rental, discount brokerage, insurance, and so much, much more.

Deregulation has simply swung wide open the door to product extension and off-balance sheet income.

From a marketing management perspective, these appear to be the major consequences of deregulation. Others could be cited, of course; for example:

- The acceptance of higher levels of risk in pursuit of profit optimization.

- The need to manage rate-sensitive liabilities as well as rate-sensitive assets.
- Greater stress on cost-control and productivity analysis.
- The closing down of bricks-and-mortar places.

Nonetheless, these five "truths" more than adequately define the basic ground rules that financial service marketers need to observe in mastering the challenging game of customer satisfaction in a deregulated environment.

Deregulation: Strategic Responses

Commercial banks and thrifts—indeed, each of the many players in the evolving financial services business—are currently working out a series of strategic responses to the fact of a more competitive environment, a less sheltered environment, a high-tech environment, and an environment in which the common imperative is to operate an Anywhere Bank, an Anytime Bank, a Selling Bank, and a Relationship Bank.

Commercial banks and thrifts, while they differ substantially on the specifics, nonetheless are hard at work in Washington and at the state level to assure *competitive equality*. This is the operating phrase and the battle cry. The drive for competitive equality *assumes* a growing inequity within the financial services industry between depository institutions and the *existing* and *potential* less regulated nonbank players. Existing means Sears, Beneficial Finance, Merrill Lynch, and Amex-Shearson in particular. Potential could be 7-Eleven and Safeway, or Ma Bell and IBM, or more American banks in the hands of foreign owners.

The drive for competitive equality assumes inequity. Some is real; some is fancied. Much is political and territorial. By the same token, many nonbank players point to the considerable advantages held by depository institutions: image, deposit insurance, 50,000 commercial bank offices alone, built-up customer loyalties, efficient back-room technologies, and so on. They claim that banks especially hold the upper hand; they, the nonbank players, must push to achieve competitive balance. Further, any discussion of competitive equality becomes confused by disagreements among and between banks and thrifts. Countless banks look no further than the savings and loan across the street in pinpointing the enemy. Merrill Lynch is some dimly perceived foe that is challenging large city banks. And while many banks and thrifts are worried about Sears, they are petrified that one day soon Citicorp will be perched on their doorstep. *Competitive equality is a many-sided issue.*

But if the issue is hazy, the three front battlefield on which this struggle is being waged are sharply defined. The troops and the arguments are marshaled in Washington and at the state level. The skirmishing has started, and the first roars of the big cannons have been heard.

Geographic expansion—the locational issue—is the first of the three fronts on which the competitive equality war is being fought. The push and shove, led largely by money center banks and regionals, is to break down what remains of historic barriers to in-state and out-of-state office expansion. It is to mitigate, if not to totally eliminate, the constraints inherent in McFadden and Douglas. At its heart, the geographic expansion battle involves the freedom to chase household accounts through effective and efficient distribution systems. Banks and thrifts can and do operate on an interstate basis on the asset side of the ledger and in pursuit of large-denomination liabilities and capital instruments. But they can't easily *chase* household and individual consumer deposits; they can't match the growth potential in interstate lending with supporting interstate consumer deposits, with "cheap money."

Product extension—the powers issue—is the second front in this war. From a depository institution's perspective, it is the power and the right—legally, operationally, and directly—to sell stocks and bonds and offer a fully competitive range of home . . . life . . . travel . . . credit . . . car . . . and valuables insurance. From a commercial bank's perspective, it is the elimination of Glass-Steagall. Much more broadly, the powers issue involves a fundamental redefinition of commercial banking's "line of commerce." *It is determining the business of banking.*

In a very real sense, savings and loans and credit unions are saying, "Let us into the commercial banking business"; commercial banks are saying, "Let us spread our wings into the securities and insurance business"; and the securities and insurance industries are saying, "Allow us to play on your turf, but keep off ours." Meanwhile, Sears and the retailers appear to be saying, "The water's great; jump in." But then Sears is there, and the others are just jockeying for position. Confusing? Yes, certainly. Still, these are the stakes today in the frontal assault on product extension.

Tomorrow, we suspect, the character of this battleground will change slightly. The powers issue in its specifics will become the right to offer accounting and tax preparation services at a fee; to handle travel arrangements for a fee; to engage directly in management consulting for a fee; to rent home and office space for a fee; and to sell, rent, or lease computer terminals and the related software packages for a fee. From a bank perspective once again: Why not? Sears expects to; so does Amex-Shearson; and so do a lot of other nonbank players in the financial services business . . . *the business all of us are in.*

Technology—the delivery systems issue—is the third front in the long war ahead for competitive equality. Its focus is the rationalization of existing as well as projectable financial service technologies. This issue affects all of the players in the financial services arena. It is not a bank or broker issue as such, but a common concern for developing realistic responses to these formidable questions:

- Where does our institution most wisely allocate precious time, effort, expertise, and dollars? ATMs and POS money machines? People-staffed office systems? At-home banking terminals and the hard-ware-software interface? Or, for that matter, a *memory card* that possesses memory, accessibility, security, and transaction power in a set of microchips the size of a dime?
- Do we share these evolving, dynamic technologies with our bank and thrift competitors? With the nonbank competition? Do we even care at our organization whose electronic banking technology our customer uses just so long as any transaction leads back to us?
- How do banks or thrifts prepare their own people to market these new high-technology modes? How, even more basically, do we in-crease their confidence level in handling more complex product lines and delivery system methodologies?
- How do banks or thrifts convince customers to accept and frequently utilize new cost-reducing and service-enhancing technologies?

How does our organization respond to these questions and so many, many others that continue to break out as "little wars" on the technol-ogy front?

The underlying competitive challenge is twofold. *First*, the technol-ogy revolution would appear to provide an edge to the bigger players in the financial services business, a chilling reality. *Second*, the down-the-road potential inherent in the technology revolution promises to invite new players to the table, an equally chilling prospect.

Summing up, these three strategic issues—geographic expansion, product extension, and harnessing technology—stand out as the major contemporary fronts on which the competitive equality struggle un-leashed by deregulation is being waged.

THE MARKETING IMPERATIVE

Strategic Planning: The First Step

The new marketing imperative is the creation of satisfied financial in-stitution customers in a deregulated environment. This is the theme of *Marketing Financial Services*.

It is not a how-to book, however, that lists 101 exciting marketing programs that might work for your financial organization because others made them work in the past. It is not about the *doing* of marketing in a functional or task-oriented manner. Rather, *this book deals largely with ideas, concepts, "strategic visions."*[4]

Marketing Financial Services is not aimed at banks or thrifts as such. It accepts a fundamental truth about competing in a deregulated environment: *we all are banks.* We are competing for success and survival in a new business, the financial services business. The clock won't be turned back.

The marketing imperative in the financial services business is anchored in soundly conceived and well-organized commitments to planning at the organizational level. Planning and marketing begin by exploring that most fundamental question: *What business are we in?* Planning and marketing then move on to those equally important, though subordinate, questions: What business are we in today? What will tomorrow be like? How do we fit into that future? If change we must, how do we accomplish it? How do we build the cultural perspective to turn change to our advantage, and how do we move from here to there in terms of concrete objectives, strategies, and tactics? How do we turn planning into marketplace accomplishments?

Part Two of *Marketing Financial Services*, The Planning Imperative, begins by distinguishing between strategic and operational planning. Strategic planning focuses on achieving organizational effectiveness when the environment becomes turbulent due to competitive, technological, economic, and other marketplace changes. It defines the direction of the financial organization. Operational planning—*marketing planning is one element in this process*—is concerned with moving the banking organization in the direction decided upon as the major output of the strategic planning process.

The second chapter in Part Two examines some important concepts in marketing planning. Markets are collective, general; customers are distinctive, particular. Marketing planning recognizes both dimensions. It also recognizes the need to act from strength—for example, to concentrate an organization's marketing efforts on those products where the market is relatively attractive and where the organization enjoys a strong competitive position. And finally, marketing planning confronts the reality that by and large financial service marketers are selling intangibles; the challenge is to create a "tangible representation" or perception in a customer's mind. A mortgage, for example, achieves a higher level of tangibility when it is positioned as a *home affordability instrument.*

The concluding chapter in Part Two integrates strategic planning, marketing planning, and "high-performance" organizational structures. Maximum performance in the financial services industry as in

any other industry is achieved only when there is a congruence between structure and strategy. Most important, we believe that the
evolving deregulated environment rewards a *market orientation*. The
organizational structures of traditional depository institutions are commonly incompatible with this orientation. Banking's traditional organizational structure stresses *operational efficiency;* in a market-oriented
environment, in a less stable deregulated environment, in a markedly
more competitive environment, an organizational structure that also is
anchored in *performance effectiveness* is mandated.

Strategic Marketing

The three chapters of Part Three share a common theme. In a deregulated environment, very few financial institutions can any longer afford
to be all things to all people. Most financial institutions must *segment*
customer markets. For each customer grouping, these institutions must
stand apart, stand for something very special; they must *differentiate*
themselves with respect to image, performance characteristics, product
lines, and the other elements of the marketing mix. For each of their
customer groupings and for all of their market segments, effective differentiation requires that they *position* themselves organizationally,
functionally, and, above all, in a synergistic manner. Segmentation,
differentiation, and positioning combine, finally, in enabling a banking
organization to succeed in the critical task of turning relatively indifferent, single-service customers into loyal, multiservice clients. *A major
goal of strategic marketing should be to attract, maintain, and enhance
client relationships.*

The opening chapter in Part Three, logically enough, deals with market segmentation, the prerequisite to effective positioning and relationship banking strategies. It focuses on the *process* employed in identifying customer groupings that are *measurable, meaningful, reachable,*
and *responsive* to marketing approaches. Unless these criteria are satisfied, much in the way of marketing practice becomes fruitless wheel-
spinning.

The second chapter in Part Three is concerned with differentiation
and positioning. It raises a series of questions:

- Just what kind of bank or thrift or brokerage firm should ours be in a
  deregulated environment?
- An all-things-to-all-people bank?
- An anytime-and-just-about-anywhere-that's-important-to-be bank?
- A cream-of-the-crop-customer bank?
- A technology pioneer bank?
- An old-fashioned people bank?

And these questions represent only the proverbial tip of the iceberg in terms of the available choices for differentiating successfully and profitably in a busy and possibly overcrowded marketplace. Positioning is a matter of making the best choices from among a growing list of available choices—the best choices for the financial organization and for its customer segments.

For what purpose? *To create a relationship.*

To some, relationship banking is merely a buzzword. Or it is perceived as fine theory, but not easily workable in the marketplace, if not impractical. We disagree, believing strongly and with sound reasons that relationship banking will dominate financial services marketing thought and practice throughout the 1980s and beyond. *It is the cornerstone of the new marketing imperative.*

Precisely how and why is the subject of the concluding chapter in Part Three. So is the more challenging task of making relationship banking work.

Implementing Marketing

Financial services marketing is both a philosophy of doing business that should permeate the entire organization and a series of functional tasks that are designed to result in customer satisfaction. Implementation—making marketing happen—is the focus of Part Four. The contents of Part Four generally follow the traditional order of marketing texts, moving from one to another element of the marketing mix: product development, price, distribution (place), and promotion—*the 4 Ps,* which any marketing practitioner will recognize and feel comfortable in responding to.

This is all that is traditional, however, since the concern of each chapter is with new directions in marketing practice, new approaches, new methods for designing products and services, pricing them, literally moving them from bank to customer, and promoting them both to the staff members that must sell products and services and to end-user customers who will be buying them. The emphasis, moreover, is on new approaches for a new business, the financial services business, in a new operating environment. The emphasis is on marketing mix approaches that will assure success and survival in the banking environment of today and tomorrow, not the approaches of yesterday that still permeate the thinking of too many financial institution managers and marketers.

One element of the marketing mix is not treated in a distinctive chapter-length form. Instead, *pricing* is interwoven throughout Part Four of *Marketing Financial Services.* This decision on our part was made for a number of reasons. *First,* and most important, pricing in the financial services business is the essence of this business, its inherent managerial responsibility. Off–balance sheet activity aside, financial institutions are chiefly involved in buying and selling money and managing the spread. The reality is that marketers work with the *price of money*, a price set by market forces well beyond the ability of marketers—or of managements—to control. The price of money is volatile; look at the roller-coaster ride the prime took during the Carter administration. The price of money is discriminate, which is why there is one price for prime corporate customers, another (prime-plus) for marginal customers, and a wide range of price structures for varying types of consumer credit options.

Second, and also because of the nature of the banking and financial services business, pricing involves hands-on efforts from many decision makers in the organization. *Third*, pricing reflects the necessary interaction of legislative and regulatory initiatives. At the time of this writing, for example, financial institution managers, the Federal Reserve Board, the Reagan Administration, and Congress were caught up in a policy struggle over tightening or easing credit, a struggle whose resolution will ultimately take concrete form through the price of money. Price is not simply what a banking organization wants to charge for its services, or even reasonably should charge, but also a matter of public policy.

For these reasons, we have elected to *integrate pricing from a marketing perspective* throughout our chapters on marketing implementation as well as in those chapters dealing with marketplace positioning and Relationship Banking. It is clear to us that deregulation, intensified competitive pressures, the advent of new cost-impacting technologies, and changes in public policy have combined to foster fresh thinking and initiatives with regard to pricing among financial institution managers and marketers.

Lessons

Lessons—Part Five, the final segment of *Marketing Financial Services*— offers a conclusion and a conviction. Summing up, so to speak, we offer our definition of the new marketing imperative for financial service institutions in a deregulated environment and speculate on the consequences for institutional performance. We also dwell on our conviction that for a long time to come banking will remain a *people business*.

This conviction does not at all detract from the breathtaking possibilities propelled by technological innovation. We believe, for example, that by the year 1990 or thereabouts most if not all of our routine financial transactions will be processed through at-home, at-work, or other place-convenience terminals. We are indeed awed by the promise of technology in the financial field. We are acutely sensitive to the very real possibility that what most of us today mean by a "bank" could be stored in microchips on a plastic card and used worldwide to facilitate personal financial transactions.

Still, banking will remain a people business.

The leaps and bounds ahead fostered by technological innovation will be more than matched by extensions in product lines and servicing approaches that will demand increasingly higher levels of customized, high-touch attention. The dependence on quality bank people will not change. If anything, it will intensify. What will change is how and where bank people perform their tasks, how they are trained and educated, and how they are motivated and compensated. What will change, moreover, is what they can do for a customer.

What might even change is how tomorrow's bankers view themselves. We hope that they will define their job as *customer satisfaction engineering.* After all, tomorrow's bankers will continue to be the frontline troops of marketing. And marketing in the financial services business, in any modern business activity, has only one purpose: *the creation of satisfied customers.* This is what our book is all about.

NOTES

1. Interview with Senator Garn on "Legislation: Review and Prospects," conducted by John M. Berry, *Financier*, August 1982, p. 32.

2. Raoul D. Edwards, "The Chase for the Household Account," *United States Banker*, October 1980, pp. 8–12, 560.

3. Thomas W. Thompson, "Commentary: The Over-Emphasis on Earnings Now," *United States Banker*, November 1983, pp. 12–14, 72.

4. The concept of a "strategic vision" was developed by John Naisbitt in his chapter on "Short Term/Long Term" in *Megatrends: Ten New Directions Transforming Our Lives* (New York: Warner Books, 1984). Naisbitt argues that "strategic planning is worthless unless there is first a strategic vision . . . a clear image of what you want to achieve, which then organizes and instructs every step toward that goal."

PART TWO

The Planning Imperative

"If we want to formulate plans that will be successful in tomorrow's world, we should study who has tended to be right more times than not in thinking about tomorrow, and who has tended to be wrong. If you do so, you may find that it was often the marketer who most clearly foresaw future business opportunities, rather than the technicians, the scientists, and the general managers.

"When you reflect on this it makes good sense, because marketing people are constantly striving to find out what people want and then to look for ways to satisfy these needs. It is an immutable fact that tomorrow's winners in our business or any business will be those who understand clearly that our only reason to exist is to create a customer, and that customers are created by finding better ways to help individuals and corporations solve their problems."

Walter B. Wriston, *retired Citicorp Chairman, quoted in the* American Banker, *September 28, 1984, p.4. From an address given to a Peat-Marwick seminar*

Strategic Planning: The Changing Managerial Focus

At a recent planning seminar for senior bank officers, a CEO in attendance commented that a great deal of what was taking place was "old wine in a new bottle." For example, he suggested that strategic planning was just a new buzzword for long-range planning. Such misunderstandings are common today, and we believe that they indicate a misunderstanding of the concept of organizational performance. Before the importance of strategic planning can be appreciated, we must understand the critical dimensions of organizational performance and why they have changed in banking. To accomplish this, we must first examine the relationship between the organization's environment and the focus of its planning efforts.

THE ENVIRONMENT AND MANAGERIAL PLANNING

There is a very important relationship between the environment that an industry faces and the managerial planning focus of the industry. Let us examine two alternative environments.

Stable Technology and Stable Markets

Industries facing such an environment are in a somewhat fortunate position, at least with respect to planning. They can assume a reasonable degree of continuity in their planning, and they can expect the trends of the past to remain pretty much the same in the future. Under such circumstances, extrapolative planning is possible. This involves extrapolating and projecting the trends of the past into the future. At present, these conditions probably hold true for the white goods industry (washers and dryers). No new technological breakthroughs for washers and dryers are on the horizon, and these products are made pretty much the same as they have always been. Finally, the markets for these products are stable. We replace our white goods every 17 years, and first-time purchasers are mostly reflected in marriage rates, birthrates, and housing starts. Thus, if planners know the relationship between these three demographic factors and sales during the past decade, they can extrapolate these trends into the future and develop fairly accurate sales forecasts for use in production and marketing during the next decade.

It is obvious that extrapolative planning assumes that (1) the trends of the past will hold true in the future and (2) the external environment will not change to any significant degree. Such assumptions are valid as long as the technology of the industry and the markets of the industry remain stable: in other words, as long as the future is expected to look like the present.

Changing Technology and Changing Markets

What happens to planning efforts when an industry's environment shifts in a very short period of time from one of stable technology and stable markets to one of changing technology and changing markets? Returning to the white goods industry, assume for a moment that there are rapid changes in the industry's technology (outside competition invents a microwave washer/dryer requiring no water or detergent) and in its markets (Americans begin wearing more disposable clothes).

If such turbulence besets the white goods industry, the planning methods previously used to develop production plans, marketing plans, and long-range corporate plans would no longer be sufficient or would be obsolete. An entirely new planning focus would be necessary. Technological and market changes would have altered the basic nature of the industry to such an extent that planning would have to focus away from the traditional products of the industry (washers and dryers) and begin to focus on redefining the entire white goods industry. New directions for the industry would have to be identified, new products and markets developed, new objectives established, perhaps even entirely new businesses launched. In its planning efforts, management would be forced to adapt to the changing environment, or the business as we know it today would cease to exist. Management would require a planning focus different from the one that was necessary in simpler times when all the business did was manufacture washers and dryers.

This hypothetical account is analogous to the situation faced by all types of financial institutions today. As shown in Chapter 1, the financial services industry has in a very short period of time shifted from a rather comfortable, stable environment to an environment characterized by changing technology, changing markets, and changing economic and regulatory conditions. These changes have altered the basic nature of the industry, so that the planning techniques that were formerly useful to it are now inadequate. We must now be concerned with being more than just a better bank, savings and loan, or credit union. We must become something different. In other words, financial institutions must be more than just *efficient*. They must also be *effective*.

DIMENSIONS OF ORGANIZATIONAL PERFORMANCE

There are two very different and very important dimensions of organizational performance; organizational *efficiency* and organizational *effectiveness*. Well-managed companies perform well along both dimensions. However, at certain points in an industry's life cycle, one dimension may be more important than the other as the major focus of managerial planning efforts.

Organizational Effectiveness

The effectiveness dimension of organizational performance focuses on the "what" of the organization—the nature and direction of the organization, what kind of organization it wants to be. This may involve new strategy—new choices involving what products and services the organization will produce and what markets and customer groups it will serve. *Effective organizations do the right things.*

Organizational Efficiency

The efficiency dimension of organizational performance focuses on "how" the organization will get where it has decided to go. This involves the efficient use of resources in the production of whatever goods or services the organization produces. Improvements in efforts result in improvements in productivity and more efficient use of the organization's resources. *Efficient organizations do things right.* Figure 2–1 summarizes the differences between planning efforts focusing on efficiency and those focusing on effectiveness.

FIGURE 2–1

Planning and the Critical Dimensions of Organizational Performance

planning that focuses on efficiency focuses on	*planning that focuses on effectiveness focuses on*
1. Efforts (improving the use of resources)	1. Results (the achievement of objectives)
2. Doing things right	2. Doing the right things
3. Inward view	3. Outward view
4. Doing better what you are doing at present	4. Relating well with your changing environment (having a clear strategy)

Shifting the Planning Focus

Reviewing our previous discussion and Figure 2–1, we can see that as long as the environment remains stable, no decisions need to be made regarding "what" the organization needs to be. Concentrating on improving the "how" is sufficient for survival and profitability. It is only when the environment changes that the "what" question becomes relevant. The problem, of course, is not to continue to focus on the "how" when attention should be shifted to the "what" as the critical dimension of organizational performance.

For example, between 1870 and 1920 the railroads were the growth industry of the world. The leaders of Europe invested in them, as did the Roman Catholic Church. By 1920 the railroads were mostly broke. This unfortunate situation was not caused by declining demand for what the railroads did. In fact, the demand for moving people, things, and information from point A to point B increased. At the same time, however, vast changes were taking place in the technology of moving people, things, and information. As is often the case, technological changes brought on market changes because they gave customers more choices. The customers chose, but not the railroads. They chose the new developing technologies of trucks, planes, automobiles, pipelines, and telephones. What did the railroads do? They continued to focus on the efficiency dimension of organizational performance, apparently deciding that the way to respond to the environmental changes was to become better railroads. They focused their attention inward, replaced equipment, developed new schedules, laid new railbeds. All of these efforts were undoubtedly good efforts. Unfortunately, they were the wrong efforts. Management was focusing on the wrong dimension of organizational performance.

What happened to the railroads is not an isolated instance. For example:

No phonograph company ever entered the radio field.

No theatrical company ever entered the movie business.

No wagon manufacturer attempted to enter the automobile business.

No steam locomotive company entered the field of diesel or electric locomotives.

And today, of course, many commercial banks, thrift institutions, and credit unions are resisting any move into the financial services business as distinct from their traditional businesses. In each of the earlier cases, management did not shift its planning focus when the environment changed. It continued to focus on the efficiency dimension of performance and ignored the effectiveness dimension. The same appears to be occurring in many financial institutions today.

The Efficiency / Effectiveness Relationship

While they are clearly two different dimensions of organizational performance, efficiency and effectiveness are also closely related. This relationship is presented in Figure 2–2, which indicates four possibilities. Let us examine each of them.

FIGURE 2–2

Relating Efficiency and Effectiveness

		3	**4**

	efficient	Not wasting resources
		Not relating well with
		   changing environment
			Not wasting resources
			Relating well with
			   changing environment

efficiency (efforts)		**1**	**2**

	inefficient	Wasting resources
		Not relating well with
		   changing environment
			Wasting resources
			Relating well with
			   changing environment

ineffective   *effective*

effectiveness
(results)

---

1. Inefficient and Ineffective This organization has no clear idea of what it wants to be and consequently does not relate well with its environment. In addition, its operations are inefficient. It is "doing the wrong things" and not doing them very well. It has an unclear strategy and inefficient operations. Unfortunately, many local and municipal governments, nonprofit organizations, and federal agencies operate in this mode. Some people place most of the American automobile industry in this quadrant. Obviously, profit-making organizations do not stay in it for long because they eventually go the way of Penn Central, W. T. Grant, and failed financial institutions. W. T. Grant illustrated poor performance along both dimensions, as the following comments indicate.[1] The first comment addresses the effectiveness dimension:

> Early on Grant seemingly could not make up its mind what kind of store it was. There was a lot of dissension within the company whether we should go the K mart route or go after the Ward and Penney position . . . the upshot being we took a position between the two and consequently stood for nothing.

The second comment addresses the efficiency dimension:

> From 1963 to 1973 Grant opened 612 stores and expanded 91 others. . . . The expansion program placed a great strain on the physical and human capability of the company to cope with the program. These were all large stores—6 million to 7 million square feet per year—and the expansion of our management organization just did not match the expansion of our stores. Our training programs couldn't keep up with the explosion of stores, and it didn't take long for the mediocrity to begin to show.

These comments clearly express the difference between the two dimensions of organizational performance. For W. T. Grant, that difference meant failure because while it did not know what type of organization it wanted to be, it decided to do things in a big way and did them very inefficiently.

2. Inefficient and Effective. This situation tells us that it is possible for an organization to be inefficient and yet be very effective. The organization has a clear idea of what it needs to be and responds well to its environment (that is, has a clear strategy) despite its inefficient operations. It is "doing the right things," but not very well. Such a situation can exist when demand is so great or the price is so high that inefficiencies in operations can be camouflaged and absorbed. However, under such conditions it is usually difficult to win over the long run because conditions usually change. Many fast-food chains were in this quadrant but met misfortune when markets became saturated and growth opportunities declined in the early 1970s. Success then depended on running an efficient chain of fast-food restaurants, a capability that many of the fast-food chains did not have. A Heublein executive's comments on the firm's acquisition of Kentucky Fried Chicken illustrate this problem:

> In the wine and liquor business, it doesn't matter what the liquor store looks like. Smirnoff Vodka doesn't get the blame if the floor is dirty. And you can control your product at the factory. We simply bought a chain of five thousand little factories all over the world, and we didn't have the experience in handling that kind of operation.[2]

This situation can also exist when an industry is highly regulated and, therefore, is legislated effective. However, as we have seen in the past with many utilities, they can have inefficient operations.

3. Efficient but Ineffective. This is a very frustrating situtation to find yourself in. A business in this quadrant is doing with great efficiency that which it should not be doing and consequently it does not relate well to its changing environment. Businesses in this quadrant are "drifting" organizations that were probably very effective at one time but have become less effective or ineffective because of environmental changes. However, they continue to be efficient in doing what they originally did. They are "doing the wrong things" but doing them very well. Many Swiss watch manufacturers are currently in this situation. They are superbly efficient in the production and marketing of traditional watches. Technological changes and customer purchases of digital watches have, however, rendered them ineffective. Many savings institutions and commercial banks are also in this situation. They, like the railroads before them and the Swiss watch industry today, must renew their search for purpose in order to regain their effectiveness. They have an unclear strategy but very efficient operations.

4. Efficient and Effective. In this quadrant are the best-managed companies and the best-managed financial institutions. These "winners" have a clear vision of what they will be in the future as well as eminently efficient operations. They are "doing the right things," and they do them very well. They have a clear strategy and efficient operations.

Two conclusions become evident from this discussion:

- Effectiveness is the foundation for success. Efficiency is a necessary condition for survival after effectiveness has been achieved.
- When an organization or an industry begins to lose its effectiveness because of environmental changes, becoming more efficient will not enable it to regain its effectiveness.

With this understanding, we can now respond to the criticism of the CEO cited at the beginning of the chapter. Strategic planning differs from all other planning activities because it focuses on the effectiveness dimension of organizational performance. Because of environmental change, financial institution executives must now be concerned with more than just the efficiency of their operations. In order to survive and flourish in the new environment, financial institutions must face the future knowing both "what" they want to be (strategic planning) and "how" they will become what they want to be (operations, marketing, and long-range planning). Strategic planning is not a buzzword. It is a planning process that is necessary in the new banking environment. Managers in financial institutions must separate the "what" questions of the business from the "how" questions.

In the financial services industry, efficient operations have histori- cally been more important than strategic thinking. This was due in part to the fact that the industry's effectiveness was, in effect, legislated. Because the "what" question was legislated, bankers needed only to concentrate on the "how" and became extremely good at it. Thus, many banks prospered even when they lacked a clear sense of strategic direc- tion. After all, when an organization's effectiveness is legislated, who needs to think much about what kind of business it should be? Finan- cial institutions did not ignore strategic planning. Until recently, they never needed it.

It is certain that financial institutions must now define themselves, not in the terms and conditions under which they were born, but rather in the terms and conditions under which they currently operate. This requirement dictates the need for strategic planning. We devote the remainder of this chapter to some key concepts of strategic planning.

SOME KEY CONCEPTS OF STRATEGIC PLANNING

Strategic planning is a management process that leads to the develop- ment of a clear purpose or mission, objectives, and strategies for the entire organization. The output of the process should be a clarity of purpose and direction. Strategic planning is truly a statement of con- viction about what kind of business we will be, how we will make money, and where we will be positioned in five years. Every strategic planning effort should address three broad questions: (1) What are the institution's strengths and weaknesses? (2) What is the institution's primary driving force? and (3) What strategic alternatives are available to the institution?

Assessing the Institution's Strengths and Weaknesses

Any judgment of what the institution should do has to be based on an assessment of what it can do. This involves an objective assessment of strengths and weaknesses by the senior management team. The results of that assessment can be extremely useful in establishing objectives. This is because establishing objectives involves identifying areas of bank performance that management wishes to evaluate and assessing strengths and weaknesses really involves evaluating organizational performance.

An obvious criterion of organizational strength is *survival*. W. T. Grant, Penn Central, and many failed financial institutions have ceased operating. Beyond survival, however, it is not easy to identify criteria for effective organizational performance. But criteria are needed in order to judge how well an institution is performing and to evaluate its strengths and weaknesses.

We suggest four broad criteria of performance. We present them as general objectives that every financial institution must achieve to ensure the ultimate objective of survival. These four criteria are *profitability*, *competitiveness*, *efficiency*, and *flexibility*. Each of these areas represents a *different* type of performance. Figure 2–3 presents the most widely used measures for evaluating performance in the four areas. Let us briefly examine each of these areas.

Profitability. Clearly, profitability is the most important area of performance because it guarantees the flow of capital necessary for new product development and expansion. The specific measures of profitability are usually expressed as return on investment or some variation of that (for example, return on equity).

Competitiveness. Competitive strength is really a substitute measure of long-run profitability. It tells us a great deal about our prospects for long-run profitability. An institution's competitive strength can be evaluated by examining two matters: (1) *growth*—the annual rate of increase in earnings per share, earning assets, total assets, volume of loans, total deposits, capital, and the organization's market share in such spheres as demand, time and savings deposits, and loans; and (2) *stability*—the extent to which the volume of demand and time deposits, earnings per share, and earnings have fluctuated in the past five years. (Remember, financial institutions must be competitive not only in customer markets but also in capital markets.)

Efficiency. To ensure long-term profitability, financial institutions must maintain certain kinds of short-term efficiencies. Measures of efficiency determine how well assets and liabilities are being employed.

Flexibility. Because financial institutions operate in a very uncertain environment, well-managed financial institutions should try to protect themselves from significant negative events by remaining flexible, both

FIGURE 2–3

Assessing Strengths and Weaknesses

some indicators of

profitability	*competitiveness*	*efficiency*	*flexibility*
Return on assets	**Growth** (annual rate of increase) in:	Earnings growth	**External**
Return on equity		Return on equity	Deposit mix
Return on earning assets	Earnings per share	Return on assets	Loan mix
Earnings per share	Total assets	Return on earning assets	Composition of investment portfolio
Return on capital	Loan volume	Percentage of total assets at work in earning assets	Borrowings
	Total deposits		
	Capital	Operating revenue as a percentage of total assets	**Internal**
	Market share:		Liquidity:
	—demand deposits	Rate of return on loans	—ratio of loans to deposits
	—time deposits	Rate of return on U.S. Treasury securities	—ratio of liquid assets to total assets
	—savings deposits	Rate of return on obligations of states and so on	Capital adequacy:
	—loans		—ratio of capital to total assets and deposits
	Stability (extent of fluctuations) in:	Ratio of service charges to demand deposits	—ratio of capital to loans, risk assets
	Demand deposit volume	Ratio of interest paid to time deposits	—debt as a percentage of capital
	Time deposit volume	Depth, age, education of critical personnel	—equity as a percentage of capital
	Earnings per share	Condition of premises, equipment, and so on	
		Ratio of net loan losses to loans	
		Ratio of total operating expenses to total operating income	
		Salaries and wages as a percentage of operating revenue and total assets	

Source: James H. Donnelly, Jr., *A Preface to Banking,* (Washington, D.C.: American Bankers Association, 1979).

externally and internally. *External flexibility* is indicated through a financial institution's deposit mix (the distribution of deposit types and maturities), its loan mix (the various classes of loans), and the composition of its investment portfolio (types and maturity structure), as well as its management's philosophy with regard to borrowings on a regular basis. Traditional measures of risk—measures of liquidity and capital adequacy—are indicators of *internal flexibility*.

What our evaluation system indicates clearly is our belief that an effectively managed financial institution must be profitable, must be able to compete, must use its resources efficiently, and must be flexible in order to adapt to changes in its internal and external environments. Corporate objectives should be developed and performance evaluated in each of the four areas. Accordingly, assessing the organization's strengths and weaknesses for purposes of strategic planning should identify strengths and weaknesses in each of these areas. For example, typical strengths might include a high return on assets, a high growth rate in total assets and in market share of time deposits, and low loan loss reserve requirements. Typical weaknesses might include low earnings per share, a declining growth rate in loan volume, widely fluctuating time deposit volume, a low capital/asset ratio, and high employee turnover.

We have seen that it is possible to produce objective measures of profitability, competitive strength, efficiency, and flexibility. We can use these measures to identify strengths and weaknesses and to evaluate performance as good or bad to the degree that the measures improve relative to past performance or relative to the performance of similar organizations. However, the measures must be used with caution. There are some important questions that must be asked about the measures that are used to evaluate performance and identify strengths and weaknesses.

1. *How stable is the measure?* A measure may be more valid at one point in time than at some other point in time. For example, growth in market share will usually be more important in a rapidly expanding market than in a stable or shrinking market.

2. *How precise is the measure?* Not only are many measures difficult to compute but in many instances there is more than one way to arrive at them. For example, depth of critical personnel or investment in employee development can be measured in a variety of ways, thus leading to different conclusions.

3. *How important is time?* It is important to evaluate the four areas in both the short run and the long run. For example, a measure of profitability or competitiveness may show it to be excellent in the short run although efficiency or flexibility are being jeopardized in the long run.

Finally, an assessment of strengths and weaknesses should examine qualitative factors that may be relevant. For example, how sound is the present organizational structure for the 1980s and beyond? The present compensation system? Internal communications? The extent of correspondent relationships?

Identifying the Driving Force

Almost every organization is dominated by a specific driving force. It may have developed by conscious design or evolved over many years, emerging from the strengths developed over time. It is the force that moves the company, and it must be identified as part of any strategic planning effort.[3] When an organization is faced with the necessity of responding to a changing environment, its specific driving force may function as either an asset or a liability. At any rate, *when the final decision about a product or market is made, the driving force will be the most critical influence on that decision.* The most common driving forces are:

Products.   The product-driven organization defines itself in terms of the products it offers. Its resources and capabilities are focused on improving these products. The product-driven organization will continue to produce and distribute products similar to those it has always produced. Ford Motor Company and Metro-Goldwyn-Mayer are generally thought of as product-driven organizations.

Markets.   The market- or customer-driven organization consciously seeks to provide a range of products directed at broad classes of customer needs in the markets it serves. IBM and Revlon are good examples of organizations that continually seek to serve the changing and evolving needs of their customers.

Technology.   The technology-driven organization produces only those products that capitalize on its technological/operations capabilities. Examples are 3M, Texas Instruments, and the U.S. Center for Disease Control.

Production Capability.   All the products of a production-driven organization are developed to take advantage of its skills and equipment in specific production processes. U.S. Steel and International Paper are driven by high-fixed-cost production processes.

Method of Sale.   In an organization driven by its method of sale, all the resources, capabilities, and products of the organization center on sales methods. Among such organizations are Mary Kay Cosmetics, Avon, Franklin Mint, Book-of-the-Month Club, Spiegel, Tupperware, and Amway.

Method of Distribution. An organization driven by its method of distribution determines its products, customers, and geographic markets on the basis of whether they can be reached through established distribution channels. Examples are American Telephone and Telegraph and Canteen Service Company.

Natural Resources. An organization driven by natural resources develops products and markets through the use or conservation of natural resources. Gulf Oil, DeBeers Consolidated Mines, and the U.S. Forest Service are driven by natural resources.

Size/Growth. Some organizations are driven by the desire to become either larger or smaller. Accordingly, they will set levels of size and growth that are significantly different from the present levels. This often leads them into new, unrelated products and markets. American Express is driven by size/growth.

Return/Profit. Some organizations are driven by the financial results of their efforts (for example, return on sales, assets, and equity). Accordingly, what such an organization does (its strategies) is determined by its desire for specific levels of return or profit. This driving force may also lead the organization into new businesses. Examples of such organizations are Gulf and Western Industries, ITT, Philip Morris, and R. J. Reynolds Industries.

Determining the driving force of the institution is critical because it determines the framework for selecting from among strategic alternatives. Recall our earlier discussion of the railroad industry and the Swiss watch industry. Each of these industries was product/operations driven when environmental changes required them to be market-driven. Given similar conditions, a financial institution must be ready to invest in acquiring the capabilities necessary to enable it to alter its driving force. For example, for years Citibank was size/growth–driven, with the objective of developing a presence in every feasible market. Profits were not its overriding objective. Having achieved this presence, it is now seeking to become a market-driven organization so as to meet the current and emerging needs of various markets.[4]

Finally, each driving force has different implications for operating decisions. For example, a market-driven financial institution needs skills and capabilities in marketing research, market segmentation, product development, product management, and sales. The management of such a financial institution may also be forced to concentrate all or most of its resources in only one part of the total market if market needs differ greatly between segments. Finally, a few financial institutions that are strongly *return/profit–driven* may eventually leave the business. A financial institution that does this may divest itself of its banking charter and demand deposits. This would enable it to form a financial services holding company that might acquire smaller local or regional brokerage firms, consumer finance companies, or insurance companies. And this, in turn, would enable it to develop regional and national sales forces and delivery systems.

The important point to remember is that to identify the driving force of an organization, ask the question: "When a decision is made about whether to add a new product or enter a new market, what factor finally determines the outcome?" When this question is answered, you will know what force drives the business. At present, we believe that the majority of financial service organizations are either operations or product-driven. Knowing an organization's driving force is critical because like it or not, it will have a profound influence on strategic decisions. Thus, knowing what drives the organization gives management the opportunity to decide whether or not it wishes to stay with the present driving force or invest the resources to change it.

Often an organization's strengths and weaknesses will determine its driving force. The most important thing is that management must be fully aware of what force moves the organization. It can then decide whether to take advantage of the organization's strengths and move with the driving force or else begin a concerted effort to alter the driving force, assuming that the organization either has or can acquire the capabilities to do so. We believe that most financial institutions will be moving away from operations and product-driving forces and toward becoming truly market-driven organizations. Whatever the case, the organization's strengths, weaknesses, and driving force will determine the range of strategic alternatives from which to choose.

Selecting a Corporate Strategy

The real purpose of assessing strengths and weaknesses and determining the driving force is to enable management to select from among numerous strategic alternatives. We present these strategies as neither conclusive nor mutually exclusive. Our major concern is finding approaches to markets and competitive strategy that are capable of being effective and producing desired performance results. We will present our alternatives in four categories:

1. Strategies for the underdog institution.
2. Strategies for the dominant institution.
3. Probable losing strategies.
4. Definite losing strategies.

Strategies for the Underdog Institution.   The major strategic concern of the underdog institution is how to increase its market share and transform a "middle-of-the-pack" position into a leadership position. We believe that for an underdog to be outstandingly successful, it must in most cases develop a truly differentiating strategy designed to build a competitive advantage. We do not believe that an underdog institutions can achieve a real degree of success by imitating the leading institution in its market. There are several alternative strategies that can be effective for an underdog.[5]

1. Vacant Niche Strategy.   This involves searching out and cultivating profitable areas of the market that larger firms are not catering to, are ignoring, or are not equipped to serve. The ideal niche would be large enough to be profitable, have growth potential, and be well suited to the institution's strengths. This may involve an industry (e.g., Thoroughbred horses) or a demographic group (e.g., career woman).

2. Specialist or Concentration Strategy.   This involves competing only in carefully chosen market segments with a limited product line rather than trying to compete for all customers with a full product line and being forced to attack dominant institutions head-on with price cuts and increased promotional expenditures. Some financial institutions are specializing in the superrich and as trustees in bankruptcy, while others are getting out of the mortgage loan and commercial loan business. Bankers Trust of New York abandoned all but the upper end of the retail market to concentrate where it believes its strengths are— in corporate and upscale banking.

3. "Ours-Is-Better-than-Theirs" Strategy.   An underdog institution possessing the right strengths may succeed by improving on the products of dominant institutions. This may involve working closely with customers to develop a better product or appealing, as some financial institutions do, to the quality-conscious or performance-oriented customer.

4. Contented Follower Strategy.   An underdog institution may be content to follow rather than challenge the dominant institution. This involves maintaining present market share and avoiding confrontations with dominant institutions by not attempting to lure customers and increase market share. It requires a strong top management and an internal profit emphasis rather than a market share emphasis.

5. Guppy Strategy. Following this strategy, an underdog institution would focus all of its competitive strength on increasing market share at the expense of smaller competitors in its market area.

6. Positioning-to-Be-Acquired Strategy. In some underdog financial institutions, management may decide that the best strategy is to join a larger organization. Thus, the major objective would be to maximize profitability measures in the short run in order to make the institution attractive to potential buyers. The danger, of course, is that such a short-run objective may be accomplished only at the expense of the institution's competitive strength, efficiency, and flexibility. If the institution is not acquired management will face the prospectively adverse results of its actions in the intermediate and long run.

In the new environment, most underdog financial institutions will probably find it difficult to win. Not losing will probably be what most underdog institutions will settle for. We believe, however, that underdogs can establish a strong competitive position. The most promising strategic guidelines appear to be: (1) compete only in carefully chosen market segments where particular strengths can be developed, and avoid attacking the dominant financial institutions head-on with price cuts and increased promotional expenditures; (2) be content to remain small, and emphasize profits rather than volume or market share; and (3) push specialization rather than diversification.[6]

An excellent example of the above guidelines and of a successful underdog strategy is provided by the Citytrust Bancorp of Bridgeport, Connecticut. By staying small and emphasizing marketing, Citytrust prospers despite its proximity to much larger competitors in New York, Boston, and Hartford. It does not seek larger customers. It develops services to small companies—those with $1 million to $25 million in sales—that the larger banks often or frequently ignore. It has also abandoned most parts of its mass-market consumer business.

Citytrust believes that it will continue to prosper and stay independent because it has found a niche, leaving the large companies to the dominant banks. Its executives state that it is a "customer-driven" bank with a "results-oriented" planning process. It seeks to develop specific products that its entrepreneurial clients need.[7]

Strategies for the Dominant Institution. As a leader, a dominant institution has a well-established and envied market position. The dominant institution's strategy should seek to harvest what has been accomplished and to either maintain or improve on its present position. At least four strategies are open to the dominant institution.[8]

1. Keep-the-Offensive Strategy. A dominant financial institution that follows this strategy is not content with being the leader. It seeks to outdo its previous levels of performance. It seeks to become known to customers and competition as the source of new products and services, innovative delivery systems, and internal systems improvements. It seeks at every opportunity to exploit the weaknesses of competitors.

2. Confrontation Strategy. A dominant institution should, in most instances, respond to an underdog's attempts to take its customers by quickly retaliating with major promotional campaigns that the underdog will be unable to match. Most price cuts should be promptly met or surpassed to neutralize any benefit to the would-be price cutter and to discourage the use of such tactics by other underdog institutions. Let the market know who should lead and who should follow.

3. Maintenance Strategy. A dominant institution cannot and should not allow any slippage in volume, market share, and customer service. It must invest in whatever human and technological resources are necessary to maintain competitive strength, efficiency, and flexibility.

4. Position-to-Be-a-Financial-Conglomerate Strategy. This is an appropriate strategy for the very few institutions with the strengths to employ it successfully and, as we mentioned earlier, with a strong return/profit driving force. Sears, Beneficial Finance, and others have formed diversified financial service organizations whose earnings are far beyond what most financial institutions achieve.

Probable Losing Strategies. In the present turbulent environment, managers of banks, savings and loans, and credit unions will be called upon to exhibit competence and skill in areas where these were not previously demanded. Under such circumstances, management, out of frustration, desperation, poor advice, or poor analysis, may be attracted to a strategy that is risky and has little chance for true success. Financial institution managers should be cautious about adopting the following high-risk/low-potential strategies.[9]

1. Me-Too Strategy. Copying or imitating the strategy of a leading institution is trying to beat a stronger opponent at its own game. Such a strategy rarely achieves meaningful results, and just as importantly, it ignores the development of the institution's own unique strategy and direction.

2. Take-Away Strategy.   An institution following this strategy seeks to gain greater market penetration by attacking other institutions head-on. The tactics used to lure customers include lower prices, more advertising, and other attention-getting gimmicks. The weakness of this strategy is that it forces retaliation and a costly battle for market share that no one wins, including the institution playing take-away.

3. "Test-the-Water" Strategy.   When new opportunities or very new products present themselves, it is usually best to either get in or stay away entirely. We are familiar with many banks that have products "available" but instruct their frontline personnel not to sell them. These and similar halfway efforts seldom result in anything except an inadequate corporate commitment, a frustrated staff, and disillusioned customers.

4. Hit-Another-Home-Run Strategy.   Often an institution that has pioneered a very successful product or promotion campaign tries to repeat the success (hit-another-home-run) by repeating the same strategy. Repeating a strategy rarely works because conditions change and the requirements for success are usually different.

5. Arms-Race Strategy.   Often financial institutions of equal size (usually underdogs) will enter into a contest for increased market share. As one institution increases promotional expenditures, initiates price cuts, and provides additional services, the others are forced to follow for defensive reasons. The result is a cost-increasing arms race. The only thing this strategy ever really accomplishes is increased costs for everyone. The customer is the only person that benefits because rarely do such battles ever produce any substantial changes in market share.

Definite Losing Strategies.   Some corporate strategies seldom, if ever, work. If an institution that uses them achieves any degree of success, that success is certainly not the result of the strategy. For obvious reasons, financial institutions should avoid these strategies.[10]

1. Drift Strategy.   When an institution's direction is not consciously designed, it evolves out of everyday decisions and actions at the operating level. You might think of such an institution as having no strategy, but it does, in fact, have one. It is the strategy of drifting.

2. Hope-for-a-Better-Day Strategy.   Where managerial inertia and tradition permeate a financial institution, poor performance is often blamed on the economy, customers, bad luck, and other factors beyond the control of management. Thus, "everything will be OK if we can just make it through these bad times." Such coasting is a sign of inept management and a shaky future.

3. Losing-Hand Strategy. Many times a financial institution that was once successful in pursuing a particular strategy will continue to follow the same course although that course is no longer viable. Instead of reformulating its strategy, management settles for cosmetic changes as a means to reverse a decline. Financial institutions following this strategy are usually victims of the success-breeds-success syndrome. "If it worked for my father, it will work for me."

4. Popgun Strategy. For whatever reasons, underdog financial institutions often believe that they can confront dominant institutions. Often they will set themselves the objective of being the leader in the community in market share within, say, five years. Thus, they will go head-to-head with leaders when they have neither a distinct differential competitive advantage (see strategies for underdog institutions) nor adequate resources to win the confrontation.

CONCLUSION

There are two dimensions of organizational performance: efficiency and effectiveness. Running an efficient organization is sufficient for survival and profitability when the organization's environment is stable. When the environment becomes turbulent because of technological, economic, regulatory, and market changes, management must shift the planning focus to the effectiveness dimension. The "what" questions of the business (What products should we make? What markets should we serve?) become more important than the "how" questions of the business.

Strategic planning focuses on achieving effectiveness, while other planning processes focus on improving efficiency. Strategic planning defines the direction of the institution. All other planning processes have as their purpose moving the organization in the direction decided upon as the major output of the strategic planning process—that is, their purpose is to implement the strategic plan.

NOTES

1. Quoted in B. B. Tregoe and J. W. Zimmerman, "Strategic Thinking: Key to Corporate Survival," *Management Review*, February 1979, pp. 9–14.

2. Quoted in Thomas J. Peters and Robert H. Waterman, Jr., *In Search of Excellence* (New York: Harper & Row, 1982), p. 292.

3. From J. W. Zimmerman, and B. B. Tregoe, *Top Management Strategy* (New York: Simon & Schuster, 1981).

4. See R. O. Metzger, "Strategic Planning for Productivity," *Journal of R* *tail Banking*, March 1982, pp 41–50. The following paragraph is adapted from this work.

5. For more detailed discussions, see Philip Kotler, *Marketing Manage-ment: Analysis, Planning, and Control*, 4th ed. (Englewood Cliffs, N.J.: Prentice-Hall, 1980), pp. 281–84; and R. G. Hamermesh, M. J. Ander-son, Jr., and J. E. Harris, "Strategies for Low Market Share Businesses," *Harvard Business Review*, May–June 1978, pp. 95–102. This presenta-tion is based on A. A. Thompson, Jr., and A. J. Strickland III, *Strategy Formulation and Implementation*, rev. ed. (Plano, Tex.: Business Publi-cations, 1983), pp. 156–69.

6. Adapted from ibid., p. 158.

7. See "Bank in Connecticut Recovers by Ignoring the Big Companies and Small Consumers," *The Wall Street Journal*, August 16, 1983, p. 35.

8. Kotler, *Marketing Management*, pp. 273–81.

9. J. Ross and M. Kami, *Corporate Management in Crisis: Why the Mighty Fall* (Englewood Cliffs, N.J.: Prentice-Hall, 1973); and Kotler, *Marketing Management*, chap. 8.

10. Ibid.

Concepts and Issues in Marketing Planning

It is easy to appreciate that a financial institution's strategic plan should be developed prior to any efforts at marketing planning. Ideally, the marketing plan should contribute to the achievement of the overall strategic plan.

It's no wonder, then, that we continually hear about a common and perplexing problem among financial marketers. It usually goes something like this: "My institution has no plan. What can I do? How can I develop a marketing plan when we have no strategic plan?" The answer, of course, is that it can be done, but certainly not within the framework that it should be done. Remember, the purpose of marketing planning is to make the institution go where it has decided it wants to go. Thus, if the institution does not know where it wants to be, any marketing plan will get it there, but it may end up somewhere it doesn't want to be. In reality, your institution is going somewhere. Five years from now, it will be someplace. The problem is that without a conscious plan, the direction of the organization is dictated by the sum total of everyday operating decisions. That direction ends up being whatever opportunity or threat the institution happens to be pursuing or avoiding at the given time. Under such circumstances, it is easy to see how marketing planning efforts can, by default or in the absence of a strategic plan, influence the institution's direction, rightly or wrongly.

The purpose of this chapter is *not* to review the basic elements of developing a marketing plan. Developing the situation analysis, establishing marketing objectives, developing marketing strategy, and determining means to evaluate results are certainly critical marketing planning activities. (In fact, the information discussed in the previous chapter as necessary for developing a strategic plan can also serve as useful input into the marketing planning process.) However, in keeping with the theme of our book, to discuss marketing at a strategic level, our purpose in this chapter is to take up *two ideas* that we believe can be extremely useful in developing marketing plans in financial institutions. The first, *product portfolio analysis*, can, as you will see, be valuable in both the situation analysis and objective-setting phases of the marketing planning process. The second is a very difficult but rarely discussed problem faced by financial marketers, namely, the fact that they deal with *intangible services*. Our discussion of that problem will be very useful in the strategy development phase of the marketing plan.[1]

MORE PRODUCTS, LESS TIME, LESS MONEY

One of the major responses of the financial services industry to environmental change has focused on the development of new deposit products and new fee-based services. And, as product lines have expanded, particularly on the deposit side, a major issue for marketers is which of the products to stress from a marketing perspective. In fact, there are several planning-related problems that are becoming more acute as financial institutions expand their product lines:

- As the number of products expands, the time available for developing marketing plans for each individual product decreases.
- When resources for marketing activities are scarce (which is usually the case), the process of deciding which products to emphasize in advertising and personal selling becomes more complex.
- Product profitability for individual products is more difficult to forecast in an environment in which new products are rapidly being added. Many new products will be interrelated with existing products on the cost and/or demand side. Also, many new products often "cannibalize" deposits that were previously applied to existing instruments.
- Current product performance is seldom an effective guide to future performance because of continual change in growth rates, competition, regulation, and other environmental forces. Therefore, some

products may provide little growth but high profitability; others may offer high growth but marginal profitability.

- Financial institutions vary in terms of their capabilities. For example, some may be more successful in offering instruments linked to trust services because of their strength in this area; others may be more advanced in electronic banking, and thus may be more efficient in managing demand deposit products.

All of these problems focus on the question of "how to manage the institution's existing product line." Multiple-product firms have faced this problem for decades. Most financial institutions are facing it for the first time. Managing a product line involves answering two questions: (1) What role should each product play in achieving such long-term objectives as profitability and competitiveness (growth and stability)? and (2) How should marketing resources such as promotional expenditures, personal selling time, and new employees be allocated across products? In industry, marketing managers often try to answer these questions through a technique known as product portfolio analysis.

PRODUCT PORTFOLIO ANALYSIS

Portfolio analysis is not a new idea to financial institutions. Few, however, have extended the idea beyond the traditional loan portfolio to include deposit products and fee services, even though deposit products and fee services do not all make the same contribution to the organization, just as there are differences in contributions of the various loan portfolio elements.

Product portfolio analysis is the process whereby the institution attempts to specify the role that each of its products should play. It provides marketers with a method for classifying products in order to determine the future contributions that each product can be expected to make and the future resources that each will require. While some subjectivity is involved, the results enable management to clarify the role that each product should play and provide direction for decisions regarding the allocation of resources across products. This final contribution is a critical one because financial institutions cannot provide equal marketing resource support for all products and therefore some means for allocating resources is needed. Applying product portfolio analysis involves several important phases.

Defining the Scope of the Analysis

In larger financial institutions having a divisionalized organizational structure, decisions must frequently be made regarding the degree of emphasis placed on institutional versus individual banking and deposit versus fee-service business. As we saw in the previous chapter, these are clearly strategic decisions. However, they involve only a few—though very important—alternatives. Our experience has been that the application of the product portfolio concept in financial institutions is most effective when it is done at a lower level of aggregation, such as all corporate services or all deposit services.

Classifying Products

The most comprehensive product portfolio planning tool is the portfolio planning matrix. It was developed by General Electric and is presented in Figure 3–1. It enjoys wide acceptance because it permits the user to consider a wide range of factors in evaluating a product. One of its important benefits is that it forces management to identify all of the institution's sources of strength and all of the factors that determine the long-term attractiveness of a market. Note that in Figure 3–1 products are classified as either high, medium, or low on two dimensions, *competitive strength* and *market attractiveness*.

Competitive Strength.   In evaluating competitive strength, the institution is forced to identify those areas in which it has specific capabilities that give it a competitive advantage in marketing a particular service or product. In addition, the process also forces the institution to identify weaknesses that must be overcome to be successful in marketing the service. Figure 3–1 presents a list of some widely applicable components of competitive strength. For example, suppose that for a particular service an institution now has the largest share of the market, that its technology for providing the service is superior to that of competition, that its costs of providing the service are lower than that of competition (i.e., its profit margin is higher), and that it has superior personnel for providing the service. If these factors are critical for success, then this service would be rated high in competitive strength.

Just as important, however, as focusing on the firm's strengths is focusing on its weaknesses. If skilled personnel are *critical* for offering the above service and the institution did not have these personnel, then its competitive strength would be moderate at best. You have identified a capability that must be developed before the institution can market this service effectively.

Market Attractiveness.   This dimension focuses on all of the market factors that may influence how the product in question will perform. Obviously, the objective is to offer those products that provide the best opportunities for the institution. Figure 3–1 also presents a list of some

FIGURE 3-1

Portfolio Planning Matrix

		market attractiveness		
		high	medium	low
competitive strength	*high*	A	A	B
	medium	A	B	C
	low	B	C	C

priority levels

A—top priority; invest resources heavily to grow.
B—selective priority; support to maintain share and earnings.
C—low priority; consider elimination or minimize resources assigned to maintain at least a minimal level of profitability.

some components of competitive strength	*some components of market attractiveness*
Institution size	Market size
Share of market	Market growth rate
Customer loyalty	Extent and types of competition
Technology	Market stability
Personnel	Regulatory uncertainty
Image/reputation	Industry capacity
Cost structure	Ratios of fixed costs to value-added
Number and quality of facilities	Cross selling potential
Financial strength	Substitution effects
Management capability	Bargaining power of customers
Capacity	Ease of switching institutions

widely applicable components of market attractiveness. For example, suppose that the market for the product is large and expected to grow, that competitive intensity is normal, and that the product's cross-selling potential is high. If these factors were considered to be important for this product, then the product would be rated high in market attractiveness.

On the other hand, suppose you determine that a particular product will be purchased by demographic groups whose numbers are declining; or that the product appeals only to a small number of large depositors, resulting in strong bargaining power for each customer; or that institutions in the market have "excess capacity" for the product, which could result in price cutting and suddenly narrowed profit margins, especially if high fixed costs are associated with the product. Any of these factors would contribute to a lower rating in market attractiveness for the product.

The basic idea behind the portfolio planning matrix is that a financial institution should concentrate its marketing efforts on those products where the market is relatively attractive *and* where the institution has a strong competitive position. In addition, the portfolio planning matrix makes it very clear that (1) because of finite resources an institution can market only a limited number of products effectively at any given point in time; (2) improving your position depends on the attractiveness of the market (some markets will simply not be worth the effort); and (3) effort alone does not guarantee success. For any product, unless the institution has a strong position to maintain or some competitive advantage to exploit, focusing on market-share objectives or increases in volume will probably result in a misallocation of resources.

Establishing Priorities

The portfolio planning matrix in Figure 3–1 is divided into three zones. When products have been classified, management has a systematic mechanism for establishing priorities in allocating resources for marketing effort.

Priority A Products. These products have been classified as either medium or high in both market attractiveness and competitive strength, suggesting that the institution should "invest and grow." These are the products that you have determined to have the greatest potential for supporting corporate objectives.

Priority B Products. These products have been classified as being medium in overall market attractiveness and competitive strength. For these products, it is usually decided to maintain present levels of market share and profitability rather than to invest and seek growth. In some cases, these products may still be marketed aggressively, but only to carefully selected market segments. For example, IRAs might be marketed only to selected groups that can be reached relatively inexpensively, such as commercial businesses wishing to establish employee retirement plans.

Priority C Products. These products have been classified as being low in both market attractiveness and competitive strength. You should give serious consideration to eliminating such products. However, you may decide to maintain them because they are still marginally profitable, because they attract a customer base that may ultimately prove profitable, or because they provide a community service that is deemed worthwhile by management.

An important final point concerning priorities is that the portfolio planning matrix does not imply that only priority A products should be included in the institution's marketing plan. The term *priority* only reflects the way in which financial and/or human resources should be allocated. Indeed, your marketing plan may include specific objectives for reducing or eliminating marketing support or raising the prices of some services in order to "export" unprofitable business.

Establishing Product Objectives

Product objectives should be the results that your marketing plan is to achieve for each product. Like all objectives, they should be specific and measurable in terms of profitability, volume, and/or market share. Figure 3–2 presents in general terms the basic types of product objectives that are most appropriate for each priority level.

Developing Marketing Strategies

At this point, marketing strategies can be developed that now have an increased chance of succeeding. In other words, you now describe the

---

FIGURE 3–2

General Product Objectives for Different Priority Levels

Priority A products
1. Maintain market share (if it is already high) or volume.
2. Increase market share or volume.
3. Increase primary demand (the total demand for the product, not just the institution's product).

Priority B products
1. Increase or maintain market share or volume, but only in selected customer groups.
2. Improve profitability even at the risk of losing market share.

Priority C products
1. Harvest profits; that is, accept the current volume level for the product and maximize the profits from that volume by not allocating any marketing resources to the product.
2. Eliminate unprofitable business.

FIGURE 3-3

Some General Marketing Strategies

Strategies for influencing primary demand
1. Show new uses for the product.
2. Obtain new users for the product.
3. Increase the rate of use/account size for the product.

Strategies for influencing market share
1. Retain current customers.
2. Export unprofitable customers.
3. Acquire newcomer accounts.
4. Acquire competitors' customers by head-to-head competition.
5. Acquire competitors' customers by differentiated competition.
6. Expand total banking relationship of present customers.
7. Shift current customers to other, higher-profit products.

"game plan" by which you will accomplish the previously set objectives. A marketing strategy should be a coordinated set of decisions on (1) target markets, (2) marketing mix, and (3) marketing expenditure level. A very important contribution of product portfolio analysis is that the information it gathers is used to make these three interrelated decisions more effective ones. Figure 3-3 presents some general marketing strategies.

Once general marketing strategies have been decided upon, specific marketing mixes and resource support must be determined. For example, a strategy of head-to-head competition would involve doing the same things that are being done by competitors but doing them better. Implementing this strategy might involve a marketing mix of more convenient locations and lower prices than are being offered by competitors. On the other hand a strategy of differentiated competition would involve offering something unique such as a special service or a different type of product and is especially appropriate for underdog institutions. Implementing this strategy would involve a marketing mix stressing product innovation and promotion.

MAKING PRODUCT PORTFOLIO ANALYSIS WORK

We believe that product portfolio analysis can contribute to good marketing planning in financial institutions. It does not, however, offer simple solutions for complex planning issues. Among the things that should be kept in mind are the following:

1. Many of the factors involved in classifying products into the matrix can only be done subjectively. For example, it is not an easy matter to quantify factors such as management capability and cross-selling potential. Since subjective assessments must be made, reliability is critical. Thus, multiple and if possible independent perspectives should be solicited. (We saw this approach work recently in a bank where 24 officers were divided into four groups. Each group was asked to develop priority levels for all deposit products. The consistency in the priorities assigned across all four groups was amazing. Consensus had not been reached for only 2 of 20 products. After discussion with the entire group, consensus was also reached for these two products.)

2. Because each product is evaluated on a series of characteristics, there is no standard mathematical procedure for developing a summary rating for either market attractiveness or competitive strength. For example, a product with only modest growth potential might be classified as a priority A product because the market is very stable and the requirements for success match the institution's capabilities. Another product may attain the same rating in spite of low profitability simply because its growth rate and cross-selling potential are very high.

3. Different institutions may give different priority levels to the same product even if they made the same evaluations of the individual components of competitive strength and market attractiveness. This is because each institution may vary in the relative importance that its management attaches to the individual components. For example, an institution with profitability problems will probably attach greater weight to the profitability component of market attractiveness than will an institution that is more concerned with growth. This illustrates why at the opening of the chapter we stated that marketing planning is likely to be more effective if the management of the institution has decided where it would like to go and what kind of institution it wants to be. It then becomes much easier to decide "how" the institution will get there.

4. In establishing priority levels, you must constrain the number of products that can receive top priority, unless, of course, you have an unlimited marketing budget. Thus, some products that might appear to be priority A products may have to be relegated to priority B because the institution cannot give true priority A attention to more than a few products in a given time frame. Forcing decisions on priorities is a great benefit of product portfolio analysis. This is extremely useful to the financial marketer because it forces management to make choices and thus increases the likelihood of marketing success because you are concentrating on activities that have a greater chance of being successful. In other words, product portfolio analysis improves the *effectiveness* of marketing planning by insuring that you are "doing the right things."

5. Top management must support the portfolio planning process at least to the extent of providing input as to the relative importance that should be attached to profitability, growth, stability, and other market attractiveness components. Top-management support is important for two reasons. First, as we have already seen, the process of setting priorities is closely intertwined with the establishment of the institution's overall objectives. Second, unless officers perceive support from top management, they will be unlikely to commit the time and effort necessary for a thorough analysis.

6. Subjective factors notwithstanding, internal and external data bases must be developed and maintained to provide precise and current information on those components of market attractiveness and competitive strength (e.g., costs) that are amenable to measurement.

7. The product portfolio process should be repeated or at least reviewed periodically to accommodate the possibility of industry changes that may rapidly change the attractiveness of a market.[2]

CONFRONTING INTANGIBILITY WITH ELEMENTS OF MARKETING STRATEGY

Financial products are intangible; they are services rather than goods. This is a fact of life that financial marketers must deal with. However, it is our belief that we can, and must, deal more effectively with intangibility from a marketing strategy standpoint. Some nonbank competitors, especially insurance marketers, are doing it, and doing it very well. We believe that part of the problem stems from the fact that we continually use frameworks developed for the marketing of physical products. While many similarities do exist between the marketing of physical products and the marketing of intangible products, some financial marketers often accept without further thought whatever conclusions result from the application of "goods-based" ideas.

For example, on the basis of the concepts developed for the marketing of goods, marketers of services are usually told that the intangibility of services creates several marketing "handicaps" for service marketers. The following "handicaps" are often cited.

1. Because they are intangible, services cannot be separated from the person of the seller. Thus, they must be produced and consumed simultaneously. In other words, goods are produced, sold, and consumed. Services are sold, then produced and consumed simultaneously. Therefore, direct sale is the only feasible means to distribute most services and location is the only major distribution decision.

2. Because they are intangible, services cannot be inventoried, stored, or transported.

3. Since direct sale is the only way to deliver a service, traditional middlemen can rarely operate in service markets. Thus, the geographic region in which the service marketer can operate is limited.

4. Because intangibles cannot appeal to the senses, promotion is extremely difficult, and since we must compete with standardized products (for example, credit is credit), product differentiation is extremely difficult, if not impossible, for marketers of services.

In comparison to physical products, these contentions are true. However, we believe that accepting these goods-based conclusions may be lulling some financial marketers into accepting these "handicaps" as facts of life. More important, we believe that it is undermining our efforts to understand what must be done to effectively market services and from developing means for using elements of marketing strategy to deal with intangibility. In fact, we believe that one of the major goals of marketing strategy in financial marketing must be to confront the problem of intangibility. In the next section, we will focus on this issue.

THE CONCEPT OF INTANGIBILITY

If we are going to try to deal with intangibility with elements of our marketing strategy, we must fully understand the concept. The concept of intangibility has two distinct meanings:[3]

- That which cannot be touched, impalpable.
- That which cannot be easily defined, formulated, or grasped mentally.

Unfortunately, both of these meanings hold true for financial services. In other words, financial services are doubly intangible. Dealing with the intangibility of financial services therefore really involves dealing with two problems. The differences between these problems may appear subtle, but for financial marketers they are important. Each problem must be attacked separately, in different ways, and with different elements of the marketing mix.

Confronting Intangibility with Marketing Strategy

In Figure 3–4 we present a framework for confronting intangibility with marketing strategy. Note that we are addressing both aspects of the concept. In other words, in developing marketing strategy, financial marketers should seek ways to make the service more palpable, that is, more tangible, and/or they should make it easier to grasp mentally. Let us examine each of these tasks.

FIGURE 3–4

Confronting Intangibility with Elements of Marketing Strategy

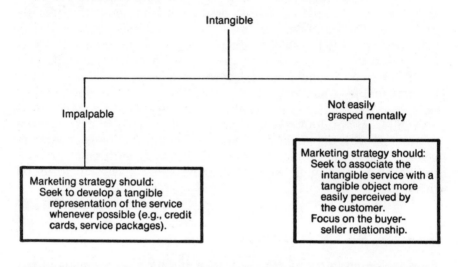

Impalpability. To make a service palpable, the marketer must make the intangible more tangible (that is, "tangibilize" the service). Since this is not possible directly, the only alternative is to *develop a tangible representation* of the service. For example:

1. Credit Cards The credit card is a tangible representation of the service of credit, although it is not the service itself. It has enabled financial institutions, in effect, to overcome each of the supposed "marketing handicaps" just cited. For example:

- It enables customers to "store" an "inventory" of credit for use at their convenience. Thus, it has enabled financial institutions to expand their geographic market by maintaining credit customers far beyond their traditional trading area.
- Because the credit card enables institutions to separate the service from the seller, inseparability is no longer a handicap and direct sale is no longer the only means of distribution for credit. The credit card has enabled financial institutions to utilize the retail merchant as a *middleman* in the distribution of the intangible of credit.
- Because a tangible representation exists, it becomes easier to differentiate the product physically and psychologically, with brand names and reseller support. The major credit cards are physically

different, with different images, customer profiles, target markets, and brand names. Also, financial institutions have been able to utilize the merchant for various types of reseller support in the form of incentive credit card promotions.

2. Service "Packages." When a customer joins the "Preferred Club" and receives a membership card, what the customer actually has is a tangible representation of a group of intangibles. With one-stop shopping, the customer now has an inventory of several financial services. By increasing the availability and convenience of several services, packages may also expand the geographic area in which the institution operates (depending on what services are included in the package). Packages may also expand the distribution of services since the buyer purchases services that might not have been purchased individually. Finally, because they are a tangible representation with a brand name, service packages make product differentation feasible.

In each of these two examples, the intangible has actually been "tangibilized." Thus, if a service can be made tangible in some way, then *impalpability* is no longer a problem and the development of a marketing strategy is much easier since the marketing "handicaps" associated with intangibility are no longer relevant (Retail bank marketers are very familiar with the unwillingness of many customers to surrender their passbook. Part of the reason is certainly the fact that they are giving up a tangible representation of their savings. On the other hand, insurance marketers usually provide leatherbound folders and fancy certificates as tangible evidence of insurance.)

In many cases, it is not possible to develop a tangible representation of an intangible service. In such cases it becomes very important that marketing strategy confront the other aspect of intangibility, that of making it easier for customers to grasp the service mentally.

Not Easily Grasped Mentally. Some of the competitors of financial institution marketers do an excellent job of confronting this aspect of intangibility. We suggest two possible strategies:

1. Association with a Tangible Object More Easily Perceived by the Customer. The objective here is to make the service more tangible in a mental sense. You want to achieve a psychological association of the intangible service with a tangible object that can be more easily perceived by the customer. Insurance marketers do this very well. For example:

"You're in good *hands* with Allstate."
"I've got a piece of the *rock*."

"Under the Travelers *umbrella*."

"The Nationwide *blanket* of protection."

Obviously, hands, rocks, umbrellas, and blankets have nothing to do with insurance, nor does the Kemper Cavalry or the shield of protection. What the insurance marketer is trying to achieve is a mental association between the intangible service and the *benefit* that the customer is seeking. The insurance marketer, in effect, makes it *easier* for the individual to grasp mentally the intangible of insurance. (The Merrill Lynch bull in the china shop or among the quickly sprouting plants achieves it for brokerage services.)

Achieving associations such as these is difficult, since not any tangible object will do. The tangible object must in some way represent the benefit that the customer seeks from the service. The importance of identifying benefits will come up again in our chapter on market segmentation. At this point, let us just say that an exact understanding of what is being purchased by the user (from the user's point of view) is essential. The insurance marketers are effective with this strategy because they know exactly what benefit the buyer seeks from insurance. Otherwise, meaningful associations would not be possible. We see no reason why other financial institutions cannot also utilize this strategy effectively. Before you do so, however, you will need a clear understanding of what benefit the customer seeks from your service, and a large dose of creativity. For example, we know of one financial institution that used plants (a growth symbol) as premiums for new deposits. In our opinion this was a very appropriate tangible object given the purpose of the promotion.

2. *Focus on Buyer-Seller Relationship.* While the intangible service may be difficult to grasp mentally, the "relationship" between the buyer and the seller is not. Thus, astute service marketers may focus on this relationship and not on the service itself. What they actually sell is this "client relationship" rather than the intangible service. The technical competence, skill, concern, and so forth, of the provider of the service does not make the service itself more tangible. However, it focuses attention on the relationship between the buyer and the seller, *which is tangible*. The insurance industry makes excellent use of this approach. The individual is encouraged to identify with the insurance agent rather than the company. The agent is presented as an all-around concerned counselor for the family (e.g., "Like a good neighbor, State Farm is there"). The securities brokerage industry also implements this strategy very well (e.g., "When E. F. Hutton talks, people listen").

We believe that the new environment will force financial institutions to appreciate the strategy, purposes, and implementation of client marketing. Your nonbank competitors do it very well. Turning customers into clients is, in our opinion, one of the many marketing challenges that financial institutions will face during the remainder of this decade. Focusing on the buyer-seller relationship is an excellent strategy for confronting intangibility. Understanding that a service marketer must focus on the buyer-seller relationship is a prerequisite to effectively implementing a strategy of client marketing. Client marketing will be the focus of chapter seven, which is devoted entirely to relationship banking.

CONCLUSION

Marketing plans should be rational approaches to a financial institution's markets and customers. This chapter examined two topics that can be useful during the marketing planning process. The first, product portfolio analysis, can help specify the role that each product should play. Simply put, it's a method to help "evaluate the kids" so as to determine which of them have the potential to grow and deserve resource support, which should be maintained at current levels of support, and which should be demarketed. The product portfolio matrix enables you to concentrate your marketing efforts on products for which the market is relatively attractive *and* the institution has a strong competitive position. We have seen that product portfolio analysis makes a great contribution to the situation analysis and to the objective-setting phases of the marketing planning process.

The concluding section of this chapter confronted the reality that financial institutions market intangibles. What we sought to do was to offer suggestions that could be used when developing marketing strategies for services. We saw that intangibility has two distinct meanings, both of which apply to financial services, and that the problems presented by each of these aspects of intangibility must be attacked separately (see Figure 3–4). Whenever possible, seek to develop a tangible representation of the intangible service. When this can be accomplished, the "marketing handicaps" associated with services become irrelevant. When developing a tangible representation is not possible, or even if it is possible, then your marketing mix must also confront the fact that intangibles are difficult to grasp mentally. We suggested two approaches for doing this: (1) associate the service with a tangible object that is more easily perceived by the customer; and (2) focus on the buyer-seller (client) relationship.

NOTES

1. Some material in this chapter was drawn from Joseph P. Guiltinan and James H. Donnelly, Jr., "The Use of Product Portfolio Analysis in Bank Marketing Planning," *Journal of Retail Banking*, Spring 1983, pp. 15–24; and James H. Donnelly, Jr., "Intangibility and Marketing Strategy for Retail Bank Services," *Journal of Retail Banking*, June 1980, pp. 39–43.

2. The reader wishing in-depth coverage of product portfolio models is encouraged to see Joseph P. Guiltinan and Gordon W. Paul, *Marketing Management: Strategies and Programs* (New York: McGraw-Hill, 1982), pp. 31–44; and David W. Cravens, *Strategic Marketing* (Homewood, Ill.: Richard D. Irwin, 1982), pp. 61–79.

3. See any standard dictionary.

Organizational Structure and Performance*

In previous chapters, we underscored the importance of strategic planning as a crucial management responsibility for dealing with the challenges and opportunities of the contemporary environment. Both strategic and marketing plans enable managers to take an active role in moving their institutions through turbulent times.

Effective managers make a difference in bottom-line performance. For example, studies of high-performance financial institutions confirm that effective management plays a major role in achieving above-average records on measures of profitability and competitiveness. Other factors such as competition, inflation, and economic growth also make a difference. But more and more, we are coming to realize that management skill, knowledge, and ability account for differences in performance among institutions facing similar market and economic factors.

---

*Prepared by James L. Gibson, Professor of Management, University of Kentucky.

One ongoing study of high-performance banks indicates that their managers set financial goals, develop long-range strategies, establish short-range profit plans, and track and reformulate plans.[1] No doubt, many managers of low-performance banks also undertake these activities, but with quite different effects. The effects are different because the real cause of performance differences is not the process or form of these managerial activities, but their content. The content of these managerial activities relates to success in pricing loans and services, minimizing loan losses, controlling manageable costs, limiting fixed-asset commitments, and maximizing investment income.

Thus, it is not enough to say that effective managers set objectives, develop both strategic and marketing plans, and track progress toward the achievement of the objectives set. These actions in and of themselves do not make the difference. They may enable a financial institution to achieve mediocrity in a systematic way, but that is all one can say. More important, one cannot say that effective managers are experts in granting credit, making investments, and pricing services. Many different employees contribute to these activities. The responsibility of management is to assure that the activities are performed at a high level of competence in coordination with related activities.

Managers are not accountable for the doing of work but for seeing that work is done. We believe that the most important managerial responsibility is to create settings that encourage and reward the best efforts of every employee. One important element of such settings is an effective organizational structure. In the pages that follow, we will describe the purposes of organizational structure and identify two different structural types. We will then suggest how financial institution managers can maximize the contribution of organizational structure to performance.

PURPOSES OF ORGANIZATIONAL STRUCTURES

Organizational structures enable financial institution managers to perform two different, and often conflicting, managerial tasks: (1) dividing work and (2) coordinating work.[2] In a sense, these two tasks suggest that managers must take apart the work of their institution and then put it back together. In fact, that is exactly what organizational structure is all about. When the work is divided into specialized jobs, the total task is "taken apart." When these jobs are linked through managerial coordination, the total task is "put back together." These two tasks are relevant ideas for understanding the importance of organizational structure.

Dividing Work

The idea of dividing work acknowledges that a financial institution needs different people to do different jobs. As an institution develops additional products and customers that are unlike those it currently provides and serves, additional division of work becomes necessary. An example of this process occurs when an institution becomes large enough to support a trust department. Management then finds that this new product involves special expertise that is different from the expertise currently available. To provide the services of a trust department, the job of trust officer is created and assigned to an individual. This new job represents further division of work among the individuals in the institution. Managers in every industry encounter the need for different skills and abilities as they develop new services and products. The important point is that there is an inevitable and direct relationship between the development of new products and customers and the need for division of work.

Coordinating Work

Coordinating work refers to the ways in which managers integrate the work of the individual jobs and units. As an institution's work becomes increasingly divided, the necessity for coordination intensifies. Different, divided jobs involve diverse actions and decisions. If left alone, individuals will tend to take actions that make sense from the perspective of their specialty but that may not be in the best interest of the total organization.

One way to integrate different jobs is through the chain of command. The purpose of managerial levels is to clarify matters of authority: who is to be doing what at what time. Another important way in which managers can achieve coordinated effort is through precise definitions of job and unit duties and objectives. If management defines the job of the institution's marketing department to include responsibility for *all* of its marketing programs, it has, in effect, integrated the marketing function into the other functional areas of the institution.

Coordinated effort can also be achieved through planning, through policies, and, in some instances, through informal understandings about who is to do what. But as a financial services organization takes on more and different activities, coordination becomes not only more important but also more difficult. It is simply easier to coordinate the efforts of individuals and units that perform the same job or the same function. Different jobs require not only different skills and abilities but also different attitudes and different ways of looking at problems. For example, marketing people and operations people not only do different jobs; they also have different perceptions of issues and problems. Managers who have sat in problem-solving meetings with representatives of the various functional units in a financial institution fully understand the difficulty of achieving integrated solutions to problems that involve numerous specialties.

The president of a midwestern bank described just such an incident to one of the authors. It seems that the bank had decided to enter the credit card business. Immediately, a feud developed between two departments over the question of which should have control of that business. Each department's manager had good reasons to support his position and was unwilling to yield to the other. The president's solution was to allow each department to have its own credit card, with the bank having two credit cards.

CHARACTERISTICS OF ORGANIZATIONAL STRUCTURES

Even though organizational structures exist for only two purposes, dividing and coordinating, they can have many different characteristics. Managers have considerable latitude when it comes to deciding how to divide and coordinate work. Those of us who have worked in various organizations know that there are many differences in organizational structures. Consequently, we have coined a number of terms that enable us to describe these differences.

We describe differences in organizational structure in both objective and subjective terms. Important characteristics of organizational structure are described by such objective terms as the number and kinds of different jobs, the number of managerial levels, the number of people supervised, the number and kinds of decisions made, and the number and kinds of committees and task forces. Subjective terms such as bureaucratic, autocratic, democratic, formal, informal, and the like also describe organizational structures. These descriptive terms enable us to compare and contrast organizational structures. And what we find is that these structures are different even within the same industry and among firms that serve the same markets with essentially similar products and services.

Those of us who work in organizations tend to think of structure in rather narrow terms, whether objectively or subjectively. We think in terms of our own job responsibilities and duties, whom we report to, whom we must please, and whether we have sufficient authority to meet our responsibilities. These characteristics refer to our particular jobs, which is a narrow, however meaningful, perspective. Financial institution managers must take a broader view. They must think in terms that define the structure itself, *not* the jobs that it comprises. We can use three terms—*specialization, centralization,* and *formalization*—to describe and analyze an organization's structure.

Specialization is the degree to which the overall task has been divided among the different jobs. Specialization can result from adding more tasks to what is already done or from further division of the present tasks. The degree of specialization is an outcome of dividing work; the more extensive the division of work, the more highly specialized is the structure.

Centralization is the degree to which the authority to make decisions is concentrated in the jobs of those in top management. As authority is delegated downward, the structure becomes less centralized, or more decentralized. The degree of centralization is the outcome of both dividing and coordinating work.

Formalization is the degree to which rules, procedures, and policies exist in written form. Written documents are the final arbiters of actions and decisions, and they are outcomes of coordinating work.

The relationships between these three characteristics and the purposes of organizational structure are shown in Figure 4–1. The figure shows that centralization is the result of both dividing and coordinating work. Specialization is the result of dividing work; formalization is the result of coordinating work.

We cannot measure absolutely any one of the three characteristics. We must be content to think in terms of relative distinctions. It is helpful to know that these three characteristics tend to be correlated. Thus, a particular financial institution tends to be relatively specialized, centralized, and formal or relatively nonspecialized, decentralized, and informal. But to establish that organizational structures are different is not very important unless we can determine whether the differences make a difference. We shall now examine the relationship between organizational structure and performance.

ORGANIZATIONAL STRUCTURE AND PERFORMANCE

The contribution of organizational structure to the performance of a financial institution is demonstrated, for example, every time an employee satisfies a customer's financial needs, makes a profitable loan, develops a new product, or devises a cost-reduction program. These examples indicate that people are doing their jobs in a competent and motivated manner. When employees do not do these things either well or at all, the chances are that the fault can be found in the organization.

FIGURE 4–1

Purposes and Characteristics of Organizational Structure

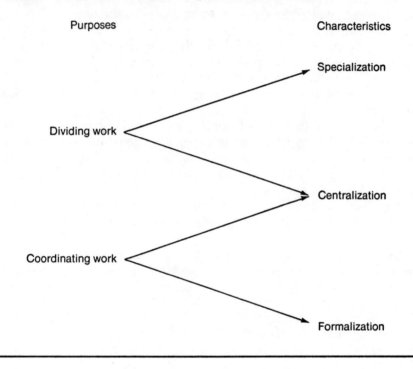

Purposes   Characteristics

An effective organizational structure enables qualified people to do their best work.

Many studies have shown that organizational structure and organizational performance are related. These studies have, by and large, taken place in industrial settings, yet the conclusions drawn are applicable in other settings. The gist of these conclusions is that *different organizational structures facilitate the accomplishment of different strategies in relation to the environments that the organization faces.* The organizational structure must be congruent with the demands of the environment and the strategy that management adopts to exploit that environment.

Spokespersons for the financial services industry have in recent years urged managers to evaluate their practices in the light of the new environment of deregulation and competition. Eugene Looper stated the issue quite well when he wrote: "The fundamental problem in management is how to overcome the past through techniques employed in the present in such a way that the future is developed."[3] In many financial institutions, managers have begun to implement management by objectives, job enrichment, and quality circles. The rationale for adopting these practices is usually stated in terms of increasing productivity, improving employee morale, and accelerating the quantity and quality of innovative ideas. But why the interest in these ends? Haven't the managers of financial institutions always been interested in productivity, employee morale, and ideas? The answer is, of course, yes. But the contemporary environment raises the stakes and the risks for success and failure. The performance edge will go to those institutions that are capable of generating timely proactive and reactive responses to changing demands. Consequently, organizational structures of the future must encourage flexible and adaptable behavior of employees. In a practical sense, this involves designing a structure that is market-oriented rather than function-oriented.

FUNCTION-ORIENTED AND MARKET-ORIENTED STRUCTURES

Many forms of organizational structures exist in the financial services industry. A specific bank, savings and loan association, or credit union will organize in ways that reflect its personnel strength, history, tradition, and even legal requirements. However, the many variations on the themes of specialization, centralization, and formalization tend toward one or the other of two general organizational types: organizations may be viewed as either *function-oriented* or *market-oriented*. In this section, we will describe these two types, but we must acknowledge at the outset the almost infinite variety that we find in the world of business organizations. The reduction of such variety to only two types enables us to make some sense of that complexity, not to deny that it exists.

Function-Oriented Structures

The identifying characteristic of function-oriented structures is the use of the functions of the particular business as the basis for identifying which departments will report to the CEO. In manufacturing companies, departments such as production, sales, finance, personnel, and engineering will be placed at the highest level in the organization. The placement of these units reflects the dominant concern of top management—to achieve efficiencies through the integration of the important functions of the business. In such organizations, the chain of command will be lengthy, with many different managerial positions and levels that supervise people doing rather narrowly specialized jobs. The driving force in such organizations is often the production department since its activities reflect the primary concern of management.

Function-oriented structures work quite well in relatively stable, predictable, and certain environments. In such environments, the dominant managerial concern is to obtain efficiency of operations. Because function-oriented structures are highly *specialized, centralized,* and *formalized,* they encourage and reward employees for "doing things right"—for being efficient. In such structures, managers can define the expected activities and decisions of individuals with great precision and detail. The scope of each employee's contribution to overall objectives is intendedly limited. Important decisions are the exclusive province of top management. The routineness of day-to-day activities enables managers to develop extensive rules and procedures to govern nearly every action and decision.

The attitude of employees is to achieve accuracy and efficiency in every department and job. Individual initiative is discouraged because detailed job specifications and procedures remove the necessity for independent judgment. Employees learn that they are paid to do their jobs according to the rules and to restrict their attention to those matters for which they are explicitly accountable.

In the context of financial services, the two basic business functions are: (1) receiving and accounting for the deposits and withdrawals of personal, commercial, governmental, and institutional customers (operations), and (2) making loans to those and other customers (loans). The use of these two functions as the basis for primary departments reporting to the CEO reflects their importance to the performance of financial institutions. As a consequence of historical practice and employee training programs, operations and loan specialists have reached exceptionally high levels of expertise and efficiency.

As the financial institution's customer and service base increases, the commitment to efficiency persists. In response to the increased workload associated with more customers and services, the institution continues to create specialized functional units. For example, trust departments and investment departments are usually the first new departments to be added once the institution passes the $50 million asset mark. With time and the acquisition of appropriately skilled personnel, an asset management department will emerge. Thus, function-oriented organizational structures become exceedingly complex and the CEO eventually becomes a referee of territorial squabbles among the competing specialties. Figure 4–2 depicts a typical function-oriented structure for a bank. Other financial services firms would have similar functional departments reporting to the CEO.

FIGURE 4–2

The Function-Oriented Structure

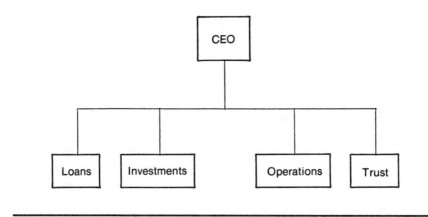

The use of the function-oriented structure is so widespread in financial institutions that industry leaders refer to it as the "traditional" organizational form. Its popularity reflects its successful achievement of efficient operations. And its success is due to its exploitation of the benefits of specialization of labor, centrally directed decision making, and highly routinized ways of getting work done. The structure is viable so long as the environment is relatively certain, predictable, and unchanging. Specialization, centralization, and formalization are most advantageous when the organization does not have to deal with unusual or exceptional environmental circumstances.

But once the environment becomes uncertain, unpredictable, and dynamic, the advantages of function-oriented structures become their disadvantages. By virtue of their emphasis on efficiency and operations, they encourage and reward fixation on the tried-and-true ways of doing things. They attract people who value certainty and closure. Adventuresome and risk-taking individuals either leave the organization or lose their zeal because they have not been encouraged. The structure does not encourage the development of individuals who can cope with the demands of a competitive environment. But the structure tends to persist so long as the customer and service base remains unchallenged.

Financial institutions often cope with the first signs of a challenge to their customer and service base by turning to the marketing function. In most instances, the function already exists, but its primary purposes are public relations and advertising. The marketing function may be elevated to an organizational level on a par with other functional units such as the operations, loans, investments, and trust departments depicted in Figure 4–2. But the marketing department is often equivalent to the other functions only on the organization chart: The operational efficiency orientation remains deeply embedded, and when key decisions are made, they reflect efficiency criteria rather than effectiveness criteria.

The appearance of marketing departments in the organizational structure of operations-dominated and function-oriented financial institutions reflects a transitional state. These institutions are in the ending stages of their commitment to operations and in the beginning stages of their understanding of and commitment to markets. How short or protracted this transitional stage will be depends on the intensity of competitive pressures and on the rapidity with which management recognizes the deficiencies of the present organizational structure. If the pressures are extremely intense and are evidenced by deterioration of the customer and service base, the function-oriented structure becomes increasingly incompatible with market-oriented strategies.

The problems of function-oriented structures present themselves in many ways. One rather common way was experienced in a large western bank that had recruited and trained a group of sales officers to call on middle-market businesses. The group was very capable and was compensated with both salary and commission. In the first week on the job, one of its members was told by a prospect that he would transfer $300,000 in deposits to the bank in exchange for a loan discount. The sales officer stated that he did not have the authority to approve the discount and would have to consult the commercial loan officer. The response of the latter was, "What's in it for me?"

The financial services industry has relied on function-oriented structures throughout its recent history, particularly since 1933. Regulation discouraged competition and aggressive market and product development and encouraged efficient operations. Over the years, the industry has developed an admiration for operations efficiency that discourages consideration of the merits of an alternative organizational structure—the market-oriented type.

Market-Oriented Structures

The defining characteristic of market-oriented structures is the elevation in status of customer and market-based departments to the top level in the organization. For example, market-oriented departments such as real estate banking, corporate banking, and consumer banking report directly to the CEO, thus reflecting their importance. An example of a market-oriented organization in banking is shown in Figure 4–3. The placement of units whose primary concern is satisfying prod-

FIGURE 4–3

The Market-Oriented Structure

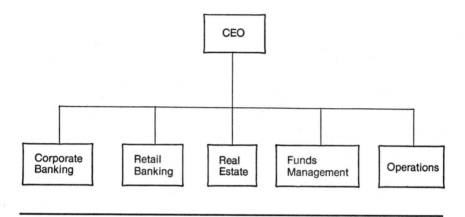

uct and customer concerns at the top of the organization reflects the priority of top management—to do the right things as reflected by being in the right markets with the right products. The organization looks outward to its markets for sources of information and insight that permit survival. The chain of command is relatively short, with fewer management positions than exist in function-oriented structures. Middle-management positions tend to disappear from market-oriented structures as individuals learn self-management and accept the overall purposes of the organization as their own.

Market-oriented structures are compatible with uncertain and changing environments. Such structures facilitate the actions and decisions that are required in order to adapt to changing environmental forces and to achieve effectiveness. These structures are relatively *despecialized, decentralized,* and *informal.* The typical job is relatively broad in scope, with considerable latitude for individual discretion in decision making. Jobs are defined in terms of expected outcomes rather than required actions. Employees understand their contribution to the overall objectives of the organization. If the bank with two credit cards referred to earlier had had a market-oriented structure, its managers would have settled the dispute according to organizational, not departmental, objectives. Decision making is done throughout the organization by individuals who have the necessary expertise. The primary criterion for participating in decision making is expertness, not position in the hierarchy. Shared understandings of expected behavior replace rules and procedures.

Market-oriented structures encourage employees to do the right thing—to be effective. Challenging the status quo and experimenting with new ways of doing things are the rule rather than the exception. Individuals are expected to seize every opportunity to satisfy customer needs and to take an interest in all aspects of the business. Adaptive and flexible behavior is the norm.

In addition to changing the bases of the departments that report to the CEO from functions to markets, the market-oriented structure introduces new jobs. Jobs such as product managers and sales representatives are created and assume important roles in decision making. Similar jobs may also be found in function-oriented structures, but they tend to attain their fullest potential in organizations that have made an unambiguous commitment to market and product development.

The role of product manager is a response to the need to create and develop new products. In such banks as Chase Manhattan, the roles of product managers have become important since deregulation. The role of product manager is widespread in industries that produce consumer goods—General Foods and General Mills pioneered the idea in the food processing industry. The product manager takes ideas and turns them into realities. Product managers reduce the chances that new products will be operations-driven but not market-compatible.[4]

Product managers are often the most visible changes in the structures of financial institutions embarking on market-driven strategies. Their duties and responsibilities vary from institution to institution. Generally, they are accountable for all activities associated with developing, pricing, promoting, selling, and servicing the new product. Once the new product is established in the product line, responsibility for these activities reverts to customer-contact people.

The other important jobs that emerge in market-oriented structures are those of sales representatives.[5] The role of sales representatives is to represent and sell the products and services of the organization to present and future customers. The sales representatives are out and about seeking new business. They also maintain offices to counsel customers regarding their financial needs. They specialize in knowing and anticipating the present and future needs of particular customer groups. The exact configuration of customer groups depends on the demographic and economic characteristics of the service area. The bank whose structure is depicted in Figure 4–3 has identified the real estate industry as a key customer group. Institutions without this orientation would not have such a unit, of course. Growing and developing markets include every class of commercial and consumer customer types. Rural and small communities have quite different customer segments, no doubt dominated by the needs of agricultural and small business customers.

Market-oriented structures are designed to take maximum advantage of shifting market and industry developments. They encourage every employee, not only sales representatives, to be problem-solving, sales-oriented, and committed to institution-wide purposes. There is no personal advantage to "protecting one's specialized turf." Decision making takes advantage of all the expertise in the organization without regard to specialty or status. The departmentalized mentality fostered by functional specialization is supplanted by organizational commitment.

The cost of market-oriented structures in comparison to function-oriented structures is, of course, loss of efficiency. Market-oriented structures do not take maximum advantage of the economies of specialization. The dominant jobs in such structures are relatively despecialized. Employees must be expert in their specialties, but they must be knowledgeable about all products, services, and operations. Strategies such as relationship banking and cross-selling require breadth of knowledge as well as unquestioned expertise in the needs of the customer and the market. In addition, the use of group decision making and delegated authority involves greater time and effort than does one-person, centralized decision making. Finally, the necessary absence of rules and procedures often involves trial and error testing of solutions.[6] These costs are inherent in the market-oriented structure, but the loss of efficiency is offset by the increase in effectiveness.

The important distinctions between the function-oriented and market-oriented organizational structure are presented in Figure 4–4.

FIGURE 4–4

Function-Oriented versus Market-Oriented Structures

function-oriented	*market-oriented*
Dominant characteristics:	*Dominant characteristics:*
Highly specialized	Highly unspecialized
Highly centralized	Highly decentralized
Highly formalized	Highly informalized
Secondary characteristics:	*Secondary characteristics:*
Detailed job description	Generally undetailed job descriptions
Lengthy chain of command	Short chain of command
Functional departments	Product/customer departments
Efficiency-oriented attitudes	Effectiveness-oriented attitudes
Compatible environments:	*Compatible environments:*
Stable, predictable, certain	Unstable, unpredictable, uncertain
Dominant values:	*Dominant values:*
Efficiency and operations inflexibility	Effectiveness and marketing flexibility

These two types should be viewed as extremes of a continuum that contains many shades of differences.

The appropriate organizational structure depends on the institution's primary strategy in relation to its environment. If adaptiveness and flexibility are the keys to performance, then managers should consider the applicability of market-oriented structures. Some observers suggest that financial institutions really have no choice in the matter and that they must undergo changes in their organizational structures.[7] The "business as usual" strategy will simply not work, and if that strategy won't work, traditional function-oriented structures won't work. But how does a manager go about the difficult process of changing an organizational structure? That question is addressed in the following section.

MANAGERS MUST MANAGE ORGANIZATIONAL STRUCTURE

The realization that organizational structure contributes to performance emphasizes the attitude that managers must manage structure. There is a tendency to permit structure to manage managers. The existing structure is inevitably a force for stability because stability is one reason for and benefit of its existence. Individuals become comfortable in their jobs as they develop competence and knowledge to perform the tasks, make the decisions, and deal with other individuals. They quite naturally resist threatened disruption to the status quo. Thus, the benefit of stability can become a liability when change is necessary.

Managing organizational change involves devising ways to overcome resistance to change. Although the details will differ from instance to instance, the general principles of successful change efforts will be the same, regardless of the specific setting. Adherence to the following five principles of change improves the odds that the actual outcome targeted by management will be realized.

Top-Management Commitment Is Imperative

The first principle is that top management must be committed to the idea that a fundamental change in structure is necessary. The evidence of top management's commitment is willingness to become actively involved in all the processes required to bring about the change. If training and retraining are required, top management is in the classroom along with other employees. If goal setting is part of the required change, top management sets goals along with everyone else. The jobs of top management are as much a part of the organizational structure as any other jobs, and changing an organizational structure involves changing all jobs in some way.

The first indication that structural changes are required is the acknowledgement by managers that they don't have the people to embark on an aggressive product or market development strategy. "We can't compete with Merrill Lynch because we don't have the horses," as many financial institution executives were heard to say. The reason they don't have the people is that function-oriented structures do not provide for such skills and talents. A seemingly simple solution to the problem would be to go out and hire sales and marketing people and graft their functions onto the present structure. But that solution is seldom satisfactory because the organizational culture has created an ingrained preference for operations, not marketing, among employees. In financial institutions throughout the country, undue strain continues to be experienced between marketing and operations because each views the other as a competitive rather than complementary force in the organization.

A firm commitment to changing structure reflects management's rejection of the quick-fix approach. Informed managers understand that structure is a principal source of employees' perceptions of what is right, what is expected, and what is rewarded. The structure of jobs and authority provides a continuous flow of information. The history of management is replete with accounts of failed efforts to bring about organizational change. The most often cited explanation for failures is that top managers were either not committed to the effort or that they did not demonstrate their commitment by word and, more important, by deed.

Organizational Strategy Must Precede Structure

The second principle states that management must define and devise strategy first and structure second. Strategy should precede structure. What may seem obvious in the abstract often becomes less obvious in reality. Strategic analysis begins with the environment and then proceeds to the distinctive competencies of the institution. But the distinctive competencies of most financial institutions have been operations-related competencies. The existing structure saw to that. An expedient and often compelling tendency is to permit the operations-oriented competency to overwhelm signals from the environment that sales and marketing competencies are required. In this instance, organizational structure is preceding strategy. Operations efficiency can be a vital resource in a product development strategy. But the order of analysis is to establish the appropriateness of the strategy and then to test the adequacy of the organizational structure.

Persistence Pays Off

The third principle requires managers to persist in their efforts to explain and promote the importance of organizational change. Persistence involves keeping on even when success seems remote. To stay the course in the face of adversity reflects persistence. Thomas J. Peters and Robert H. Waterman, Jr., in their publishing phenomenon—*In Search of Excellence*—reestablish the importance of managerial personality as a factor in business success. Managers instill the organizational values and mold the organizational culture. IBM's T. J. Watson, Jr., Dana Corporation's René McPherson, and AT&T's J. D. deButts are examples of individuals who have created high-performance organizations through sheer force of will and persistence. A lesser individual than deButts, for example, might have been intimidated by the enormous change required to turn AT&T from an operations-driven telephone utility to a market-driven communications business. To make that strategic change, AT&T had to change one out of every three jobs. When one considers that AT&T employed a million people, the magnitude of deButts' responsibility can be appreciated. The organizational change at AT&T will no doubt be the largest such change in American industrial history. However, the financial services industry has witnessed similar massive overhauls of structure. The most publicized one has been Citicorp's reorganization to meet what its former chairman, Walter Wriston, described as "the greatest financial revolution in American history."[8] The change involved nearly all of Citicorp's 52,000 employees.

Highly visible managers who unfailingly articulate the meaning and importance of the institution's plan for the future are indispensable elements of success. Their persistence reflects the importance of the undertaking.

Reward and Reinforcement

The fourth principle is to reward the behavior called for by the new strategy and structure. Management can dispense a variety of monetary and nonmonetary rewards. It is imperative that those rewards be channeled to the individuals whose performance is consistent with the strategy. This principle, similar to the preceding three, is deceptively simple. But common knowledge and common sense inform us that pay, promotion, status, and privilege are historically founded and tradition-bound. The existing reward system reflects all that the management has previously considered valuable. Moreover, the system has built-in safeguards to protect employees from changes in criteria. Yet criteria must change and the system must change. It makes little sense to expound the importance of being customer-oriented but promote on the basis of teller error-rates. The implementation of this principle requires managerial courage, as well as persistence.

Compensation and promotion present particular difficulties in market-oriented structures because of the shortened chain of command. There are fewer gradations of authority and, consequently, fewer opportunities for upward promotion. Compensation plans must be more carefully drawn to reflect real contributions to strategic objectives among employees at the same managerial level. It is possible in relatively "flat" organizations to spread out what have been traditional management perks such as time off for personal business, club membership, and expense accounts. When the prevailing attitude toward compensation reflects accomplishment rather than authority, rewards can be distributed in more imaginative and instrumental ways.[9]

Change Takes Time

The fifth principle acknowledges the importance of time. Significant change is not achieved overnight. Organizational change takes time because it involves reeducating existing personnel to accept the new behavior. If time is not allowed, the seeds of eventual failure are sown. As a commercial for an auto maintenance product puts it: "You can pay me now or pay me later." If in the interest of expediency, an organizational change is forced upon employees, they are unlikely to buy it. And the enthusiasm of top management is unlikely to persuade them that the change is good for them.

The exact manner in which a financial services organization changes from operations-oriented to market-oriented strategies must necessarily reflect local circumstances. Changing the organizational structure must likewise reflect local circumstances. *Perhaps the only circumstance that pervades all firms in all industries is that once strategy has been defined and devised, its realization is made possible by the organizational structure.*

CONCLUSION

The foregoing discussion stresses the importance of matching organizational structure and organizational strategy. Maximum performance is attained when there is a congruence between structure and strategy. Because the financial services industry has confronted a relatively unchanging and regulated environment for the past 50 years, a form of organizational structure has evolved that enables it to achieve operations-oriented strategic objectives. The contemporary environment has shifted to one that rewards market orientation, and the traditional organizational structure is incompatible with that orientation. A prime responsibility of managers is to assume an active role in the transformation of their organization's structure. Making this transformation will require commitment, talent, and time.

NOTES

1. William Ford and Dennis Olson, "Profitability: Why Do Some Banks Perform Better than Others?: An In-Depth Analysis," *Bankers Magazine*, October 1978, pp. 38–45.
2. James L. Gibson, John M. Ivancevich, and James H. Donnelly, Jr., *Organizations: Behavior, Structure, Processes*, 5th ed. (Plano, Tex.: Business Publications, 1985).
3. Eugene Looper, "Framework for Managing a Multiunit Organization," *Magazine of Bank Administration*, July 1979, p. 43.
4. John H. Shain and Francis X. Shea, "How Product Management Can Work in Banking," *ABA Banking Journal*, July 1981, pp. 100–102, 109.
5. Mary E. Bird and W. D. Beynon, "Organizing the Productive Bank," *Magazine of Bank Administration*, November 1979, pp. 30–35.
6. Donald Jacobs, Joseph Moag, and Robert Duncan, "Developing New Models of Bank Organization Design," *Journal of Contemporary Business*, Summer 1977, pp. 1–13.
7. R. D. Shapiro and L. V. Durland, Jr., "Changing the Organization," *National Underwriter—Life and Health Insurance*, June 26, 1982, pp. 17, 26.
8. Alena Wels, "How Citicorps Restructured for the 'Eighties," *Euromoney*, April 1980, pp. 13–24.
9. Rick Kemmer, "Managing Group Behavior in Your Bank," *Magazine of Bank Administration*, September 1980, pp. 44–45.

PART THREE

Strategic Marketing

"Nichemanship, which has now become an industry buzzword, is based on several principles. It
recognizes that the market is not homogeneous
and certain subgroups are more profitable than
others. It acknowledges that resources are limited and must be focused. It also recognizes that
consumers have become more sophisticated
and, with the availability of more appealing
choices, are beginning to expect more than just
the basics. Clearly the concept is taking hold."

William J. Klaisle,
"Developing a Niche Strategy,"
Bank Marketing, *December 1983*

5

Market Segmentation

This chapter begins a three-chapter sequence on important aspects of strategic marketing. As you will see, relationship banking and market positioning are the subjects of two of the chapters. It is important to understand that a prerequisite to effectively implementing relationship banking and a sound positioning strategy is a clear understanding of the concept of market segmentation. Market segmentation is the subject of this chapter.

Ask a financial marketer what market segmentation is, and he or she will probably say something like "Marketing your products to specific groups of customers." Although this statement is certainly true, unfortunately it tells us absolutely nothing about what market segmentation really is and what it involves. More important, if the depth of the financial marketer's understanding of the concept of market segmentation is represented by the statement, then effective relationship banking and positioning strategies are unlikely to result from that understanding.

This chapter is included here because we find misunderstanding among financial marketers of the concept of market segmentation. Perhaps such misunderstanding exists because on the surface the concept appears easy to understand and has great commonsense appeal. We often find misunderstanding among people who think that this is the case. The objective of this chapter, therefore, will be to communicate a clear understanding of the concept of market segmentation—to make clear what market segmentation really is and what it really involves. Only on the basis of such an understanding can one effectively implement such applications of market segmentation as market positioning and relationship banking. Thus, this chapter focuses on knowledge and the next two chapters focus on the application of that knowledge.

Market segmentation may be the critical marketing skill for financial institutions in the new environment. In fact, the primary reason for attempting to understand customer needs and behavior is to provide bases for effective segmentation and a large portion of marketing research is concerned with segmentation. From a marketing management point of view, selecting the appropriate target market is of paramount importance to the development of successful marketing strategies. Simply put, yesterday segmentation was merely helpful for financial institutions; today and tomorrow it is either segment or die.

THE PROCESS OF MARKET SEGMENTATION

The logic of market segmentation is quite simple: market segmentation is based on the idea that a single product can seldom meet the needs and wants of *all* customers because customers are usually too numerous, widely scattered, and varied in their buying requirements and buying practices. Typically, customers vary as to their needs, wants, and preferences for products and services, and successful marketers adapt their marketing strategies to fulfill these preference patterns. For example, even a simple product such as a credit card meets different preferences (credit, convenience, prestige, independence) of various customers. While a single product cannot meet the needs of all customers, it can almost always meet the needs of more than one customer. Thus, there are usually *groups of customers* who can be served well by a single product. If a particular group can be served *profitably* by a financial institution, then it is a viable market segment and the institution should develop a marketing mix to serve that group or market segment. In most cases, different institutions will be in the best position to serve particular segments of the market. Therefore, instead of competing everywhere, an institution should identify the most attractive parts of the market that it can serve effectively. Identification of those parts of the market is, hopefully, the output of the process of market segmentation.

From a practical standpoint, the process of market segmentation involves dividing a market into groups of similar customers and selecting the most appropriate group or groups for the institution to serve. We break down the process of market segmentation analysis into six steps,

FIGURE 5–1

The Process of Market Segmentation

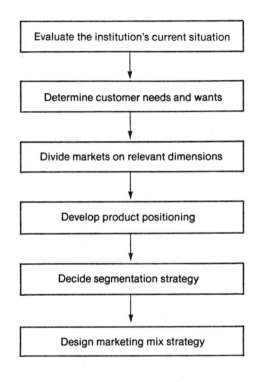

as shown in Figure 5–1.[1] While we recognize that the order of these steps may vary, depending on the institution and the situation, there are few, if any, times when market segmentation analysis can be ignored. In fact, even if the final decision is to "mass-market," that is, remain an "all-things-to-all-people bank" and not segment at all, that decision should be reached only *after* a market segmentation analysis has been conducted. Then, at least the decision will be based on a sound analysis rather than solely on the fact that the institution has always been such an institution. Thus, market segmentation analysis is a cornerstone of sound marketing planning and decision making.

Evaluate the Institution's Current Situation

As emphasized in our planning chapters, a financial institution must conduct a complete situation analysis when embarking on a new or modified strategy. At the marketing planning level, such an analysis aids in determining the objectives, opportunities, and constraints to be considered when selecting target markets and developing marketing strategies. In addition, marketing management must have a clear idea of the amount of financial and other resources that will be available for developing and executing a marketing plan. Thus, the inclusion of this first step in the market segmentation process is intended to be a reminder of the tasks that must be performed prior to such marketing planning steps as objective setting.

Determine Customer Needs and Wants

Successful marketing in general and successful segmentation in particular depend on discovering and satisfying needs and wants of existing or potential customers. In some cases, this idea is quite operational. For example, suppose a bank holding company with a great deal of capital wants to diversify into new markets. A bank in this situation may seek to discover a broad variety of unsatisfied needs. In most cases, however, an organization's current business domain specifies the boundaries of its need satisfaction activities. For example, a retail-oriented institution may seek more efficient means for serving the total financial needs of its customers.

As a practical matter, new technology often brings about an investigation of customer needs and wants for a new or modified product or service. In such situations, the institution is seeking the group of customers whose needs and wants can best be satisfied by the new or modified product or service. Further, at a strategic level, customer needs and wants are usually translated into more operational concepts. For example, customer attitudes, preferences, and benefits sought, which are determined through marketing research, are commonly used for segmentation purposes.

Divide Markets on Relevant Dimensions

In this important step, which is often considered to be the whole of market segmentation, customers are grouped on the basis of one or more similarities and treated as a homogeneous segment of a heterogeneous total market. Thus, markets are viewed, not as homogeneous, but as heterogeneous wholes made up of homogeneous segments. Three critical questions must be considered here:

1. Should the segmentation be a priori or post hoc?
2. How does one determine the relevant dimensions or bases to use for segmentation?
3. What are some bases for segmenting retail and corporate markets?

These three questions must be answered if a financial institution is to conduct a true segmentation analysis.

A Priori versus Post Hoc Segmentation. Real-world segmentation usually follows one of two general patterns.[2] An a priori segmentation approach is one in which the institution has decided on the appropriate basis for segmentation *in advance* of doing any research on a market. For example, a corporate marketer may divide the market on the amount of company sales and a retail marketer may divide the market on the basis of income or net worth. Segmentation research is then conducted to determine the size of each of the groups within the chosen basis and their demographic and/or psychographic profiles. Thus, one bank has segmented its retail customers a priori on the basis of income and net worth as follows:

1. *Upscale market.*   This segment is made up of executives/professionals who comprise the top 10 percent of the bank's clients. Their net worth is at least $250,000, and their income is at least $50,000 a year. Special attention is given to the top 1 percent, identified as preferred clients. Their income tops $100,000; their net worth is more than $1 million; and they have deposits of at least $25,000.

2. *Middle market.*   This segment is made up of the next 20 percent of the bank's clients. It consists of professionals with deposits of $5,000 or more.

3. *Mass market.*   This segment is made up of the remaining 70 percent of the bank's customers. It consists of consumers who are seeking convenience.

In this example of a priori market segmentation, the bank decided in advance the appropriate basis for segmentation and then conducted marketing research (in this case, focus groups) to help it define the products and services that each segment needed and the appropriate means for delivering them. The result was a retail banking group organized around three departments, each serving one of the segments.

Post hoc segmentation is an approach in which customers are grouped into segments *on the basis of research findings*. For example, an institution may interview a sample of corporate treasurers to find out what these people believe they need in the way of financial services and then group customers according to the responses and use these groupings as the basis for market segments.

There is no doubt that financial services companies use a priori segmentation to a much greater extent than post hoc segmentation. This may be due in part to the fact that post hoc segmentation requires more sophisticated and costly marketing research and analysis.

Both approaches are valuable, and which should be used depends in part on how well the institution knows the market for the particular product in question. If through previous research and experience a financial marketer has successfully isolated a number of key market dimensions, then an a priori approach based on them may provide more useful information. In the case of segmentation for entirely new products, a post hoc approach may be useful for determining key market dimensions. However, even when a post hoc approach is used, some consideration must be given to the variables to be included in the research design. Thus, some consideration must be given to the relevant segmentation dimensions regardless of which approach is used.

Relevance of Segmentation Dimensions. Unfortunately, there is no simple way of determining the relevant dimensions for segmenting markets. Certainly, selecting the appropriate dimensions or bases on which to segment particular markets requires managerial expertise and experience. In most cases, at least some initial dimensions can be determined from previous research, purchase trends, and managerial judgment. For example, suppose a financial institution wished to segment the market for a retail cash management package account that included an unsecured line of credit and discount brokerage capability. Clearly, several dimensions, including income and net worth, come to mind for initial consideration. At a minimum, these variables should be included in subsequent segmentation research.

The most market-oriented approach to segmentation is based on the *benefits* that the potential customer is seeking. Thus, consideration and research of the benefits sought by customers is the "ideal" approach. Then, demographic and psychographic information can be used to enrich the marketer's understanding of the benefit segments. At this point, let us discuss the most useful bases for segmenting markets, including the benefit approach.

Bases for Segmentation. A number of useful bases for segmenting retail and corporate markets are listed in Figure 5–2. Although this is by no means a complete list of possible segmentation variables, it includes the most widely used bases for segmenting markets for consumer goods and industrial goods. We have adapted them for use in this book. In fact, as the following quotation from an international banker indicates, these bases may also have wide applicability in that sphere of banking:

> The rapid shifts within the banking industry (U.S. and worldwide) and the significantly different risk characteristics of international busi-

FIGURE 5-2

Some Suggested Bases for Segmenting Retail and Corporate Markets

retail markets

Demographic

Age	Occupation
Sex	Education
Family size	Religion
Stage in family life cycle	Race
Income (net worth)	Nationality

Psychographic

Social class—lower-lower, upper-lower, lower-middle, upper-middle, lower-upper, upper-upper

Lifestyle—traditionalist, sophisticate, swinger

Personality—compliant, aggressive, detached

Cognitive and behavioral

Attitudes—positive, neutral, negative

Benefits sought—convenience, return, prestige

Readiness stage—unaware, aware, informed, interested, desirous

Perceived risk—high, moderate, low

Innovativeness—innovator, early adopter, early majority, late majority, laggard

Involvement—low, high

Loyalty status—none, some, total

Usage rate—none, light, medium, heavy

User status—nonuser, ex-user, potential user, current user

corporate markets

Source loyalty—purchase from one, two, three, four or more institutions

Size of company—total sales, sales relative to industry

Loan needs—small, medium, large

Usage rate—light, medium, heavy

Purpose of loan—working capital, expansion, venture capital

Type of business—manufacturer, wholesaler, retailer, SIC categories

Status—New customer, occasional, frequent, noncustomer

Attribute importance—rate, convenience, reliability, service, reputation

Location—geographic considerations, home office location

ness transactions have changed our markets and those of our clients dramatically. Some form of independent market research is required to provide the proper base for analysis of those changing markets.

Market segmentation—by geography, product, client type, and size—should be carefully examined since current organizations are often based on segmentation which is no longer valid. It is entirely possible that the trade patterns of your bank's natural client base has changed over the years. In our region (the mid-Atlantic) the emergence of smaller companies into the flow of international trade is a reality which must be addressed by long-range planners. The needs of this sector are radically different from those of major multinational exporters who have dominated this market in the past.[3]

Let us now examine the more market-oriented modes for segmentation: *benefit segmentation* and *psychographic segmentation*. These bases are singled out here because as more sophisticated bases than simple demographic and geographic bases become necessary for market segmentation in financial services, these market-oriented modes will become more widely used.

Benefit Segmentation.   The belief underlying this segmentation approach is that the benefits that people are seeking from a given product or service are the basic reasons for the existence of true market segments. This approach bases market segments on the reasons *why* people buy the product, not on a mere description of *who* (income, net worth, age) will buy the product. Thus, it is a market-oriented approach.[4]

Examples of benefit segmentation are presented in Figure 5–3 (toothpaste) and Figure 5–4 (banks). In Figure 5–3, the first segment is particularly concerned about flavor and product appearance, the second seeks the benefit of white teeth, the third is oriented toward decay prevention, and the final segment is interested only in price. The most

FIGURE 5–3

Benefit Segmentation of the Toothpaste Market

	the sensory segment	the sociable segment	the worrier segment	the independent segment
Principal benefit sought	Flavor, product appearance	Brightness of teeth	Decay prevention	Price
Demographic strengths	Children	Teens, young people	Large families	Men
Special behavioral characteristics	Users of spearmint-flavored toothpaste	Smokers	Heavy users	Heavy users
Brands disproportionately favored	Colgate	Macleans, Ultra Brite	Crest	Cheapest brand
Lifestyle characteristics:	Hedonistic	Active	Conservative	Value-oriented

Source: Adapted from Russell I. Haley, "Benefit Segmentation: A Decision-Oriented Research Tool," *Journal of Marketing*, July 1968, pp. 30–35.

FIGURE 5-4

Benefit Segmentation of a Retail Banking Market

	Front-runners	Loan Seekers	Representative Subgroup	Value Seekers	One-stop Bankers
Principal benefits sought	Large Bank for all Good advertising	Good reputation Loans easily available Low loan interest	No differences (about average on all benefits sought)	High savings interest Quick service Low loan interest Plenty of parking	Wide variety of services Convenient hours Quick service Encourages financial responsibility Convenient branch
Demographic characteristics	Young Rent home	More transient More blue-collar		Tend to save more	Older
Lifestyle characteristics	High ability to manage money	Liberal about use of credit Positive about bank loans		Conservative overall lifestyle Conservative about use of credit Low propensity toward risk taking	Conservative about use of credit Positive toward checking account
Percentage of sample market	2.3	14.8	34.3	25.9	22.7

Source: Adapted from Roger J. Calantone and Alan G. Sawyer, "The Stability of Benefit Segments," *Journal of Marketing Research*, August 1978, p. 400.

important thing to note here is that although there are demographic differences, personality differences, lifestyle differences, and differences in brand preferences among the four segments, the most important variable for market segmentation is benefits sought. The reason for this conclusion is that the other differences are caused by the benefit segmentation differences, not vice versa. With this kind of understanding, marketing strategies (products, names, flavors, packages, advertising, etc.) can be developed for whichever segment the manufacturer is seeking to penetrate. Thus, manufacturers know what segments they will pursue before they develop their marketing strategies. Obviously, this increases the chances for success.

Figure 5–4 presents a benefit segmentation approach for retail banking services in a particular market area. Note that this study identified four distinct groups based on the benefits sought and labeled the groups front-runners, loan seekers, value seekers, and one-stop bankers. Note also that demographic and lifestyle information was used to enrich the profile of the segment but not as the basis for the segmentation. The benefits sought formed the bases of the segmentation.

Benefit segmentation is clearly a market-oriented approach to segmentation that seeks to identify consumer needs and wants and to satisfy them by providing products and services with the desired benefits. This approach is consistent with the philosophy of a market-driven financial institution.

Psychographic Segmentation. Whereas benefit segmentation focuses on the attributes desired by the customer, psychographic segmentation focuses on the personal attributes of the customer. Thus, psychographics is a segmentation variable that uses customers' attitudes, interests, and options, and it typically follows a post hoc model. Generally, a large number of questions are asked concerning customers' lifestyles, activities, interests, and opinions, and then customers are grouped together statistically based on their responses. Figure 5–5 presents a sample of the types of questions that are used in psychographic research.

The basic rationale for using psychographic variables as bases for segmentation is to enrich the description of market segments beyond demographics. Psychographics tell us about attitudes and lifestyles allowing the financial marketer to differentiate between "homebodies" and "swingers," between feminists and women with traditional values, between those who admire Ralph Nader and those who identify with Archie Bunker.[5]

An example of the output of a psychographic study is shown in Figure 5–6. The study was conducted by the Newspaper Advertising Bureau and focused on the male market. As you can see, it identified eight psychographic segments. Further analysis of these segments showed

---

FIGURE 5-5

Some Typical Questions Used in Psychographic Segmentation Research

1. My greatest achievements are still ahead of me.
2. I often watch the newspaper advertisements for announcements of department store sales.
3. Five years from now, my family income will probably be a lot higher than it is now.
4. My children are the most important thing in my life.
5. I will probably have more money to spend next year than I have right now.
6. I think I have more self-confidence than most people.
7. It is good to have credit cards.
8. I don't like to take a chance.
9. A woman should not smoke in public.
10. If Americans were more religious, this would be a better country.

Sources: G. Homan, R. Cecil, and W. Wells, "An Analysis of Moviegoers by Life-Style Segments," in *Advances in Consumer Research*, ed. M. J. Schlinger (Association for Consumer Research, 1975), p. 219; and A. C. Burns and M. C. Harrison, "A Test of the Reliability of Psychographics," *Journal of Marketing Research*, February 1979, p. 34.

---

that such things as products used, magazine readership, and television viewing behavior varied greatly across segments. For example, beer and cigarette use was found to be highest in groups 5 and 7, while air travel was highest in groups 6 and 8. Groups 5 through 8 are more likely to read *Playboy* magazine than are groups 1 through 4. This type of segmentation yields a tremendous amount of information about customers and is based on the idea that the more you know and understand about your customers, the more effective your marketing will be.

Develop Product Positioning

By this stage of the segmentation process, a financial institution should have a good idea of the basic segments of the market that could be satisfied with a particular product. The next step is to position the product in the minds of customers.

As we noted earlier, we will devote an entire chapter (Chapter 6) to a discussion of positioning. At this point, let us just say that in positioning a product, the marketer must consider its offering relative to that of competition. For example, in Chapter 2 we saw that positioning depends on whether the institution is a leader or an underdog. Underdogs usually should not attempt to position their product directly against the market leader. The main point here is that in segmenting markets, some segments that may appear to be approachable might be forgone since competitive products may already dominate those seg-

FIGURE 5–6

An Example of Psychographic Segmentation: The Male Market

Group 1: "The Quiet Family Man" (8% of total males)

He is a self-sufficient man who wants to be left alone and is basically shy. Tries to be as little involved with community life as possible. His life revolves around the family, simple work, and television viewing. Has a marked fantasy life. As a shopper, he is practical, less drawn to consumer goods and pleasures than other men.

Low education and low economic status; he tends to be older than average.

Group 2: "The Traditionalist" (16% of total males)

He is a man who feels secure, has self-esteem, follows conventional rules. He is proper and respectable, regards himself as altruistic and interested in the welfare of others. As a shopper, he is conservative, likes popular brands and well-known manufacturers.

Low education and low or middle socioeconomic status; the oldest age group.

Group 3: "The Discontented Man" (13% of total males)

He is a man who is likely to be dissatisfied with his work. He feels bypassed by life, dreams of better jobs, more money, and more security. He tends to be distrustful and socially aloof. As a buyer, he is quite price conscious.

Lowest education and lowest socioeconomic group; mostly older than average.

Group 4: "The Ethical Highbrow" (14% of total males)

This is a very concerned man, sensitive to people's needs. Basically a puritan, content with family life, friends, and work. Interested in culture, religion, and social reform. As a consumer, he is interested in quality, which may at times justify greater expenditure.

Well educated, middle or upper socioeconomic status; mainly middle-aged or older.

Group 5: "The Pleasure-Oriented Man" (9% of total males)

He tends to emphasize his masculinity and rejects whatever appears to be soft or feminine. He views himself as a leader among men. Self-centered, dislikes his work or job. Seeks immediate gratification for his needs. He is an impulsive buyer, likely to buy products with a masculine image.

Low education, lower socioeconomic class; middle-aged or younger.

Group 6: "The Achiever" (11% of total males)

This is likely to be a hardworking man, dedicated to success and all that it implies—social prestige, power, and money. Is in favor of diversity, is adventurous about leisure-time pursuits. Is stylish, likes good food, music, and so forth. As a consumer, he is status conscious, a thoughtful and discriminating buyer.

Good education, high socioeconomic status; young.

Group 7: "The He-Man" (19% of total males)

He is gregarious, likes action, seeks an exciting and dramatic life. Thinks of himself as capable and dominant. Tends to be more of a bachelor than a family man, even after marriage. The products he buys and the brands he prefers are likely to have "self-expressive value," especially a "man of action" dimension.

Well educated, mainly middle socioeconomic status; the youngest of the groups.

Group 8: "The Sophisticated Man" (10% of total males)

He is likely to be an intellectual, is concerned about social issues, admires men with artistic and intellectual achievements. Socially cosmopolitan, broad interests. Wants to be dominant and a leader. As a consumer, he is attracted to the unique and fashionable.

Best educated and highest economic status of all the groups; younger than average.

Source: W. D. Wells, "Psychographics: A Critical Review," *Journal of Marketing Research,* May 1975, pp. 196–213.

ments both in volume and in the minds of customers. Figure 5–7 illustrates a useful application of the concept of positioning in financial services advertising.[6]

Decide Segmentation Strategy

The institution is now ready to select its segmentation strategy. There are four basic alternatives. First, it may decide not to enter the market. Analysis to this point may have revealed that there is no viable market niche for the institution's offering. Second, management may decide not to segment the market but instead to offer the product to the mass market. There are at least three situations in which this alternative may be appropriate: (1) the market is so small that marketing to a portion of it is not profitable; (2) one group makes up such a large proportion of the sales volume that it is the only relevant target; and (3) the institution's product is the dominant product in the market, and targeting to a few segments would not increase volume or profits.[7]

Third, the institution may decide to market to one segment, or fourth, it may decide to market to more than one segment and to design a separate marketing mix strategy for each segment. In any case, the institution must have some criteria on which to base its segmentation decisions. The criteria of a viable market segment are that it is measurable, meaningful, reachable, and responsive to marketing.

1. Measurable. For a potential segment to be viable, the institution must be capable of measuring its size and characteristics. For example,

---

FIGURE 5–7

Using the Concept of Positioning in Financial Services Advertising

A product can be positioned:

1. By attributes	"Our Money Market Account Is an Inflation Fighter"
2. By price/quality	"Our Gold Card Is Worth It"
3. By competitor	"We Are the Small Bank That Puts You First"
4. By application	"Our Platinum Account Is for the Investment-Minded"
5. By product user	"Our Unsecured Line of Credit Is for Those Who Have Earned It"
6. By product class	"Santa's Account Is a Special Savings Account"

an objection to segmenting on the basis of social class is that social classes are difficult to define and measure. It is much easier to define and measure income classes.

2. Meaningful.   A meaningful segment is one that is large enough in size and growth potential to justify the expenditure of marketing dollars, and to offer long-run profits for the institution.

3. Reachable.   In some cases, large segments exist that cannot be reached feasibly through promotional or delivery efforts. For example, it might be too costly for a small financial institution to reach a group of corporate treasurers by either personal selling or advertising, or the institution may be unable to reach a group of retail customers profitably with its present delivery system. In both cases, these segments are not reachable.

4. Responsive to Marketing.   If the response of a segment to changes in marketing strategies is no different from that of other segments, there is no need to treat it separately. For example, if all savings customers had the same degree of price consciousness, there would be no need for differentially priced or tier-priced deposit products. If all customers had the same degree of service consciousness, there would be no need to offer different levels of service. This simply means that it is easier to sell to a segment when it differs from other segments on several marketing mix dimensions (product, price, promotion, distribution).

Design Marketing Mix Strategy

The financial marketer is now in a position to complete the segmentation analysis by finalizing the marketing mix to be used for each segment. The selection of the target market and the design of the marketing mix go hand in hand, and thus many marketing mix decisions should have already been carefully considered. For example, the segment selected may be price sensitive, so some consideration has already been given to price levels, and the product positioning phase has many implications for promotion and delivery decisions. Thus, while we place the design of the marketing mix strategy at the end of the segmentation analysis, many of these decisions are made in conjunction with various earlier steps of the analysis. In any case, at this point a marketing mix strategy (product design decisions, pricing decisions, promotional decisions, and distribution decisions) is developed for each of the selected market segments.

CONCLUSION

A critical element in the marketing planning process is the identification of target markets. The purpose of this chapter was to provide an overview of the process of market segmentation. As we have seen, an understanding of market segmentation is a prerequisite for the two chapters that follow: market positioning and relationship banking.

We have seen that market segmentation is the process of dividing a market into groups of similar customers and selecting the most appropriate group or groups for the institution to serve. We presented segmentation analysis as a six-step process: (1) evaluate the institution's current situation; (2) determine customer needs and wants; (3) divide markets on relevant dimensions; (4) develop product positioning; (5) decide segmentation strategy; and (6) design marketing mix strategy.

Again, what we have provided is merely an overview of segmentation analysis. We have intentionally avoided offering extensive examples of possible customer breakdowns that a financial institution might construct in assessing its existing and potential customer base. Application is emphasized in the following two chapters of Part Three.

NOTES

1. The process depicted in Figure 5–1 is a generally agreed-upon model of the market segmentation process, although some may include or exclude a particular element. This chapter is drawn from J. Paul Peter and James H. Donnelly, Jr., *A Preface to Marketing Management*, 3d ed. (Plano, Tex.: Business Publications, 1984), chap. 5.

2. Yoram Wind, "Issues and Advances in Segmentation Research," *Journal of Marketing Research*, August 1978, pp. 317–37; and Paul E. Green, " A New Approach to Market Segmentation," *Business Horizons*, February 1977, pp. 61–73.

3. L. A. Caldwell, "Strategic Planning Will Help Define Your Role in International Banking," *American Banker*, September 28, 1983, pp. 2, 6.

4. Russell I. Haley, "Benefit Segmentation: A Decision-Oriented Research Tool," *Journal of Marketing*, July 1968, pp. 30–35; and Russell I. Haley, "Beyond Benefit Segmentation," *Journal of Advertising Research*, August 1971, pp. 3–8.

5. Peter Bernstein, "Psychographics Is Still an Issue on Maidson Avenue," *Fortune*, January 16, 1978, pp. 78–84.

6. The idea for this figure was stimulated by David A. Aaker and J. G. Stansby, "Positioning Your Product," *Business Horizons*, May–June 1982, p. 62.

7. Shirley Young, Leland Ott, and Barbara Feigin, "Some Practical Considerations in Market Segmentation," *Journal of Marketing Research*, August 1978, pp. 405–12.

6

Market Positioning

Many financial institution executives are wondering, "Just what kind of institution should ours be?"

- An all-things-to-all-people institution
- An anytime-and-just-about-anywhere-that's-important-to-be institution
- A cream-of-the-crop–customer institution
- A technology pacesetter institution
- Or perhaps, just an old-fashioned people institution

These questions and many others like them represent the positioning choices confronting financial industry managers and marketers as they grapple with the challenging and often terrifying new realities of deregulation, ever-intensifying competition, a proliferation of high-technology products and service delivery mechanisms, and a more demanding but also more enlightened customer base.

In a world where we all are banks (First National, Community Savings and Loan, Sears, Beneficial Finance, Safeway, and Merrill Lynch)—where, indeed, we all are consumer banks—very specifically, what kind of bank should ours be? How do we stand apart? How do we differentiate successfully, profitably, one from the other in an over-crowded marketplace? From so many available choices, which are the best for our banking organization? Throughout the remainder of this chapter, we shall use the term *banking organization* to generically embrace all financial service providers that are operationally capable of satisfying basic consumer and business customer needs. *In today's financial service industry, after all, they are all banks.*

A PLACE IN THE SUN

To begin with, positioning strategies in an era of deregulation and major financial industry restructuring must be viewed as a pluralistic approach to the marketplace. Positioning involves much more than identifying one or another empty niche and devising marketing programs that will facilitate seizing it. Positioning—simultaneously, concurrently, in a complementary fashion—entails

- *Institutional* positioning—deciding whether to operate on a national, regional, or community basis; within the retail or wholesale arenas, or both; and as a generalist or a specialist.
- *Product line* positioning—deciding what products and services to offer customers and, for that matter, whether to develop those products on a proprietary basis or to "lease" them.
- *Distribution or delivery system* positioning—determining the most efficient mix of manned (people) and unmanned (machines and electronic interface) mechanisms for reaching out to customers.
- *Price* positioning—determining which services to sell wholesale and which retail; seeking out the kind and proportion of fee-based income, and constructing "package-priced" components.
- *People* positioning—matching what the customer wants with the right level of staff expertise, knowledge, training, motivation, and compensation.
- *Customer* positioning—determining which major segments as well as subgroups or niches of the total customer universe to concentrate on—those best customers that your bank can best serve and those open spots that don't belong to someone else.
- *Profitability* positioning—from the bank's perspective, determining which blend of customers and product and service offerings will maximize return on equity or return on assets.

The critical point is that positioning must be viewed in a pluralistic sense. You don't position your financial institution as a regional retailer of basic consumer services (e.g., transaction accounts, savings and investment instruments, household credit, and career and retirement planning services) without concurrently and comparably positioning your product line, pricing, distribution, and staffing structures.

POSITIONING CHOICES

A growing body of positioning literature based on the implications of financial industry reform and deregulation has emerged in recent years. This literature commonly reflects an awareness that competitive strategies are in a state of transition rather than completeness or finalization. Even at this writing, it remains a time of change, seeking, and experimentation. It is a time of many choices and multiple opportunities. It is a time for testing and sensing the new financial services environment—what has already happened and what seems likely to happen during the 1980s.

Most of the contemporary positioning literature is rather general. Broad choices and categories are presented. You can become "bank type" A, B, or C. You can operate as a generalist or specialist vendor. The literature tends toward limited either/or selections. It stresses generalized *strategic* concerns rather than *tactical* positioning approaches. The correct strategy might be positioning as a "financial supermarket" as contrasted with a "special-services-provided-by-special-people boutique" (or the other way around, or someplace in the middle). But what is the correct assortment of tactical alternatives related to competing as a "supermarket" or a "boutique"? What are your most effective people choices, pricing choices, product choices, and delivery system choices? These are the chief concerns of this chapter.[1]

We believe that, at the very least, a financial organization, must *simultaneously* strive to become a relationship bank, an investors' bank, an everywhere bank, and a selling bank. These are the minimal positioning requirements in the battle for institutional success and survival. Let us look at them more closely.

- *Relationship banking* concerns viewing customers as clients; emphasizing client retention and enhancement, not just new customer acquisition; and attempting to satisfy total needs rather than bits and pieces of a need.
- Becoming an *investors' bank* involves moving well beyond the transaction, savings, and credit services for which the institution is best known and focusing service development work in the areas of *investment instruments* and *personal financial planning.*
- The need to become *an everywhere bank* is linked to demands to preserve "client time" rather than waste it. An everywhere bank is one that is *accessible* where and when the client wants to be

served. The institution not only saves the client time, but it is also timely and thus saves the client money.

• And finally, becoming *a selling bank* requires that depository institutions overcome a long-standing "distaste for selling." This "matters a great deal in the 1980s. The increasingly complex investment and financial planning services that financial institutions will be marketing to consumers . . . cannot be marketed only by placing advertising and taking orders."[2]

Few financial organizations can avoid being all of these "banks" simultaneously to all or most of their customer base. These characteristics represent the fundamentals that the customer will insist on: to be treated as a client, a person, and not just as a set of numbers; to be offered the widest possible range of necessary financial service options under one roof; to be dealt with during "customer time," not just banking hours; and to be served by an institution that reaches out with customer-adapted offerings. With this general framework in mind, we can now examine more fully the specific elements of positioning.

THE ELEMENTS OF POSITIONING

Figure 6–1 presents the critical components of a positioning strategy. While it does not include all of the choices open to competitors in the financial services business, we believe that it outlines the major op-

---

FIGURE 6–1

The Elements of Positioning

I. **Institutional positioning**
   Structural decisions and options
   Functional decisions and options
   Managerial decisions and options

II. **Marketing mix positioning**
   Delivery systems decisions and options
   Human resources decisions and options
   Product line decisions and options
   Pricing decisions and options

III. **Customer markets positioning**
   Locational considerations
   Line-of-business considerations
   Customer need evaluation criteria
   Institutional profitability evaluation criteria

---

tions. We do not suggest that choosing from among these tactical options is an easy process. The process requires a major commitment to the marketplace and customer research; a thorough understanding of the impact—or at least the probable impact—of competitive, technological, customer lifestyle, economic, and regulatory changes on financial institutions; and considerable senior management soul-searching. As often as not, the best positioning choices will require giving up what senior management desires for what it may realistically hope to achieve. Positioning decisions may also unsettle the executive suite by requiring the employment of new manager types to administer new approaches to success and survival. In addition, positioning may mandate such changes as having a bank abruptly begin to sell off the far-flung network of bricks-and-mortar offices that it has spent several decades in building or having a depository institution abandon traditional forms of sales staff compensation in favor of commission selling.

Listing and carefully researching the options is a comparatively easy process. So is designing specific programs to implement them. It is actually choosing the right road, yet remaining flexible enough to shift gears as challenge threatens or opportunity beckons, that calls for optimal organizational courage, insight, and imagination.

Positioning is not a crapshoot in which a financial institution can gamble and lose, then come back to the table another day. Positioning can be amended, enhanced, altered, modified, and tinkered with to reflect environmental changes. But management doesn't easily walk away from its decisions and draw up entirely different battle plans. Finally, positioning is a step-by-step process. You decide the strategy and work toward it. You *evolve* your position in the marketplace and in a customer's mind. You don't say, "Yesterday we were business-oriented, and starting today we're going to be consumer-oriented." The consumers just won't believe it, and they probably won't buy it either. Moreover a commercial bank does not easily or quickly become a leading vendor of home affordability instruments after having, year after year, chased mortgage customers to the savings and loan down the street.

INSTITUTIONAL POSITIONING

Structural Decisions and Options

- National retail and corporate banking organization.
- National retail *primarily* or corporate *primarily* banking organization.
- Regional multistate retail and corporate banking organization.
- Regional multistate retail *primarily* or corporate *primarily* banking organization.

- Regional organization *networked* with similar regional organizations to reflect a national operating presence.
- National or regional *franchisor.*
- National retail and/or corporate banking organization operating exclusively in selected metropolitan markets or special trade markets.
- National or regional *specialist* banking organization or *franchisor* organization, specializing in selected retail and/or corporate financial programs.
- Independent community banking organization, applying a broad or very narrow definition of the term *community.*
- Franchisee community banking organization.

Some of the labels assigned in this listing of structural choices merit explanation. A *regional* organization, for example, is an interstate banking organization that is primarily active in a specific geographic region such as the Northeast, the Southeast, or the Southwest. *Networking* suggests formal linkages through credit participations, product sharing, shared telecommunications programs, and the like, among noncompetitive regionals from different geographic markets. A *franchisor* employs the McDonald's or Wendy's expansion models along lines that have been developed by California's First Interstate Bancorp and First Nationwide Savings. What exactly we mean by *community* is itself a critical issue facing countless community-oriented banks, thrifts, brokerage firms, and credit unions. Is "community" a town or several towns and smaller cities within a demarcated geographic area, even a multistate area? Or is it a grouping of municipal employees from several states or all members of the national auto workers union?

Excluded in this listing of structural choices is the *international banking* option, which is of course, available to both American financial institutions operating abroad and to foreign banking organizations considering or seeking to expand an American presence. For the purpose of simplification, we have also limited the primary activities of national and regional banking organizations to either retail or corporate banking. Wider options, such as trust banking or concentrating on small business or venture financing as a corporate activity, will be cited in other segments of this chapter.

Functional Decisions and Options

- Retail and corporate banking generalist orientation.
- Retailing or corporate orientation primarily.
- Trust banking orientation primarily.
- Functional specialist (e.g., mortgage lending, factoring, venture financing, energy industry lending).

- Systems and servicing specialist (e.g., vending retail trust software packages, vending home information systems, vending asset-liability management models).
- Broker orientation (e.g., gathering loan and/or deposit accounts with pass-on orientation).

Many financial organizations, we believe, will broker substantial portions of their customer accounts. They will pass through large-denomination savings or investment deposits, for a fee or in recognition of the overall account relationship value, as a community bank helps the customer search for the highest and/or least risky yields. Likewise, many banking organizations will elect to operate as mortgage initiators, passing on home lending credits to other organizations for investment purposes or to the investor market as pass-through securities.

Managerial Decisions and Options

Market commander	"The best defense is a strong offense."
Competitive market follower	"As number two, we must try harder on every major front."
Noncompetitive market follower	"We'll just watch what the big guys are doing, then copy and stamp our brand on their best ideas."
Market innovator	"We're the guerrillas of the financial services business. We maximize new products and services short run, getting out when the market gets too crowded and the discount pricers give us too much of a run for our money."
Market specialist	"We provide something or perform just a bit better than any of our competitors. We keep an edge by having the best programs and people."
Market nicher	"There are pockets in the marketplace with distinctive unmet or undermet needs that we can go after profitably, with exactly the right rifle shot for each niche. There will always be people who want a gold Rolls-Royce with zebra-skin seats."
Market creator	"We don't sell anything really. We create products and service systems—better mousetraps—and others pay a fee to sell them for us."

Fundamentally, we perceive managerial positioning as a response to the marketplace. The banking organization manages its human and financial resources and its operational capabilities with the customer in mind. The customer can be the "mass market," a distinctive segment of individuals or business firms, or, for that matter, other financial service vendors.[3]

The critical requirement expressed in this analysis of *institutional positioning* is that banking organization managements concurrently consider *structural* or locational posture, the major *functional* activities that are to be performed or provided, and *managerial* style. The following "marketing mix" positioning choices largely amplify these integrated institutional approaches. Given an organization's choices with respect to structure, function and managerial style, what then emerge as its best tactical alternatives in designing a delivery system, establishing a product line, matching people with product management and product delivery, and pricing?

MARKETING MIX POSITIONING

Delivery Systems Decisions and Options

High-technology pioneer	A leader in systems development and implementation
High-technology follower	A reactor to innovation and market demands, serving a broad customer base with the proven latest and best
Selective high-technology utilizer	A reactor to innovation and market demands, but applying technology systems effectively to narrowly defined but high-profit-market segments
Low-technology traditionalist	Primarily a "people bank in a people business," yet employing necessary cost-reducing and service-enhancing technology systems
High-low–technology sharer	Primarily a people bank, but employing necessary cost-reducing and service-enhancing technology systems on a shared, purchased-time, or leased basis
Technology avoider	Extensively a people bank, with a minimal commitment to cost-reducing and service-enhancing technology

Technology embraces traditional back-room activities as well as cash machines, point-of-sale terminals, home banking terminals, the hardware, and the interfacing software. Technology also embraces plastic— the bank card and the value-adding amenities associated with it. This means both the card now used by most financial institution customers and evolving "chip in a card" technologies.[4]

Providing card services, moreover, may be further broken down on an organizational basis into innovator, distributor, and issuer categories. Looking ahead, we suspect that most banking organizations will be less concerned with card "brands," card amenities and characteristics, and terminal access use than with whether or not a card transaction ultimately leads back to the customer account. What's important, after all, is who the customer believes is issuing and handling bank card activity.

We have also employed the term technology to mean a financial institution office, in the sense that an ATM or even a home banking terminal in the form of a customer-activated phone, television screen, and personal computer is a de facto place for transacting financial business. Similarly, if a computer terminal in the briefcase of a financial institution officer calling on a corporate client can be telephonically linked to a financial institution headquarters during negotiations with the client, that computer terminal is also an office, a place for doing business.

Finally, there is bricks-and-mortar: tens of thousands of full-service and limited-service branches, Edge Act offices, loan production offices, storefront facilities, mobile branches, offices on moored boats, offices in discarded windmills and Pullman coaches, and just a teller-in-a-booth at a supermarket or at an industrial plant on a Friday payday.

The employment of bricks-and-mortar alternatives remains a critical element in any organization's delivery system positioning strategy. Since the end of World War II, locational expansion along traditional people-staffed branch office lines dominated the retail banking scene. Only in recent years has there been a marked shift to electronic machine systems. This trend will continue.

Even so, traditional as well as technology-complemented branch offices will remain as integral a part of an institution's delivery system as paper entries (checks) in the payments system. Branches in the traditional sense won't be blown away by the winds of change. But they will be given a better fit with respect to organizational needs and customer needs within a delivery system that is anchored in ever-expanding high-technology modes. This discussion is elaborated on further in Chapter 9, "Delivering Financial Services."

It is customary these days to think of the financial industry's future as technology-dominant. Such thinking is flawed in many key respects. Many banking organizations simply will not be able to afford being high-technology pioneers, facilitators, or followers. For that matter, many preferred customers may themselves prove to be technology avoiders, insisting on doing business with competent people at people-based locations. High-tech will generate a demand for high-touch.

Human Resources Decisions and Options

- People-intensive, high-touch banking.
- Technology-intensive, low-touch banking.
- Mix-and-match banking.
    Technology-intensive for most customers and locations.
    People-intensive for selected customers and locations.
- Expertise-intensive, highly specialized, highly personalized banking.
- Low-touch, low-technology "convenience store" banking.

Current expansion patterns suggest that medium-sized and larger regional banking organizations will generally opt for *mix-and-match banking.* They will utilize technology modes to provide basic services (transaction activity, savings mechanism, and consumer lending) in a more cost-efficient manner, and they will employ their better-skilled, better-paid and better-motivated human resource cadres to market more complex arrays of product lines to preferred customer segments.

Personal banker programs, modeled on that of the widely regarded Wachovia Bank (North Carolina) prototype, will be employed to implement this positioning approach.[5] Assuming intensifying product line, price, delivery system, and promotion program similarity among financial service industry vendors, the desired goal of achieving institutional differentiation will be determined largely by *people quality.* It is sufficient to point out here that *quality* personal banker or corporate account executive programs will not be achieved through upgrading tellers and branch managers in some cosmetic fashion. Implied are major commitments to creating and maintaining levels of excellence in high-touch, bank-to-customer interaction. This key point—people quality—is the major theme of Chapter 13.

Expertise intensive banking implies only heightened degrees of customer and product line segmentation, the cream-of-the-crop positioning favored, for example, by Bankers Trust of New York. Moreover, through interactive telecommunications, "expertise" will become more readily available to more banking organizations in the future. A country bank in a small town in rural North Carolina, for example, will lease expertise, paying a consultation fee, by playing middleman between a customer seeking export-financing advice and a human "knowledge base" in London or New York. From the customer's view, the country bank becomes the expert by administering the required consultation; from the bank's view, the satisfied customer remains the bank's customer.

Low-touch, low-technology "convenience store" banking is just that— the 7–Eleven stores of the financial services industry employing minimally skilled people to cash checks, deposit funds through simply operated and maintained POS terminals, and lend small sums. Safe-deposit boxes and even computer-assisted short-form tax preparation assistance might be provided, and utility payments will probably be processed. Most important, these "stores" will provide maximum time convenience.

Product Line Decisions and Options

- Full-service provider.
- Basic service provider and selected service specialist.
- Basic service provider and selected service broker
- Basic service only provider.
- Selected service only provider.

These product line selections apply to retail, corporate, trust, and, where applicable, international banking markets. Some banking organizations, moreover, may decide to be *full-service providers* in the retail markets and to manage a lesser product line in the corporate or trust fields. By the same token, an organization might elect to offer full service to one segment of its customer market and a lesser product line to the balance of its customer market. Basic services have already been defined as embracing transaction accounts; household savings accounts; minimal risk, higher-yielding investment accounts; consumer lending; debit and credit card administration; small business lending; safe-deposit box rentals; and so on. It is important to recognize, however, that over time deregulation and expanding technologies will most likely actuate *additional basic services*: short-form tax preparation, home terminal rentals, term life and other personal insurance programs, and household budget counseling.

An example of a *selected service specialist* or *broker* is the organization offering an extensive range of home affordability instruments that it tailors or *handcrafts* to customer specifications and distinctive customer capacities (i.e., present income levels versus earnings stream potential). The home affordability instrument as a specialized activity might include not only the mortgage plan but also advice on landscaping, interior decorating, home restoration, and home selling. The specialist provides these services directly through an in-shop capability; the broker arranges for this skill indirectly, though in a way that stamps the organization as the provider, in name if not in fact.[6]

Finally, *product line positioning* will require creating a flexible matrix within a matrix. The continual pushing, shoving, hurrying drive will be to expand accepted definitions of full service and basic service and to develop areas of specialization in pursuing the goal of institutional differentiation. Deciding exactly *who* are the best retail or corporate customers in terms of *their* needs and, from the institution's perspective, our human resources, technological capabilities, and profitability requirements will exert unrelenting pressure to enlarge and modify product lines.

Shifts in *institutional* or *delivery system* positioning will no doubt be cautiously determined and slowly introduced. This will be less true for shifts in *product line* positioning, which must be highly responsive: quickly changed, quickly put in place, quickly supported, and very quickly made to happen in the marketplace. Product definition is where the financial services business will be most susceptible to reform and radicalization in the years to come.

Pricing Decisions and Options

Prime rate traditionalist	Price is indexed to risk and maturity factors and to overall economic conditions.
Relationship banking pricer	Price recognizes rewarding proven client relationships with loan, deposit, or service price incentives.
High-volume, thin-spread discounter	Price is based on "making it up on volume" as either a funds gatherer, credit provider, or fee-based service provider.
Low-volume, wide-spread risk takers	Price is again linked to volume, but it recognizes higher degrees of deposit risk (volatility) and credit risks are recognized.
Product value pricer	Price recognizes the value of a specific product item to the customer as a primary determinant.
Total package pricer	Price recognizes the value of each item within a "bundle of services" and is discounted appropriately for the purchase of the entire package or major segments.
Prestige pricer	Price recognizes that the specialist merits a premium for highest product quality, convenience quality, or servicing (high-touch) quality.
Bargain basement pricer	Price recognizes earnings minimization to achieve customer market penetration and/or successful new product introduction.

Loss leader pricer	Price is set below profit requirements to attract new or expanded customer segments and "make it up" on greater business volume.

Very few banking organizations will adopt a single *price positioning* approach. The approach adopted will differ among retail and wholesale markets and among specific customer groupings. It will be affected by momentary product line capacities. It will also be affected by momentary rather than long-range expansion policies. Pricing, moreover, will be based on an organization's technological capabilities, the intensity and skill of its human resources, and its commitment to one or another area of specialization. Finally, all financial organizations will remain "prime rate traditionalists" in the sense that their pricing will reflect current economic conditions. Pricing will recognize scaling within economic indices and with organizational goals much in mind.

CUSTOMER MARKETS POSITIONING

Locational Considerations

- International.
- National.
- Regional.
- Local or community.

Line-of-Business Considerations

- Consumer lines of business.
- Trust lines of business.
- Corporate lines of business.
- International lines of business.

These are broad categories, each of which a marketer must further segment. For example, trust customer markets would clearly embrace *wealth builders* as one distinct group and *wealth passers* as another. *Retirement planners* could well be a third numerically substantial and prospectively profitable segment. Similarly, corporate customer markets would be divided into such viable segments as national account, middle-market, small business, and financial industry correspondent customers. Going further, small business customers might be split out as entrepreneurship prospects requiring a wide range of financial, managerial, and marketing assistance or growth prospects chiefly needing venture capital.

Customer Need Evaluation Criteria

- Demographic variables (e.g., income, sex, age, profession).
- Psychographic variables (e.g., social status, lifestyle expectations).
- Growth potentiality variables (e.g., prospective household earning power, prospective "family" needs).

Institutional Profitability Evaluation Criteria

- Customer transaction volume (account stability).
- Average customer balances (deposits).
- Average customer balances (loans).
- Usage of fee-based services.
- Length of customer relationship (loyalty).
- Number of total customer services provided (consistency).
- Community importance of customer.
- Potential customer net worth.

Customer markets positioning is far too complex a topic to approach in any definitive manner in this chapter. All that we have attempted to suggest here is a structural approach to customer identification and segmentation. Further, we have argued that customers per se as well as specific customer groupings (e.g., premium retail customers, preferred retail customers, wealth-building trust customers, or middle-market corporate customers) will be evaluated from two distinctive perspectives: *first*, the essential worth or value of the customer (e.g., net worth, current income or earnings potential, age, profession, social status, or lifestyle expectations); and, *second*, the relative value of that customer to the banking organization in terms of profitability criteria. Is the customer a stable one who maintains a high average deposit balance; utilizes bank credit and meets payment schedules promptly month after month, year after year; uses fee-based services; and exhibits "loyalty" characteristics? Clearly, it is up to each banking organization to develop well-researched and realistic *customer evaluation* and *institutional profitability evaluation* criteria.

Customer positioning chiefly recognizes that in an era of deregulation and intensifying levels of competition very few banking organizations can be all things to all people. Only a few can and will be. Only a very few will possess a national and international presence as providers of extensive financial services to retail as well as corporate and trust customers.

Many organizations will elect to become providers of "some things" (basic or selected services) to all people but "more things" to some and even more to a few. Other organizations will opt to become providers of preferred (top 20 percent of the market) or premium (top 5 percent of

FIGURE 6–2

Suggested Community Bank Positioning Integration

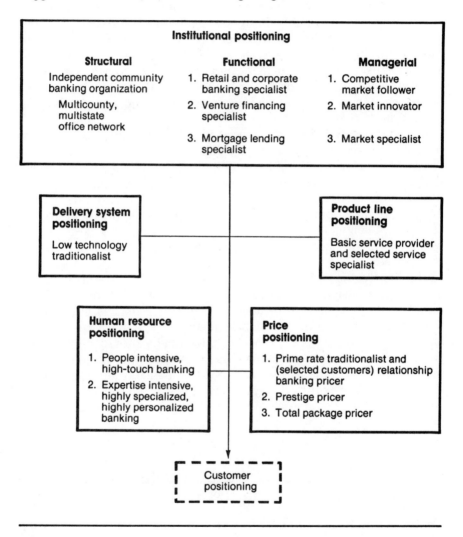

the market) customers. And still others will be on the lookout for special customer niches within the marketplace—for example, newly degreed dentists or women MBAs and other distinctive customer types that a financial services provider can nourish along to eventual preferred or premium customer status. These determinations are discussed more fully in the next chapter.

Putting It Together

Figure 6–2, indicates how one banking organization (a community bank) might integrate its positioning choices. This community bank would function locally—possibly throughout several countries and even across state boundary lines—as a retail and corporate banking generalist. It would offer the most customary household and business finance offerings. Concurrently, however, it might elect to also operate as a specialist in venture financing and mortgage lending. In the case of venture financing, it might determine that it possesses the level of expertise and an appropriate capital structure for widely extending its geographic horizon.

The community bank's managerial philosophy would be in accord with these objectives. We can only suggest, however, that the actual degree of competition within its multicounty, multistate environment will necessitate its becoming a competitive market follower as contrasted with a slightly lower profile. Delivery system, product line, human resource, and price positioning likewise would be in accord with fundamental institutional positioning strategies. The decisions taken would fit together—blended, integrated, designed to create a stronger whole.

And finally, the community bank is structured with the customer in mind. In this instance, it is evident that the organization would be directing its "customer satisfaction engineering" efforts along three lines: (1) a universe of community members seeking a competitive range of fairly priced basic services conveniently provided by skilled personnel; (2) a diverse target market of small business entrepreneurs seeking growth capital as well as growth guidance from expert financial managers and willing to pay a price premium for dollars, guidance, and expertise; and (3) a relatively homogeneous target market of home buyers.

CONCLUSION

Making the *right* positioning choices from among the wide range of alternatives presented represents a critical step toward success and survival in the era of deregulation.

We suspect that as often as not the right decisions—the most reasonable and easily integrated choices for a banking organization and its customer base—will not always be the most satisfying ones. Few organizations will delight in a decision to trim sails and accept a less grand future. Few will perceive the idea of sound, profitable, customer-satisfying, but necessarily limited opportunities as a desired state of affairs. Not all managers and marketers will relish departing from traditional banking practices and sailing into the murkier, deeper, and riskier waters of the financial services business. Some of these bank managers and marketers will complain, "We're no longer bankers—we're becoming appliance dealers." Others will insist, "It's too risky, too dangerous—we're going to get ourselves and our customers in a lot of trouble."

This is not just the thinking of commercial bankers. Similar concerns linger among credit union, brokerage firm, savings and loan, and finance company managers. Such views are instinctive reactions to change. Yet change also necessitates acting, and this need will push-pull responsible managements into reasonable positioning decisions.

The second step in becoming the kind of banking organization that yours should be in a deregulated environment involves developing the necessary *tools* for implementing positioning choices. This step entails consistent, continuing, and integrated programming. Full-page, four-color ads in major print media proclaiming product management expertise provided by highly skilled personal bankers at "First National: The One that Cares" must be implemented in practice by expert-in-fact personal banker cadres, telephone operators courteously and skillfully handling customer inquiries, fully and candidly descriptive periodic customer statements and product literature, and mistake-free backroom operations. *Positioning encompasses the promise and the delivery.*

Beyond this, there is a third crucial step: *image communications.*

Positioning, as we have seen, recognizes that most financial institutions must move away from being "all things to all people" and toward a more limited role in the marketplace. A natural consequence of this inexorable transition is *dislocation*—dislocation among existing staff members and, most important of all, among customers.

Your organization must accommodate the expectations of customers and staff members: what they think of your organization now and what they realistically should expect from it over time. In this regard, a banking organization may be required to modify not only its line of business and service delivery systems but also an image of old-fashioned, business-oriented, friend-of-the-rich, dull, and unimaginative. *Your organization becomes how it is perceived in the marketplace.*

And you work at creating this perception through words, actions, and achievements. Avis closed the gap with car rental leader Hertz by "trying harder." Its advertising slogan was implemented by ongoing, consistent performance. Avis *proved* that it tried harder.

Positioning, to sum up, is a set of marketplace strategies and tactics. It is also communicating a reasonable image to the marketplace. The top-performing American financial institutions in the years ahead will be successful at both tasks.

NOTES

1. Most helpful in understanding positioning choices available to financial institutions are Jon C. Poppen, "The Future of Consumer Financial Services," *Consumer Banking Digest* (American Bankers Association), October 1982, pp. 6–13; and McKinsey & Co., "Capitalizing on Opportunities Created by Deregulation of the Banking Industry" (Chicago, 1982).

    Also see the following analyses of the McKinsey study: Robert A. Krane, "A World without Regulation Q—Issues Confronting Us," an address at the American Bankers Association National Conference on Marketing, Compliance, and Planning, San Francisco, California, May 24, 1982; and Donald C. Waite III, "Deregulation and the Banking Industry," *Consumer Banking Digest* (American Bankers Association), December 1982, pp. 13–19.

    Valuable insights into financial institution positioning strategies are also found in William T. Gregor and Eileen M. Friars, *Money Merchandising: Retail Revolution in Consumer Financial Services* (Cambridge, Mass.: Financial Industry Services Group, Management Analysis Center, Inc., 1982); *Financial Services Innovation and the American Consumer* (New York: Hudson Strategy Group, Hudson Institute, 1982); Robert I. Lipp, "The Response by U.S. Banks to Competition from Non-Banks," an address to the European Financial Marketing Association, Monte Carlo, March 22, 1982; and Raoul D. Edwards, "The Survival of the Community Bank," an address to the Independent Community Banks of North Dakota, Jamestown, September 15, 1982.

2. Leonard L. Berry, "The New Marketing," an address at the national convention of the Bank Marketing Association, Phoenix, Arizona, October 25, 1982.

3. An excellent discussion of managerial positioning is offered in an interview with Sig Front, senior vice president and international marketing executive, Sheraton Corporation, in *United States Banker*, May 1983, pp. 17–18, 22, 26.

4. An excellent analysis of "value-adding features" associated with credit and debit cards as well as a thoughtful discussion of new bank card technologies and strategies can be found in "Card Strategies," September 1983, a position paper developed for clients of National Card Control, Inc., Richmond, Virginia, a leading wholesaler of card amenities and card registration services.

5. Raoul D. Edwards, "Relationship Banking and the Long Steady Haul: A Look at Wachovia Bank and Trust," *United States Banker*, April 1980, pp. 54–56.

6. Thomas W. Thompson, "Commentary: Home Affordability: Reviving Centerpiece in a Client Relationship," *United States Banker*, June 1983, pp. 6, 8, 10. This article considers in detail the component elements of a Home Affordability Instrument, including the integral parts: a core service, related services, and complementary services.

Relationship Banking

For many years, financial services marketing was preoccupied with attracting new customers to the institution. Premium programs, new branch locations, weekend hours, free checking campaigns—the focus was on acquiring *new business*. This was yesterday—when the financial services business was a relatively simple business, when there were healthy spreads between the cost of funds and the price of loans, when customers had to deal with banks to have a checking account and thrifts were protected by the "rate differential," when interest rates were stable and the economy strong, and when it was hard *not* to make money.

Today, when the financial services business is no longer a simple business, when there are no longer healthy spreads, when customers no longer have to deal with banks, when the thrift differential is all but meaningless, when interest rates are volatile and the economy uncertain, when it is harder to make money, easier to lose it—today, financial marketers are beginning to think about marketing in a fundamentally new way. The realization is taking hold that marketing is about *having customers*, not merely *acquiring customers*. Many financial services marketers now recognize that attracting new customers is only the first step, that making existing customers better customers is marketing too.

It is in this transition of financial services marketing thought—still very much under way at this writing—that the idea of relationship banking has become popularized. To some, relationship banking is merely a buzzword, absent of any lasting significance. We disagree, believing that relationship banking will dominate financial services marketing thought and practice throughout the decade and beyond. We think of it as a cornerstone marketing concept for today and tomorrow.

WHAT IS RELATIONSHIP BANKING?

Relationship banking concerns viewing customers as clients, stressing client retention and improvement just as much as new client acquisition, and focusing on the satisfaction of total financial service needs rather than on bits and pieces of a need. In a sentence, relationship banking is *attracting, maintaining, and enhancing client relationships.*[1]

Relationship banking is fundamentally different from order-taking banking. Figure 7-1 summarizes some of the key differences. In order-taking banking, the emphasis is on selling the service or services that the customer requests—the emphasis is on the moment, the immediate situation. In relationship banking, the emphasis is on establishing a

---

FIGURE 7-1

Some Differences between Order-Taking Banking and Relationship Banking

order-taking banking	relationship banking
Focus is "customers"; attraction of new customers is the goal	Focus is "clients"; attraction of new customers is viewed as an intermediate step
Emphasis on selling a service	Emphasis on establishing long-term relationship
Need satisfaction approached from standpoint of the "part"	Need satisfaction approached from standpoint of the "whole"
Primary sales contact through processing-driven clerks	Primary sales contact through marketing-driven professionals
Profitability assessed on individual services	Profitability assessed on total relationship

---

long-term, multiple-service relationship; on satisfying the totality of the client's financial service needs; on minimizing the need or desire of clients to splinter their financial business among various institutions.

Order-taking banking is processing-intensive—completing forms, moving the queue, being efficient. Relationship banking is service- and selling-intensive. Good service is important in keeping the business; good selling is important in building it up. Both are important in transforming indifferent customers into loyal clients.

The "client" notion is perhaps the most basic difference between order-taking and relationship banking. It presents a genuine challenge to any financial institution aspiring to be a "relationship institution." Customers may be nameless to the institution; clients cannot be nameless. Customers are served as part of the mass or as part of larger segments; clients are served on an individual basis. Customers are statistics; their needs are reflected on computer printout summaries. Clients are entities in and of themselves; specifics about them—background data, services used, special requirements—are captured in a data base. Customers are served by anyone who happens to be available; clients are served—at least for nonroutine needs—by the professional banker who has been assigned to them. Customers have no strong reason to feel an allegiance to a given financial institution; clients perceive that they have a personal relationship and are therefore more likely to feel an allegiance.

Relationship banking is not a "gimmick"; it cannot be "this year's thrust." It is a philosophy about how a financial institution should be run; it is an objective, a strategy, an outcome. It is relevant to financial institutions of all sizes and to both wholesale and retail markets. Ultimately, the potential for relationship banking depends on quality of service. Lasting relationships are not made with financial institutions that are sloppy, inconsistent, uncommitted. Relationship banking is *not* an easy state to attain or maintain. Unless the senior management of an institution *really* wants it to happen, it doesn't have a chance. It doesn't have a chance because the resource reallocations, the reorganizing, the shifts in marketing approach, the training commitments—and all of the other pieces that need to be put in place—materialize only when there is deep-down, genuine top-management *commitment* and *perseverance*.

BENEFITS TO THE INSTITUTION

If relationship banking is so hard, why bother? There are several parts to the answer. First, everyone—or so it seems—is going after the best *customers* of banks and thrifts. Yesterday Sears was where we bought underwear, auto parts, and washing machines. Merrill Lynch sold stocks and bonds. Prudential Life was only an insurance company. American Express was a travel and entertainment card. And Kroger sold food. This was yesterday. Today traditional distinctions are blurring and a new, bigger, intensely competitive financial services industry has emerged. And traditional and nontraditional competitors are in a race to get to the center of the client relationship—to be not only a survivor with the good customer but also the primary institution.

Clearly, marketing to *protect* the customer base has become exceedingly important to traditional financial institutions. Relationship banking, with its emphasis on existing customers—on serving and selling, on achieving a sense of allegiance—is a way to achieve the customer protection goal.

In a 1982 speech reprinted in *American Banker*, Norwood W. "Red" Pope, a well-known bank marketing executive, told a story about Al McGuire, a former basketball coach at Marquette University who became an announcer on NBC basketball telecasts. It seems that McGuire was upset that CBS had outbid NBC for the rights to televise NCAA championship games. All season, the games had been on NBC. Tournament time arrived, and NBC was left out. Upset by these events, McGuire was quoted as saying: "It's like getting all the dances with the girl, but when it comes time to take her home and get in the rumble seat, it's CBS that is touching the soft spots."[2]

Pope concluded the speech by suggesting that the banks had been going to the dances with their customers all these years—buying the ticket and corsage, having the suit cleaned, borrowing the car—but now newcomers who had not paid their dues, who had not been restricted by regulation, were grabbing the girl and heading for the rumble seat. Relationship banking is the banking response required by these new realities.

Another reason to bother with relationship banking is the need to compensate for narrower lending spreads by selling more services per customer in general and more fee services in particular. In commercial lending, for instance, the combination of increased loan competition from nonlocal banks, the entry into commercial lending by thrifts, the growing inclination of corporations to borrow from one another rather than banks, and the need of many financial institutions to significantly expand lending because of the extra funds attracted through deregulated instruments have all contributed to declining interest margins.

The key to the narrow-spread problem is whether the institution can make up for spreads no longer available on loans by selling more nonlending services. Relationship banking is, of course, oriented to fulfilling total financial service needs, not just credit needs. Accordingly, in a relationship institution the idea of making money without money—of selling expertise, systems, service—is viewed not as a sideline activity but as a central activity.

The argument for relationship banking is also bolstered by a close look at how financial institutions increase market share. Basically, there are three avenues. One is to attract new customers to the institution. Another is to sell existing customers more. The third is to reduce customer turnover. The relationship institution works all three avenues. It seeks new customers, and then it seeks to transform them into long-term, multiple-service clients. For the type of business that is desired, relationship banking is a market share strategy.

Ignoring the potential of relationship banking can be wasteful since it will frequently cost more to acquire new customers than to sell additional services to existing customers. For example, an institution spending $500,000 on advertising to attract new customers could conceivably gain less in net additional profitable business than another institution spending $300,000 divided among new customer advertising, a telephone campaign to existing customers promoting specific services, and staff training to improve service quality.

FIGURE 7–2

Wachovia Proves that Personal Banking Works

Wachovia Bank, N.A., an $8.0 billion statewide banking organization headquartered in Winston-Salem, North Carolina, continues to successfully make personal banking and, more broadly, relationship banking happen.

Wachovia was a "late starter" in providing discount brokerage services in its southeastern market. Nonetheless, it quickly made up for lost time. One North Carolina competitor, whose bank was an early entrant into discount brokerage, said, "They just blew the rest of us away. . . . It was one of the fastest successful starts with a new product ever."

Wachovia is not stating exactly how well it did. However, senior vice president James Brewer, a key individual in developing and managing Wachovia's personal banker program, explains that "when we began offering discount brokerage in October [1983], we set a goal of 5,000 accounts for the following three months," or by year-end. He admits that "we exceeded it by a good margin."

A Virginia bank executive, who manages his holding company's discount brokerage program, terms that "good margin" two or three times as much as Wachovia reasonably should have expected.

Recently voted one of the three best-managed banking organizations in the nation, Wachovia is the "granddaddy" of personal banking. Its extensive personal banker program began in 1973.

Why was Wachovia so successful with discount brokerage? A major reason was its personal banker program, those clientlike relationships built up over the past decade. As Brewer points out, discount brokerage was simply easier to sell to clients than to customers.

"Our personal bankers are a sales force, and they proved themselves again with discount brokerage."

The transition from order-taking institution to relationship institution is not an easy one. There is nothing automatic about it. It is easier to talk about relationship banking than to do it. Nonetheless, the potential of relationship banking is *real*. To write relationship banking off as a buzzword is to miss the essential point: in a hotly contested financial services industry, the "old marketing"—using splashy ads, premiums, and locations to drive customers through the door and then processing them as anonymous faces in the crowd—the old marketing is no longer enough. Protecting good customers, making them better customers, increasing fee income, and increasing market share require becoming proficient in the art and science of client marketing. The strengths of relationship banking are clearly illustrated in Figure 7–2.

DOES THE CUSTOMER WANT RELATIONSHIP BANKING?

An objection sometimes raised to relationship banking is that while it may be a good thing for the institution, customers would prefer to deal with multiple institutions. This enables customers to avoid becoming overly dependent on one institution and to avoid having any one institution know too much about them. Undoubtedly, these and other negatives hold true for some customers. They do not necessarily hold true for most customers, however. For example, in a 1982 nationwide study of consumers with yearly incomes above $15,000, 68 percent of the respondents indicated interest in having all of their financial services managed as a single relationship rather than buying services from various suppliers.[3]

Clearly, some consumer segments will be more interested in relationship banking than will other segments. We have been studying financial service consumers for years, and we find that at least three consumer orientations are profoundly important today. Many consumers have all three orientations.

First, there is the "get-my-money's-worth" orientation. Consumers with this orientation are value-conscious shoppers who seek the best value for the price paid. Such consumers pay more for a Maytag washing machine because they believe that its quality justifies the higher price, and they pay less for unbranded table napkins because they do not believe that the quality of such napkins is materially different from that of branded napkins. In either case, their perception of a product's quality helps shape their purchase decision.

Second, there are "time-buying" consumers. These consumers believe that there is insufficient time to do all that they want to do; they perceive a "poverty of time." Time-buying consumers respond to opportunities to preserve time on activities that they must perform so as to allow more time for activities that they want to perform. Time-buying consumers are convenience-minded.

Third, there are "I am an individual" consumers. These consumers are fiercely protective of their "individuality." Frequently they assess service quality by the extent to which the service is personalized. What seem to be "little things" to a branch manager—recognizing customers and referring to them by name, telephoning customers rather than bouncing their checks, sending customers personal notes thanking them for their business—turn out to be "big things" for the "I am an individual" consumer.

In theory, relationship banking has something to offer consumers with each of these orientations; it is a particularly powerful approach for consumers who have all three orientations. The key, of course, lies in the execution. If the financial institution calls what it does "relationship banking" but in fact practices something else, then the get-my-money's-worth consumer, who is a shopper, will find a better alternative. If the institution, on the other hand, puts together the right combination of services, expertise, and pricing incentives, then it has an excellent shot at value-conscious consumers. Similarly, there are potential timesaving benefits for time-buying consumers if a financial institution can help people deal efficiently with the confusing proliferation of financial services while providing quick and convenient access to funds when they need funds and to expertise when they need expertise. Finally, relationship banking offers "high-touch" to I-am-an-individual consumers, which is the essence of what they seek.

There is, in brief, much potential for relationship banking when we view the financial services business from the vantage point of consumers. What about the wholesale customer? Here the appeal would seem to be more dependent on a customer's situation at a certain point in time. To be sure, establishing relationships with one or more financial institutions can yield important benefits to wholesale customers. Such relationships could mean greater assurance that credit will be available when needed and that the financial institution will assign talented personnel to the account and extend favorable rates and terms. Also, the financial institution with which such relationships have been established is more likely to become knowledgeable about the wholesale customer's needs.

These potential benefits, however, will be more valuable to some customers than to others. A 1983 article by Moriarty, Kimball, and Gay points out some of the factors affecting the perceived value of banking relationships to wholesale customers:[4]

Competition.   Firms having numerous banking alternatives are less likely to value specific banking relationships.

Need for credit.   Firms needing large amounts of bank credit value banking relationships more than do firms having primarily deposit relationships or having access to the commercial paper market.

Need for noncredit services.   Firms requiring complex noncredit services, for example, international cash management systems, will value banking relationships more since fewer banks will be able to satisfy these needs.

Need for flexibility.   Firms with unconventional or complex businesses will value banking relationships more because such relationships assist them in securing the customized services they need.

Financial health.   Less strongly capitalized firms, firms with poor earnings and firms perceived to be in risky businesses will value banking relationships.

Attitude toward financial function.   Firms preferring to buy financial services rather than produce them "in-house" will place a higher value on banking relationships.

Because not all wholesale customers value financial institution relationships, relationship banking is not an appropriate strategy for all customers. A firm with little current need for bank credit and with confidence in its ability to secure credit in the future if needed will probably place a low value on banking relationships. Such firms tend to be more aggressive in buying unbundled services from various banks on the basis of price or quality rather than on the basis of long-standing relationships.[5]

Nor is relationship banking appropriate for all consumers. Some consumers do not have the array of financial service needs that justify a banking relationship on either their part or the institution's. Other consumers, as noted, have a preference for dealing with multiple institutions.

So relationship banking is not for all customers. We believe, however, that it is a potent idea for most financial institutions for some of their customers, and especially for their better customers. Attempting to compete in a deregulated financial services industry without the loyalty and multiple-service commitments of clients—and without any formal strategy for developing clients—strikes us as an inadequate response to some harsh competitive realities faced by all financial institutions save those that have decided to be strictly "specialty houses," that is, to sell a specialized service to numerous customers rather than various services to the same customer.

FIGURE 7–3

Key Elements of Relationship Banking

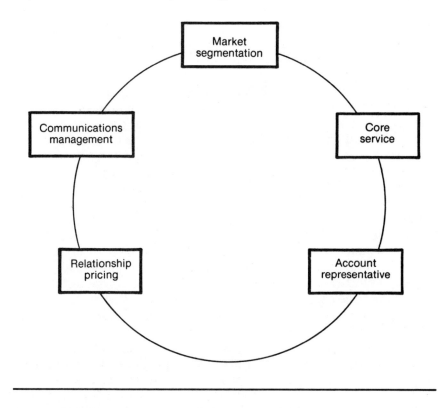

THE ELEMENTS OF RELATIONSHIP BANKING

Implementing relationship banking is not easily done. It requires a strategic approach in which five key elements must not only be present but must be carefully coordinated with one another. These elements are portrayed in Figure 7–3 and discussed in the following sections.

Market Segmentation

Relationship banking requires that a financial institution become a *segmenter* institution. Lasting client relationships require performance at a superior level, which, in turn, necessitates the focusing of resources on specific market segments.

Being a segmenter institution does not mean closing the doors to all customer prospects falling outside the boundaries of selected market segments. Rather, it means that the institution makes a strategic commitment to developing *in-depth* knowledge of the needs of selected segments and then, based on that knowledge, finding innovative ways to attract and keep a "more than normal" share of business from them.

Being a segmenter institution means searching for niches, openings in the market, underserved groups of consumers or organizations. It means looking for market opportunities that the financial institution has the expertise, resources, and willingness to serve. It does not necessarily mean doing what competing institutions are doing.

In our work in financial services marketing over the years, we have learned several important things about segmenting financial markets. First, we have learned that two of the key segmentation variables for consumer markets are income and life-cycle stage. Higher incomes encourage a *broader* set of financial service needs. Changes in the life-cycle stage give rise to a *different* set of financial service needs. The importance of income and life-cycle stage as segmentation criteria is underscored by research done in 1979 on financial "supercustomers": those who maintain a combined total of $25,000 or more in all bank and thrift institution accounts. Supercustomers, who represented only 8 percent of all customers but supplied 39 percent of the deposit dollars, were found to be significantly older than average customers (more than one in five were over 65 years of age) and to have much higher incomes than average (32 percent had annual incomes greater than $35,000, compared to 15 percent of all banking customers at that level).[6]

Second, we have learned that there is no one "upscale" market segment. There are various upscale market segments that can be quite distinct in their needs. One reason for this diversity is the life-cycle factor. Whereas above-average income is a constant in any definition of *upscale*, stage in the life cycle is not. A young, single attorney, a dual-career, middle-aged household, and a retired executive may all be above-average in income, yet have quite different financial service needs because of life-cycle influences. Accordingly, it is far more appropriate to think in terms of upscale market segments than in terms of "the upscale market."

Third, upscale segments are *not* the only game in town. That commercial banks have routinely lost money on a high percentage of depositors in years past is more a function of banking's high-cost delivery system and inept pricing than a function of any inherent unprofitability in nonupscale customers. We believe that in the next several years some striking success stories will be associated with segments not generally regarded as attractive at present. Why? Because while the financial services industry focuses its attention on upscale segments, some enterprising institutions will capitalize on the lack of attention being paid segments assumed to be unprofitable. These enterprising institutions will benefit from a *less-congested* competitive arena while pursuing profitability through sensible pricing, multiple-service relationships, and cost-reducing technologies. We are not suggesting that banks and thrifts forget the supercustomer. What we are suggesting is that banks and thrifts *not* forget everyone else. We like the spirit of a banker friend who recently mused: "Run the nonupscale out of the bank? No way I want to do that. What I want to do is figure out a way I can earn one more dollar a month of fee income from my 70,000 demand deposit customers."

The income pyramid in Figure 7–4 is one way to visualize the segmentation challenge in consumer banking. In this illustration, there are four broad income levels, with the base of the pyramid representing the lowest level (and the most households) and the tip of the pyramid representing the highest level (and the fewest households). The key is to identify segments *within* these levels that are characterized by profit potential, underserved financial service needs, and a fit with the institution's expertise, resources, and long-term strategic direction. (Chapter 5 covers the segmentation selection process in greater detail.)

The hypothetical institution in Figure 7–4 has identified five relationship segments (RS) within the consumer market: high-income professionals, preretired households with incomes above $45,000, dual-career professional households in the $25,000 to $75,000 income category, retired households with incomes above $25,000 and young single and married households that are essentially just starting out and have incomes below $25,000. Several of these segments fit into adjoining income categories. For all five segments, the institution will develop special programming designed to provide the superior need-meeting capability required for relationship banking; it will seek a more than normal share of business from these segments. In addition, by being generally competitive on rates, service quality, locations, and the like, the institution will continue to try to attract its "normal" share of business from the rest of the market.

Each financial organization must create its own realistic and workable approach to segmentation and then program accordingly to reasonably selected segments. You just don't pull segments out of a hat and claim them for your own. Relationship banking requires the marketer to clearly understand why he or she wants this segment, why it is valuable to the organization, before taking the steps that follow.

Core Service

Another key element of relationship banking is a core service around which a relationship can be built. The ideal core service attracts new

FIGURE 7–4

The Segmentation Pyramid

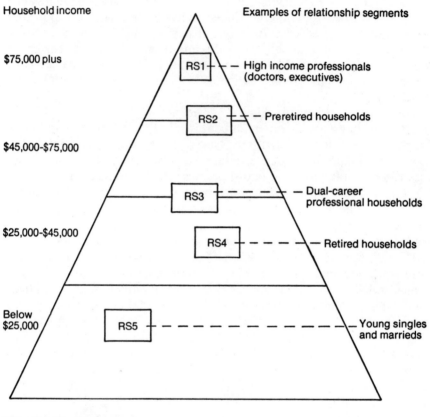

RS = Relationship segment.

customers by satisfying *central, unmet needs* of the market segment; cements the relationship through its quality, multiple component parts and ongoing nature; and encourages relationship enhancement by providing a base from which additional services can be sold. Well-conceived "packages" of services are particularly promising in meeting these criteria. Service packages can be tailored to the needs of specific market segments. They have (by definition) multiple component parts; they facilitate cross-selling; they can be a source of fee income; and they would normally be ongoing rather than discrete. The core service

FIGURE 7–5

Core Service Illustrations

core service	*relationship segments*
Level I financial planning service, including initial comprehensive financial plan, annual financial "checkups," tax preparation, credit line, and asset management services. Fee-based.	High-income professionals
Level I financial planning service with special retirement planning features. Fee-based.	Preretired households
Level II financial planning service offering cash flow analysis, budgeting assistance, insurance analysis, investment analysis, financial record keeping, tax preparation, estate planning, and other services on a "menu" basis. Explicit pricing; fee-based.	Dual-career professionals households
Senior citizen service package, including reduced service charges, free will review, merchant discount program, financial seminars, travel program, and other retirement-age services. In exchange for demand and time deposit accounts.	Retired households
Mortgage loan package, including guaranteed loan availability, home improvement credit line, appraisal services, and housing-related seminars (e.g., home maintenance, home decorating). In exchange for demand and time deposit accounts or fees.	Young singles and marrieds

as a package, then, would actually be a cluster of services marketed together as one entity.

Figure 7–5 illustrates the connection between relationship market segments and core services, using the segment examples from Figure

7–4 and examples of service packages that might be developed for each of them.

Although Figure 7–5 is meant to stand on its own as an illustration, several aspects of the figure warrant comment. One concerns the emphasis on financial planning. The other is a mortgage loan package proposed for the "young singles and marrieds" segment. Concerning the former, numerous surveys in recent years have revealed personal financial planning to be an important consumer need. Millions of get-my-money's-worth consumers need someone to help them put into motion a cohesive, intelligent financial program, someone to explain, to demystify, to present the pros and cons of alternative courses of action.

Financial planning is a major opportunity for financial institutions. A well-executed financial planning service meets all the criteria of the ideal core service. In addition, there is evidence that consumers who use financial planning services are well above average in the total number of financial services that they buy.[7] This is the good news. The bad news is that successfully providing financial planning services will not be an easy goal for banks and thrifts to achieve. In many institutions, the staff expertise and operational systems required for this type of service are not well developed. Being a lender does not necessarily assure all the preparation that one needs to be a financial planner. Nor are most financial institutions properly organized for this purpose. In banks, the trust department is generally one business and the retail bank another business. There is a "wall" between the two. Turf problems tend to be formidable—we would even say senseless—in most situations.

Nevertheless, considerable motivation for solving these problems is provided by the prospects of marketing a needed core service around which a fee-producing client relationship can be built. One way banks can establish successful programs for offering financial planning services is to merge—in part or as a whole—the retail trust and retail banking organizations so that financial planning packages which include services from both "organizations" could be delivered through broadly trained, "generalist" personal bankers. In effect, these personal bankers would be in a position to bring *all* the resources and services of the institution directly to their clients.

Another way to achieve successful programs is to make specific efforts to reduce the labor intensiveness of financial planning, for example, by using microcomputer software and by having clients perform some of the labor themselves, such as completing a financial goals questionnaire and their own financial statements.

Still another way is to focus on analysis, education, and the explanation of alternatives, with the consumer ultimately making the decisions that need to be made.[8]

Just as financial planning addresses a need of middle- and upper-income segments, so the home mortgage—or, better said, more realistically stated, the *home affordability instrument*—addresses a need of young single and married households. Developing a core service package around the residential mortgage holds more appeal for a financial institution than is apparent at first glance. First, there is more protection today against the hazards of long-term lending through adjustable-rate instruments and there is the potential of selling off mortgages in the secondary and pass-through markets. Second, home ownership encourages demand for *related* services such as insurance and for *complementary* services such as home information/entertainment/banking systems. Third, there are the numbers. Many members of the "baby boom" generation of the 50s and early 60s will be trying to buy their first home during the 80s. They represent a critical market for tomorrow that can be drawn to the financial institution that helps them become homeowners today. The main challenge is to make mortgage lending profitable enough by offering flexible financing approaches and by using it as a core service around which a full-fledged—and lasting—relationship can be built.

The home affordability instrument as a core service, as a pedestal for a wide range of existing and potential related and complementary services, is more fully exemplified in Figure 7–6.

One final point about the core service: it must be more than a "sunshine" commitment. A true relationship involves a commitment by both parties. A financial institution cannot manage a relationship on its terms only and expect to maintain the relationship. The institution needs to stand by the client even if this means forgoing short-term profit opportunities that could arise from a reallocation of funds. Relationship banking is not for institutions that are unwilling to take a long-term approach to profitability.

The Account Representative

A third key element of relationship banking is the account representative. The account representative is the liaison between the institution and the client, the relationship banker who knows the client's requirements and has the competence and authority to satisfy them. The account representative provides the "high-touch" response capability that is necessary if a relationship is truly to exist.

The function of the account representative is to transform customers into long-term, multiple-service clients; to cultivate the relationship; to

FIGURE 7-6

The Home Affordability Instrument: A Core Service Pedestal

What the customer wants:	the core service	related services	complementary services
	Flexible rate, maturity, and payment schedules	Vacation property rental, purchase, or time-sharing	Tax preparation, and related bookkeeping-accounting services
	Amortization of initial expenses (settlement costs, etc.)	Housing-as-investment advice	Purchase or rental of home information, education, and entertainment systems
	Simple refinancing or equity drawouts	Home restoration advice	Wide range of insurance options
	Relocation expense financing	Architectural advice	Budget counseling and debt management services
	Home safe advice	Fee-based home appraisal services and home-related legal services	Education financing
	Bridge lending	Home-related insurance coverage	Safekeeping of personal-household valuables
	Preauthorized credit line for home repair and modernization	Single monthly payment schedule combining home payments with home-created payments: utilities, taxes, etc.	Travel planning and financing
			Divorce planning, retirement planning, and survivor benefits planning

keep the relationship *intact*. When the client requires nonroutine service, needs advice, has a question or a problem, an individual assigned to the account is available. Account representatives administer the accounts that have been assigned to them; they sell and cross-sell; they keep their clients informed.

Account representatives are also in a position to "customize" relationships. By learning about the specific backgrounds, characteristics, and needs of clients, and by capturing these data for use as needed, account representatives can frequently tailor services—and personalize service—for specific client situations. In so doing, they give clients—especially "I am an individual" clients—a reason to remain clients rather than "starting over" with another institution. (The downside risk here is that some clients may follow account representatives who change institutions. This risk is minimized to the extent that the entire relationship banking program is strong, not just its account representative component.)

A sophisticated form of account representation in consumer banking is the "personal banker." For clients, personal bankers open new accounts, cross-sell services, make loans, provide information and answer questions, and cut red tape in the institution when a problem occurs. A specific difference between personal bankers and other forms of account representation is the personal banker's lending authority; personal bankers are bankers in every way.[9]

In some personal banker programs, all retail customers are assigned personal bankers. Within these programs, selected personal bankers may work exclusively with a given market segment, for example, doctors and dentists. In other programs, only certain classes of customers are assigned personal bankers. The latter approach will grow more rapidly than the former as more institutions vigorously pursue a segmentation strategy.

Although there have been a number of reports from banks attributing profitable deposit and loan growth to their personal banker programs, personal banking is *not* for every institution. The allure of personal banking should not mask the variety of implementation challenges that it poses. If the wrong personnel are selected as personal bankers, the program will fail. If the right people are selected but they are without adequate support staff, they will become expensive clerks. Turnover of personal bankers tends to be a problem in the best of programs. Keeping personal bankers motivated—and growing—after they master the fundamentals of the role is also a challenge.

Given these and other problems—not to mention cost—why even consider such a step? The answer is that true relationship banking is simply not possible without personal banking or some variation of it. Machines and clerks—no matter how necessary for routine banking—

FIGURE 7–7

Success Factors for Personal Banker Programs

Senior management commitment

Personal banking involves a change in an institution's culture, philosophy, and organization. Without deep commitment from top management, failure is inevitable.

Automation

If personal bankers are to practice relationship banking they must be able to determine what services a client already uses. Only automated systems can supply personal bankers with the client information they need and managers with a basis for evaluating each personal banker's productivity.

Effective staffing

Careful selection of personal bankers can moderate turnover later. Personal bankers need to have the analytical skills to make sound credit decisions, the entrepreneurial skills to "build a clientele," the time management skills to survive unpredictable daily schedules, and the people skills to put clients at ease.

cannot alone create and maintain genuine client relationships. It is not possible to have a relationship when the only party to the relationship is the customer. A good personal banking program is a means of differentiating the institution, of building the critical high-touch response capability into a high-technology financial services environment, of materially increasing cross-selling performance, of providing "I am an individual" consumers with a banker, not just a bank.

Figure 7–7 summarizes the requirements of a successful personal banker program.[10] These requirements must be met if the potential benefits of personal banking are to be realized.

Relationship Pricing

Another key element of relationship banking is pricing services in such a way that clients are encouraged to consolidate much or all of their business with one institution. This approach, known as "relationship pricing," is based on the old marketing idea of a better deal for better customers. If good customers receive a better deal, the theory goes, there will be incentive for other customers to become "good." Not surprisingly, this is what tends to occur.

FIGURE 7-7 *(concluded)*

Continuous training

First-rate personal bankers will want to continue to grow on the job. It is important that training and education be an ongoing process.

Precise role definition, proper office layout

Personal bankers often become inundated with paperwork and clerical duties. Precisely defining the roles of personal bankers and their support staff—and arranging the layout of facilities to reinforce these definitions—should enable personal bankers to devote attention to matters requiring their level of expertise and support personnel to handle routine matters.

Adequate compensation/career advancement structure

If personal bankers cannot achieve satisfactory salary increments and promotions within the personal banker career track, then high turnover is virtually assured. A career ladder system incorporating promotion opportunities within personal banking and offering competitive income and promotion potential is necessary.

Ongoing internal/external marketing

With personal banking, the institution is marketing a philosophy of doing business. That philosophy should be marketed to personnel before it is marketed to the public. With both groups, marketing should be ongoing, not just a big introductory splash.

A Citibank executive was quoted in 1981 as saying: "Our research shows that consumers will consolidate much if not all of their banking with you if there is a tangible advantage to them, and if that advantage can be easily understood."[11]

At that time, Citibank was charging two percentage points lower interest on installment loans for customers having both checking and savings accounts at the bank. For residential mortgages, the differential between noncustomers and customers was one percentage point.

Lower loan rates—or service fees—are one way to encourage relationships. Another alternative in a deregulated era is to pay more interest for more funds. We can expect much innovation with this alternative—for example, paying each client a "custom" rate depending on an appraisal of the total relationship or awarding bonuses for funds held with the institution for certain lengths of time.

Still another form of relationship pricing is service augmentation, that is, building "extras" into the service to differentiate it from the service available to lesser customers or noncustomers. For meaningful results with service augmentation, the extras need to be valued by clients and not readily available from competitors. When this is the case, loyalty is encouraged. The Texas bank that at this writing is making available its private plane as well as other amenities to high-balance depositors is using service augmentation.

Relationship pricing is equally applicable to both wholesale and retail banking. Indeed, it has long been common practice in wholesale banking to offer the most favorable rates to the best customers. Not so in retail banking, where it took relaxation of usury laws, deregulation, and growing acceptance of relationship banking in the early 1980s to encourage institutions to think in relationship pricing terms.

Regardless of the customer (wholesale or retail) or the form that relationship pricing takes (lower rates on loans, lower fees on services, higher rates on deposits, augmented services), the objective remains the same: to encourage client loyalty by rewarding it. Most important of all, with relationship pricing as Figure 7–8 illustrates, clearly you reward clients where it really counts: *in the pocketbook.*

FIGURE 7–8

Relationship Banking: An International Perspective

The importance of paying attention to the whole customer relationship is now widely recognized. Strong emphasis is placed on the cross-selling of services and the development of packages that meet the needs of particular segments of the market. To encourage the use of an array of services from the same institution, relationship pricing can be used. . . . In fact, relationship pricing is an effective way of securing a maximum contribution to the recovery of overheads by individual customers. . . .

Relationship pricing and relationship banking will in some sense act as a gateway to the market for ancillary services—and it is these that are likely to hold the key to the future of branch networks and the emergence of financial supermarkets. As payment services will become little more than electronic message switching and as deposit taking and lending will become a matter of electronic scorekeeping, ancillary services are likely to become increasingly important. They may in fact develop from being additional revenue-earning activities to being, eventually, the entire *raison d'etre* of branch networks.

Source: *Dimitri Vittas,* senior consultant, Committee of London Clearing Bankers' Research Group, in "Facing Up to the Pricing Dilemma," *Retail Banker International,* October 31, 1983, p. 10. Mr. Vittas is also coauthor of *The Retail Banking Revolution,* a detailed assessment of worldwide trends in the consumer financial services business.

Communications Management

The final key element of relationship banking is communications management: preparing relationship personnel to administer, to inform, to sell, while preparing clients to handle their financial affairs most effectively. Communications management is information-intensive; it involves the development of knowledge and the building of competence.

The importance of effective communications management in relationship banking is summed up by the truism that financial institution personnel cannot sell and clients will not buy what they don't understand or, for that matter, what they don't believe in. Also, no client wants a relationship with an incompetent and uncommunicative banker.

Communications management has two interdependent dimensions. The first is a commitment to staff education and training that will transform personnel into account representatives—persons who are *knowledgeable* about the service line, the marketplace, client characteristics and needs, and matters of money and who are *skillful* in executing the various roles associated with their particular jobs.

The second is a commitment to client education. Client education is premised on the assumption that knowledgeable customers make better customers—customers who will recognize and respond to quality and who are less likely to be influenced by competitor gimmickry. Client education is neither public relations cosmetics nor image advertising blitzes. Rather, it may involve financial newsletters designed for specific professional, business, or consumer segments; videotapes that explain complex services to corporate clients and prospects; a money management type of magazine for consumers; a business management seminar series for small business clients; advertisements that present in simple English the pros and cons of newer, more complicated financial instruments; educationally oriented literature that is available in banking offices; client-accessed terminals in banking offices providing information on various services; even computer software—financial tutorials and simulations—that businesses and households can work through on their microcomputers.

External communications that help clients better manage their financial affairs, that help protect or increase their financial strength, encourage the building of relationships. Relationship banking requires an atmosphere of trust; it requires institutional credibility. These qualities are nurtured through an orientation to inform. Communications management is treated in greater detail in Chapter 11, "The New PR: Communications," which discusses prospective programs for reaching relationship *clients* as one major public of financial institutions.

CONCLUSION

The highly competitive financial services industry of the 1980s requires financial institutions to make the difficult transition from order-taking banking to relationship banking. Relationship banking is attracting, maintaining, and enhancing client relationships. In relationship banking, attracting new customers to the institution is viewed as an *intermediate* step in the marketing cycle; the objective of relationship banking is to serve these customers as clients, selling them five or seven or nine services for a long time instead of one or two services for a short time.

Relationship banking offers potential benefits for the institution and customer alike. Given the tenor of the times, it is an appealing idea. An appealing idea, however, is not enough. To put the idea into practice, some cornerstone elements are needed. The elements that we suggest in this chapter—segmentation, the core service, account representation, relationship pricing, communications management—are the ones we believe to be vital. These are the elements that allow the idea of relationship banking to become a reality.

NOTES

1. Leonard L. Berry and Thomas W. Thompson, "Relationship Banking: The Art of Turning Customers into Clients," *Journal of Retail Banking,* June 1982, pp. 64–65.
2. Quoted in Norwood W. "Red" Pope, "Price Is the Main Key to Relationship Banking," *American Banker,* May 26, 1982, p. 17.
3. As reported in "What the 'Emerging Affluent' Want," *American Banker,* September 13, 1982, p. 8.
4. Rowland T. Moriarty, Ralph C. Kimball, and John H. Gay, "The Management of Corporate Banking Relationships," *Sloan Management Review,* Spring 1983, p. 7.
5. Ibid., pp. 8–9.
6. Susan Snell, "Who Are the Supercustomers, and Why Are They Smiling?" *Compendium,* vol. 1, no. 2.
7. "What the 'Emerging Affluent' Want," p. 8.
8. G. Lynn Shostack, "What Ever Happened to Total Financial Planning?" *American Banker,* September 22, 1982, p. 16.
9. Berry and Thompson, "Relationship Banking," p. 70.
10. The material for this figure is based on Leonard L. Berry, "Success Requirements for Personal Banking Programs," *Journal of Retail Banking,* Winter 1982, pp. 1–7.
11. Quoted in Michael Schroeder, "New York Banks Advance Two-Tiered Consumer Pricing," *American Banker,* August 10, 1981, p. 14.

PART FOUR

Implementing Marketing

"To me, there are two royal roads to bankruptcy in the new arena of very competitive consumer financial services: one is paved with pride— that's the root cause of blindly trying to 'go it alone,' to make everything yourself in this vastly more complex and expensive world."

"The second road to ruin is paved with expediency clothed in the mistaken belief that successful, new-generation marketing means that offering a new service quickly is more important than the quality of the customer attention behind it. The shortcut to profitability that detours around excellent customer service is an eight-lane highway to nowhere."

Louis V. Gerstner, Jr., *vice chairman, American Express Company, from an address: "Fact and Fantasy in the Emerging World of Consumer Financial Services," at the Texas Bankers Association Annual Convention, Dallas, May 14, 1982*

Developing New Financial Services

This chapter introduces Part Four of our book, "*Implementing Marketing.*" In this chapter, we focus on developing new services: its importance, categories of new services that might be developed, the implications of developing services rather than goods, the need to foster a climate for innovation in the organization, and the need to work out a systematic approach to new service development. We close out the chapter by identifying success factors in new service development.

Both internal and external factors drive new service development efforts in financial institutions. Most institutions seek to grow, to increase earnings, to build market share. They are not content to "stand still." And even if they were, "standing still" in a market as dynamic and competitive as financial services inevitably means "being left behind." The fundamental truth of marketing—its one unshakable constant—is that markets continually change. New services are a principal means of responding to such change. To be overly conservative in developing new services, or to be unwilling to make the resource and organizational commitments required to be successful, or to "leave the job up to the regulators,"is to encourage bigger and bigger gaps between what the market wants to buy and what the institution has to sell.

Minimizing these gaps—having available to sell what the market wants to buy—is at the heart of the marketing challenge; it is what marketing is all about.

The new service development function has always been important to financial institutions. It is services, after all, that are marketed. Services generate revenue; everything else generates cost. In today's financial services industry, however, the new service development function has shifted from merely being important to being *critical*. The growing emphasis on strategic planning is leading banks, thrifts, and other financial institutions into entirely new businesses for which services must be developed. Deregulation is creating new service possibilities that heretofore were prohibited. Implementing relationship banking programs requires the development of core services tailored to the needs of selected market segments as the last chapter discussed. Intensifying competition means that some services will have to be developed strictly for defensive purposes, that is, to prevent the loss of good customers. Narrow lending spreads mean greater stress on fee-producing services, which will have to be developed.

Virtually every force for change that is reshaping the financial services business underlines the growing significance of the new service development function. Some financial institutions will "manufacture" most or all of their new services; others will buy certain services from producing institutions and then "retail" them to their own customers. This chapter focuses on "manufacturing." We wish to make clear, however, that a given institution need not be a manufacturer to be an aggressive marketer of new services.

TYPES OF NEW SERVICES

Just what is a new service? In actuality, a range of possibilities exist, as the following classification scheme suggests.

1. *Major Innovations.* These are *fundamentally* new services that typically involve new technology, a sizable investment, considerable risk, and significant potential. These services are not only new to the institution; they are also new to the market. They are "high-stakes services" in every sense of the phrase. This category is particularly important to institutions seeking to profit from major innovations by franchising them to other firms, by marketing them to specialized market niches over large territories, and/or by using them as core services around which to build relationship banking programs.

2. *New Service Lines.* This category refers to a service line that is new to the institution but not to the market. In effect, the institution enters a business in which other companies already compete. The potential for obtaining revenue from nontraditional sources, enhancing the value of relationship packages, and cementing client loyalties, among other possible goals, provides the rationale. The newness of the line to the institution and the presence of existing competitors add to the risk. This will be a priority category throughout the 1980s as many financial institutions—manufacturers and retailers alike—seek to be one-stop financial service providers for key market segments. Hence, we see financial institutions adding—or thinking about adding—insurance services, real estate brokerage services, financial counseling services, securities brokerage services and a host of other service lines.

3. Additions to Existing Service Lines. This category applies when the institution adds a new service—usually a variation of an existing service—to a service line already in place. This is the category that has traditionally accounted for most new service development activity in banking and thrift institutions. The rationale: to attract additional business by more *precisely* meeting the requirements of given market segments.

Sometimes known as "line-stretching" or "product proliferation," adding services to existing lines usually involves less downside risk—and less upside potential—than the new service categories previously discussed. The required investment is generally low, and the technology and marketing approaches to be used are familiar. For institution and customer alike, little new learning is required.

Like the American automobile industry, which has gotten into the habit of producing an endless variety of cars, America's banks and thrifts have been guilty of *oversegmentation*. The inclination has been to add rather than to eliminate services. The result in many institutions is unwieldy service lines, confusing to both employees and customers. However, a *shift in emphasis is occurring*. A growing number of institutions are simplifying their lines, eliminating redundancies, cleaning out services that have not been selling. We anticipate a continuation of this trend. Well-managed financial institutions will continue to add new services to existing lines; they will, however, be more selective than they were in the past, concentrating efforts on the services that will result in the greatest returns.

4. Modifications of Existing Services. In this category, the institution alters an existing service. A new service is created from an old one. The intent is to bolster the appeal of the service by improving its performance, adding enhancements, making it simpler or more convenient to use, lowering its delivery cost and passing these savings on to the customer, or in some other way. Service modification is an important category for the future. Management can improve many services already on the market if it wants to do so. The risks are confined to the devoting of extra resources to a service that may prove unwarranted by the ensuing market response. The potential rewards—satisfied customers who remain customers longer, who buy other services from the institution, and who spread favorable word-of-mouth advertising—will justify the risks much of the time.

THE NATURE OF SERVICES

The fact that financial institutions develop and market services, rather than goods, presents some distinct challenges. *The goods firm produces and markets objects—for example, automobiles, neckties, industrial machines. The services firm produces and markets performances—for example dry cleaning, investment advice, transportation.* Critical differences exist when the task at hand is to make and market a performance rather than an object. Chapter 3 discussed these differences in the context of marketing strategy. In this section, we relate them to the new service development function.

Intangibility

Services are, in essence, intangible. Unlike goods, they cannot be seen, touched, smelled, tasted, tried on for size, stored on a shelf. Services are used by customers, but they are not possessed. Money is spent, but there is nothing tangible to show for the expenditure. The traveler spends hundreds of dollars on airfares, taxi fares, hotel rooms, and restaurant meals and yet returns from the trip with little more than memories and dirty laundry. The college student spends thousands of dollars for an "education" that is invisible to the naked eye.

Although most service performances are supported by tangibles—the airplane in the case of airline transportation, for example—the essence of what customers buy when they buy a service is a performance that another party renders for their benefit. What the financial services customer really buys is not the checkbook but a convenient, relatively safe, and easy-to-understand means for transferring funds. The checkbook, the monthly statement, the office facilities—these are tangibles associated with the service, but they are not the service. The service is the collective efforts of financial institutions that result in funds being debited from one account and credited to another because the payor fills out and signs a piece of paper (a check). Without this collective effort—this performance—the checkbook and all the other tangibles are essentially worthless

One way to grasp the meaningfulness of intangibility in a marketing context is to first stroll through a fashion department store such as

Bloomingdale's or Macy's and then to enter a banking, savings and loan, securities brokerage, or insurance firm office. In the department store, there will be goods everywhere—colorful goods, goods that are interesting to look at, goods that can be touched, goods that, in many instances, will sell themselves. The department store will be full of things; there will be much to see. Not so with the financial institution, which will be mostly empty, save for furnishings, forms, and people No products sit on shelves to be touched or inspected. The contrast is striking. Back-to-back visits to the two types of institutions are recommended for anyone who believes that the notion of intangibility is just so much academic nonsense.

Because the service of the financial institution is itself invisible, customers tend to be especially attentive to that which is visible—the service facility, the appearance of service personnel, the equipment used in performing the service, account statements, stationery, logos—for clues about the service's nature and quality.[1] A key challenge in developing new financial services is to design the tangibles associated with the service in such a way that they reinforce the overall positioning strategy. This task can be labeled "managing evidence." Banker Lynn Shostack writes: "Evidence must be as carefully designed and managed as a service itself, for it is evidence that provides the clues and the confirmations (or contradictions) that the consumer seeks and needs in order to formulate a specific mental 'reality' for the service."[2]

A financial institution does not want to deliver a new financial planning service for consumers in run-down branch offices with tattered furnishings and limited privacy; it does not want to introduce a new EFT service with a bland plastic card; it does not want to sell a new corporate cash management service with 22-year-old salespeople right out of college.

Inseparabiltiy of Production and Consumption

Whereas a good is manufactured in a factory, then sold and then consumed, for many services the sequence is reversed. First the service is sold, and then it is produced—or partially produced—in the presence of the customer. Frequently production and consumption are inseparable, which means that the customer must be present for the service to be performed. The customer must be present for a dental exam, must be in the taxi to receive a taxi ride.

Services can be performed directly for the customer (for example, a continuing education course, airline transportation, a haircut) or for the customer's property (for example, mail service, car washing, gardening). Generally, services performed for the customer require that the customer be present during service production.

The key implication of inseparability is that, in effect, the customer is *in the factory*. In the barber's chair, in the airline seat, or in the banking office, the customer witnesses the production of the service firsthand. How service personnel conduct themselves, how they act, even how they dress, can greatly influence the customer's level of satisfaction with the service. Accordingly, a key issue in developing new financial services is *orchestrating* the behaviors of contact personnel so that the service actually rendered will be what its developers *and* the customer want it to be.

Potential for Variability

The inseparability characteristic would not be so important in matters of service design if most services were not so labor-intensive. It is labor intensity that contributes to the variability that customers often experience when they purchase services. The extensive involvement of human beings in the production of a service introduces a degree of nonuniformity in the service that is generally not present when equipment dominates the production process. Films shown in movie theaters, automated car washes, and telephone communications are examples of equipment-based services that are relatively standardized. For people-based services such as health care, education, business consulting, and banking, it is a different story. Variability occurs because service personnel differ in their technical and interpersonal skills, in their personalities, and in their attitudes toward their work. Indeed, the *same* service worker may provide differing levels of service quality from one service situation to the next.

Comparing the standardized services delivered through automatic teller machines with the variable services delivered by human tellers makes the point. If the ATM is up, it performs uniformly for all customers, regardless of the time of day, the length of the queue waiting for service, or an individual customer's attitude or appearance. Automatic teller machines do not become angry with a supervisor, do not have prejudices, and do not have personal problems that affect job performance. The shifting of function from personnel to machines, as in the case of ATMs, does not mean that all customers will like or use the machines; it does mean, however, that those who do use the machines will receive a more standardized service.

Given the potential for variability that labor-intensive services encourage, a central consideration in designing new financial services is whether the service should be people-based or equipment-based. The success of McDonald's in using technology and automated systems to minimize the opportunity for human error in producing the service is legendary. Knowing when to offer "high-touch" and when to offer "high-tech" can pay off richly in the development of financial services.

NURTURING INNOVATION

The new service development function is more likely to flourish in organizations that place a premium on innovation. Many factors can get in the way of organizational innovativeness, and in the absence of concerted efforts to nurture the innovative spirit, these factors will succeed in reining it in. The innovative spirit resides within individuals; it can bubble up or stay put, depending on the organizational climate in which individuals work. Innovation is not something that top management can call forth when needed; it cannot be turned on and off like a water faucet. Rather, the challenge is to develop a climate for innovation that stimulates creative thinking and rewards doing something with the thinking. Thinking in and of itself is not enough. As Levitt points out: "Creativity is thinking up new things. Innovation is doing new things."[3]

The financial services industry is undergoing an "innovation shift" from traditional technologies and markets to nontraditional technologies and markets.[4] *All* of an institution's creative resources should be called upon during this transition era. As Rosabeth Kanter argues in *The Change Masters*, the grass roots of companies teem with ideas if only the ideas are given an opportunity.[5] Whereas marketing department personnel should be innovative themselves, a key marketing department role concerning innovation is helping to create a climate for innovation *throughout* the organization. It is as important for marketing department personnel to be innovative in encouraging innovation as it is for them to be innovative in their own right.

Creating a Climate of Trying

Creating a *climate of trying* requires more than management rhetoric or exhortations; deeds are what counts. Personnel throughout the organization need to feel confident that their ideas are valued and will receive full consideration. The role of staff (legal, marketing, planning) needs to be clarified in a manner that facilitates entrepreneurial thinking rather than stifling it. If, in actuality, staff groups are the decision makers and line groups the advisers, and a "we" versus "they" climate prevails, then the factors that allowed this condition to occur must be dealt with.[6]

The atmosphere in the organization should be such that employees do not fear career damage if the ideas they propose are rejected, or are accepted but fail, or step on someone's toes. To unleash the innovative spirit, management must *tolerate failure*. Personnel who author new ideas that succeed should be rewarded in a manner appropriate to the significance of the innovation. Monetary and nonmonetary recognitions should be visible for all to see. At 3M, a company praised in the literature for its entrepreneurial culture, venture groups bringing a new product to a million dollars in profitable sales are treated as though they had just won the Super Bowl. "Lights flash, bells ring, and video cameras are called out to recognize the entrepreneurial team that is responsible for this achievement."[7]

Performance reviews for all the managers should include innovations that their unit of responsibility has sponsored to strengthen the company over the long term. Performance reviews should not be restricted to short-term results since typically innovation costs money before it makes money.

Innovation Fund. Management can demonstrate tangible support for innovation through an innovation fund, a pool of dollars that is available to support the development and testing of innovative projects. The fund could conceivably support any type of innovation—for example a new service requiring unfamiliar technology, a new operational process, the design of a new information system. The fund should be reserved for truly innovative projects, and relatively few levels of approval should be required for an award to be made.[8]

Levi Strauss maintains an in-house venture capital fund to encourage new product ideas from middle managers. That fund is supplemental to existing divisional budgets, prompting managers to make proposals without the fear of having to cut back on other projects due to insufficient funding.[9]

Idea Seeding. Stimulating personnel to think beyond the "what is" in the organization is the objective of idea-seeding activities. For example, a financial institution could publish an internal newsletter recognizing innovations and innovators within the company and calling attention to especially interesting and provocative ideas that have been expressed about the financial services business. The institution could also sponsor in-house workshops or lectures in which *outsiders* (academics, consultants, analysts, journalists, etc.) present their ideas about the financial services business. Idea seeding works best when as many personnel in the organization as possible are included. Creativity is *not* the exclusive property of higher-level executives.

Rules of Risk. One method for management to nurture a climate of trying is to think through the types and levels of entrepreneurial behavior that it wishes to encourage and to publish these expectations internally. These "rules of risk" define the company's risk posture, the kinds of risks that are acceptable, the kinds of risk-taking behaviors that are expected. The rules serve as guidelines, reminders, and motivators concerning risk taking and innovative thinking in an individual employee's work. Different sets of rules can be developed for managerial and nonmanagerial positions.

In a 1979 speech, the president of the Polaris E-Z GO Division of Textron presented the "rules of risk" used in his organization. They are reproduced in Figure 8–1 to illustrate the concept. Naturally, each institution needs to formulate rules of risk to fit its own situation.

Organizing for Innovation

Chapter 4 covers organizational structure and strategy issues in detail. Our concern in this section is with structural arrangements that facilitate new service innovation. In this regard, three strategies warrant consideration: organizing along market lines, decentralization, and venture groups.

Market Managers. The strength of product manager organizations is also its weakness: product managers focus their energies on the product

---

FIGURE 8–1

The Polaris/E-Z Go "Rules of Risk"

1. Always attack the market aggressively but realistically. Never roll the dice on a double-or-nothing gamble. In other words, stay hungry—but don't get greedy.

2. Always have a fallback position that you regard as secure. Use it if your risk plans do not work as well as you thought they would.

3. Always clearly calculate the upside rewards, the odds of success and the cost of failure. If either the odds or the cost indicate a substantial degree of risk without a commensurate upside reward, stop everything and reassess your position.

4. Don't be afraid to fail, particularly if you have satisfied yourself that you did everything possible to succeed and that the failure was caused by an outside force that was both unpredictable and uncontrollable.

5. Don't hesitate to abort your risk program, particularly if you feel that it has suddenly crossed the boundaries between a good risk and a shaky risk. Take your losses early.

6. Management is expected to be innovative and to take the risk necessary to maintain market leadership, and it should not be penalized if a good risk fails.

7. Management will ultimately be penalized for a failure to take risks. The failure to generate leadership programs that inevitably require risk will result in a stagnation of the company's product development and/or marketing programs.

Source: D. F. Myers, "Balancing Risk Interests of the Individual and the Company," a presentation to the 1979 Marketing Conference of the Conference Board, New York City, October 1979.

or product line for which they are responsible. Giving existing products ongoing attention is necessary. Unfortunately, the central question that should continually be raised—"What does the market need that we do not offer at present"—frequently falls through the cracks.

Our bias is in favor of managing markets, not just products. The market manager's mandate is to serve the market by whatever means are necessary, including brand-new services, improvements in existing services, and new or improved marketing methods. The market manager's role is strategic rather than tactical. Market managers concentrate on what needs doing rather than on what is already being done.

The ideal arrangement in larger institutions is for product managers to report to market managers. In many smaller institutions, the market manager will need to do the product manager's job. Even in these instances, the position should be titled "market manager" to signal the critical new service development function that needs to be performed.

Decentralization. We believe that more and better new services will result when responsibility and authority for new service development is decentralized into line divisions rather than housed within a centralized marketing department. To be sure, this thinking flies in the face of traditional organizational arrangements in which the marketing department does marketing and other departments do other things. Our view is that marketing is everyone's job in the organization; the role of the marketing department is not so much to do the institution's marketing as to assist others in the organization to be successful marketers.

In the case of new service development, centralized marketing department personnel might perform marketing research services, serve as members of new service development groups, and assist in formulating new service marketing plans. Responsibility and authority for developing new services, however, should reside in the division that will be marketing them. The line is closest to the customer. With profit and loss accountabilities, the line has a big stake in the array of services that it has available to sell. Many of the problems that occur in traditional organizations—"The marketing department doesn't understand our requirements," or "The marketing department pays more attention to other divisions," or "The marketing department isn't coming up with enough good ideas"—would occur with less frequency if line divisions, in effect, had to do more of their own marketing.

Venture Groups. One organizational form that is consistent with efforts to organize along market lines and to decentralize service development is the venture group. Venture groups are nonpermanent teams with the mandate to pursue innovation within some predefined, but invariably broad, scope. Their charter may be to help the institution get into the cash management business, or to search for new financial services that will assist people in retirement, or to explore new opportunities in electronic banking. Jolson writes: "A venture team is essentially an intracorporate task force . . . to nurture growth businesses under hothouse conditions of concentrated devotion, imagination, flexibility, and relative isolation from the day-to-day priorities of running established operations."[10]

The venture group is considered a key part of 3M's success in fostering innovation. Venture groups at 3M consist of members from the technical, manufacturing, marketing, sales, and, possibly, financial areas of the business. The assignments are voluntary, and they are full time for as long as the venture group is in existence. The group stays together through the new product's introduction into the market.

DEVELOPING NEW SERVICES SYSTEMATICALLY

Risk is inherent in the development of new services. Resources are invested in anticipation of returns sufficient to justify the investment. The relevant issue in new service development is therefore not how to avoid risk but, rather, which risks should be assumed? Taking a systematic approach to new service development, rather than a haphazard approach, helps in making these decisions. We present such a systematic approach in this section. Figure 8–2 lists the steps.[11]

Strategic Guidelines

A crucial first step in the new service development process is management's definition of the *strategic roles* that new services should play and the *priority market segments* that new services should attract. Absent this step, considerable resources and energy may be devoted to new service ideas that are unrelated to the institution's strategic direction or, worse, in conflict with it. Stated differently, the exploration and screening stages should be *guided* if new service development work is to be supportive of the institution's strategic plan. Figure 8–3 presents examples of strategic roles for new services. (See Figure 7–4 in the previous chapter for segment examples.) Each institution must, of course, define its own set of strategic roles and priority segments. Research documents the importance of management articulating clear and consistent strategic guidelines to guide the new product development effort.[12]

Exploration

The purpose of the exploration stage is to generate new service ideas. The search for new service ideas should be formalized, ongoing, and

FIGURE 8–2

New Service Development System

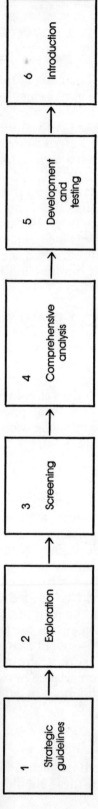

1	2	3	4	5	6
Strategic guidelines	Exploration	Screening	Comprehensive analysis	Development and testing	Introduction

FIGURE 8-3

Examples of Strategic Service Roles to Guide New Service Development

1. Capitalize on deregulation.
2. Encourage full-fledged client relationships.
3. Take advantage of the large network of branch offices.
4. Increase the proportion of noninterest income to total income.
5. Defend the market share of transaction services.
6. Build the institution's reputation as a preeminent source of financial information.
7. Reduce the labor intensity of routine service delivery.
8. Enhance the institution's image as an innovator among key publics (customers, prospects, employees, analysts, investors).
9. Serve priority segments in unique, hard-to-duplicate, ways.
10. Increase flexibility and versatility in meeting the specific borrowing requirements of key customers and prospects.

proactive. The alternative is to assume that good ideas will arise despite the absence of an organized effort.

A key to success in exploration is the assignment of responsibility. The process needs to be managed; somebody must be in charge. This individual may be a market manager, a product development officer, a venture team leader, or the head of a new services committee, but accountability needs to be pinpointed for the work to be done at the level and with the continuity that is required. The task is to *continually* tap external and internal sources of new service ideas.

External Sources. The new service ideas having the most potential will invariably be those that address important, unmet wants of target markets. Accordingly, a key source of ideas is the target market itself and a key means of tapping this source is marketing research. Although customer prospects are generally unable to describe the new services that they would like, they can discuss their financial concerns, their levels of satisfaction with existing services, and the strategies that they use to manage some aspect of their financial lives. Convening small "focus" groups of customers and prospects representing specific target markets (for example, treasurers of small manufacturing firms or consumers nearing retirement) for the purpose of such discussions can be a fruitful source of *clues* concerning new services that might be developed and old services that might be improved.

Systematically monitoring service innovations within various sectors of the financial services industry can also spark ideas. Monitoring a wide variety of industry media, subscribing to selected out-of-town newspapers, and participating in "peer institution" exchange groups, among other endeavors, can lead to imitation that is innovative in a given geographic market or to innovative imitation, that is, an improved version of what is imitated.

Internal Sources. Soliciting input from employees can also be a rich source of ideas, especially if the employees perceive it to be worthwhile to make suggestions. One technique, brainstorming, involves calling together small groups of employees—usually executives with diverse backgrounds—and presenting them with a general problem statement. For example, a brainstorming group might be asked to deal with the following issue: "Consumers need help in planning their financial affairs. How can we address this need in a way that is affordable to consumers and profitable to us?" Brainstorming offers the potential of "idea synergy"; that is, the discussion triggers fresh thinking that might not have occurred had the discussion never taken place.

Having customer contact personnel complete periodic questionnaires and holding group interviews with them are among the techniques that can be used to capture recurring customer feedback about existing services or unmet needs. Making it easier for employees to suggest new service ideas is another option. A simple form can be developed on which employees can suggest new ideas. The form might require a brief description of the proposed service, identification of the customer segment for which it is intended, and an indication of its advantages over existing services. The proposer can be rewarded in a manner consistent with the idea's progress through the service development system.

Contact personnel are "boundary spanners" with empathy for both the institution and the customer. Because these personnel are physically and psychologically close to the customer, they can be a valuable source of information about customer wants.[13] To overlook this resource during the exploration stage is to miss a key opportunity. The seeds of good ideas can be anywhere in an organization; it's important to have a wide net during the exploration stage.

Screening

The purpose of the screening stage is to determine which of the new service ideas identified in the exploration stage warrant further consideration. Each idea is screened on the basis of predetermined criteria to separate promising ideas from those not meriting additional evaluation. Ideally, screening incorporates the following characteristics:

1. Service ideas within a given category (e.g., consumer services, wholesale services) are screened on the basis of preestablished, uniform criteria.

2. The screening is done by a group (for example, a new service development committee) rather than by just one person. Members of the group represent various functional areas and types of expertise.
3. The screening is inexpensive. Information needed to screen new service ideas is either known to one or more of the screeners or easily gathered. Empirical research is the exception rather than the rule.
4. The screening criteria reflect management's strategic guidelines for new services. Also, all relevant company policies are considered during screening. The ideas surviving screening are consistent with the strategic direction and policies of the institution.
5. The screening is conducted in phases, with lower-cost screens (to eliminate unpromising ideas) coming before higher-cost screens.

Figures 8–4 and 8–5 illustrate the multiphase characteristic of screening. The sample questions in Figure 8–4 reflect strategy and policy considerations and can be answered yes or no. If the idea survives, it is then evaluated against a second set of criteria (Figure 8–5), which cover a range of values, are weighted, and are more time-consuming and expensive to assess.

Comprehensive Analysis

The importance of screening is underscored by the nature of the step following it, which is an intensive analysis of the service idea. A faulty

---

FIGURE 8–4

Examples of First-Phase Screens

	yes	no
1. Can the service be marketed through our existing distribution points?	×	
2. Is the service hard to imitate?	×	
3 Can the service be marketed through our existing sales force?	×	
4. Will the service contribute to relationship building?	×	
5. Is the service compatible with existing operations resources?	×	
6. Is the service consistent with our "top of the line" image?	×	
7. Is the service equipment-intensive rather than labor-intensive?		×
8. Is it possible to build a proprietary market niche?	×	
9. Will the service generate noninterest income?	×	
10. Is the service reasonably simple to understand?	×	

Minimum score to advance to next phase is six "yes" answers.

FIGURE 8–5

Examples of Second-Phase Screens

criteria	raw score			weight	total score
Extent of target market need for the service	below average 1	average ②	above average 3	×2	4
Potential profitability (ROI)	below average 1	average ②	above average 3	×2	4
Likely emergence of competition	within 6 months ①	6 months– 1 year 2	more than 1 year 3	×1	1
Service life cycle	1 year 1	1–3 years 2	3+ years ③	×1	3
Compatibility with strengths of company	less than average 1	average 2	greater than average ③	×2	6
					18

Minimum score to advance is 16.

screening process increases the probability of spending considerable time and funds analyzing the wrong ideas. The comprehensive analysis stage involves a detailed examination of a service's operational, marketing, and financial feasibility. The market is analyzed; the service is precisely defined; key operations and implementation issues are raised and addressed; a marketing plan is developed; and financial forecasts are made. In this stage, unlike the previous stage, empirical research is the rule rather than the exception. Figure 8–6 illustrates the components and recommended sequence of the comprehensive analysis stage. In reviewing Figure 8–6, keep these characteristics in mind:

1. The steps should be followed sequentially so that information gathered in one step can be applied toward the next step. One would not want to design a marketing strategy before conducting the market analysis, for example, and accurate financial forecasts are unlikely in the absence of a marketing plan. The operations feasibility analysis requires that a detailed description of the service be available.

2. The service idea should pass muster at each step before moving to the next step. It makes no sense to develop a marketing plan for a

service that is not operationally feasible. This is another reason for addressing the steps sequentially.

3. Authority and accountability for managing the overall process should be clear-cut.
4. Input should be sought from those who will be called upon to produce the service and those who will be called upon to sell and deliver it. Reactions, criticisms, and suggestions should be sought from those "closest to the action."

Development and Testing

Development and testing involves actually producing the service (development) and obtaining market feedback under real-world condi-

---

FIGURE 8–6

The Comprehensive Analysis Stage

1. **Market analysis**
   Environmental analysis
   Market size analysis
   Competitive analysis
   Market need analysis

2. **Definition of service**
   How service works
   Features
   Benefits
   Relation to existing lines
   Tangible appearance, if any

3. **Operations feasibility analysis**
   How service will be produced
   Key operations issues and how they will be addressed
   Time lag

4. **Marketing plan**
   Marketing objectives
   Market segments
   Positioning strategy
   Pricing strategy
   Promotion strategy
   Delivery strategy

5. **Financial forecasts**
   Costs
   Volume
   Profit
   Payback period

6. **"Go/no-go" recommendation**

---

tions (testing). Prior to this stage, the service idea is an "idea on paper"; the service itself has yet to be actually performed. If the idea survives comprehensive analysis, the service needs to be developed (e.g., data processing programming, delivery system enhancements) so that it can be performed under test conditions. Actually developing the service may expose new problems or glitches that must be resolved. The service can only add value to customers and profits to the institution if it is *performable*. Everything is theoretical until the service is developed.

If the new service can indeed be developed, a related step—obtaining market feedback—would normally be taken prior to a *final* decision concerning whether or not it should be introduced. Test markets and use tests are two possibilities.

In test marketing, the service is actually marketed in selected territories ("test markets") to obtain feedback. The purchasers of the service are unaware that a test is under way, and their responses to the service simulate therefore "real-world" conditions. Whereas focus group participants say that they will or will not buy the service, test market participants actually make a buying decision. Test market research should produce reliable data if conditions in the test market are representative of conditions in the overall market.

Test marketing also provides an opportunity to experiment with alternative marketing tactics and evaluate the overall marketing strategy while the service is still in limited distribution. Test marketing, in short, can be useful in determining whether to market the service *and* how to market the service.

This is the good news. The bad news is that test marketing "tips off" the competition, possibly shortening or even eliminating "lead time" advantages that the testing institution might have enjoyed otherwise. If the decision to use test markets is made, a variety of data should be gathered, including data on the following: who is buying the service, why they are buying the service, how satisfied they are with the service, how they learned about the service, how aware customer prospects are of the advertising for the service and how well they understand the advertising, and what customer prospects regard as the optimum pricing level for the service.

A variation of test marketing is use testing. In this case, the service is actually performed for a group of users who are aware that a test is under way. They may or may not pay for the service. The users may be customer prospects, or they may be employees of the financial institution that is testing the service. Although some real-world properties are lost in use testing—especially when the service is performed free—it does provide feedback from actual users and it can be simpler, quicker, and less expensive than test marketing.

We believe that some form of market testing is essential for major new services (as opposed to refinements or enhancements of existing services). Because the costs involved in performing the service for a few may appear to be close to the costs involved in performing the service for many, the tendency is to forgo more testing at this stage in the development of a service. However, as Shostack points out, such logic is fallacious. She writes:

> Instead of a pilot test, actual market introduction is often the first real test of functionability and market acceptance. By that point, mistakes in design are harder to correct and service modifications needed in order to improve acceptance or operating efficiency are more laborious to implement. There is simply no substitute for a proper rehearsal.[14]

We submit that it is better to be second with a good service—one that is fully thought through, tested, and debugged—than it is to be first with a faulty service. We do not advocate what some call "analysis paralysis." However, "shooting from the hip" makes no sense either.

Marketing Introduction

Once the feedback from development and testing is incorporated into the service and its marketing plan, training is completed, and a monitoring system is in place, the service is ready—finally—to be introduced. Aside from the introductory marketing of the service, the central tasks are to (1) assess the organizational and market response to the service in the context of what was anticipated, (2) immediately "fix" any breakdowns and problems that occur, and (3) begin to design and develop an improved service—before a competitor does.

MAXIMIZING NEW SERVICE SUCCESS— 12 BIG IDEAS

The foregoing sections suggest the complexity and challenge that are associated with successfully developing new services. Whereas new regulatory freedoms, isolated instances of genius and innovation, even luck, can lead to specific service successes, ongoing success in new service development—developing a stream of successful new services— requires strong senior management commitment, time, money, and other resources. One does not create a productive new service development program on a shoestring!

The following new service development guidelines summarize the spirit of the previous sections:

1. Develop a plan to nurture organizational innovation. Work at creating a climate of trying; don't leave it to chance.
2. Establish a formal, step-by-step system for finding and developing new service ideas. Don't rely on magic.

3. Create an *aggressive* system. Seek out new ideas; don't sit back and wait for them to materialize.
4. Invest in developing sound *screening criteria* so that you don't have to invest in intensively evaluating weak ideas.
5. Make sure there is a *market* for the new service before spending money on actually developing it.
6. Give complete specifications on what the customer prospect wants to the technical personnel who will be developing the service.
7. Attempt to develop a *superior* service. Don't rely on cosmetic or artificial differences. Give customer prospects a good reason to buy the new service.
8. Solicit input and feedback from contact personnel *when* the service is being designed, not afterward.
9. Develop a marketing plan before test marketing; use the test market to *test* the marketing plan rather than to find a marketing plan.
10. *Sell* contact personnel on the new service before asking them to sell it to customer prospects. Provide evidence of the service's superiority, of its benefits, of the prospect's buying interest.
11. Lead from *strength*. Don't market the service until it is ready to be marketed. Care about quality.
12. Render the service obsolete with improvements before the competition does this for you.

CONCLUSION

Virtually every force for change rocking the financial services business underscores the importance of the new service development function. Financial institutions can no longer afford a casual approach to the development of new services. Deregulation has placed a premium on fresh thinking and genuine innovation. To delegate the new services function to legislators and regulators—or to give it lip service but not resources—is not the ticket in the years ahead.

In this chapter, we suggested a classification scheme for new services, discussed some of the key issues involved in the development of intangible products (services), stressed the need to nurture an organizational climate for innovation, presented some strategies for doing so, and outlined a six-stage new service development system. We emphasized that the new service development function should be *systematic, managed, market-driven, objective, aggressive,* and *ongoing.* Although a given financial institution may have fewer or more than six stages—and may label them differently than we did—the above attributes need to be in place for the new service development function to realize its potential.

NOTES

1. Leonard L. Berry, "Services Marketing Is Different," *Business,* May–June 1980, pp. 26–27.

2. G. Lynn Shostack, "How to Design a Service," in *Marketing of Services,* ed. William R. George and James H. Donnelly, Jr. (Chicago: American Marketing Association, 1981), p. 223.

3. As quoted in Thomas J. Peters and Robert H. Waterman, Jr., *In Search of Excellence* (New York: Harper & Row, 1982), p. 206.

4. Patricia W. Meyers, "Innovation Shift: Lessons for Service Firms from a Technological Leader," in *Developing New Services,* ed. William R. George and Claudia Marshall (Chicago: American Marketing Association, 1984), p. 12.

5. Rosabeth Moss Kanter, *The Change Masters: Innovation for Productivity in the American Corporation* (New York: Simon & Schuster, 1983).

6. Edward E. Lawler and John A. Drexler, "Entrepreneurship in the Large Corporation: Is It Possible?" *Management Review,* February 1981, p. 9.

7. Lewis Lehr, chairman of 3M, as quoted in Peters and Waterman, *In Search of Excellence,* p. 229.

8. Lawler and Drexler, "Entrepreneurship in the Large Corporation," p. 11.

9. "Making Managers Compete: Levi Strauss & Co.'s Secrets," *Boardroom Reports,* August 15, 1983, p. 4.

10. Marvin A. Jolson, "New Product Planning in an Age of Future Consciousness," *California Management Review,* Fall 1973, p. 26.

11. This model was influenced by the one appearing in: *New Products Management for the 1980s* (Booz-Allen & Hamilton, Inc., 1982), p. 11.

12. See ibid., for example.

13. Benjamin Schneider and David E. Bowen, "New Services Design, Development and Implementation and the Employee," in *Developing New Services,* pp. 82–101.

14. G. Lynn Shostack, "Service Design in the Operating Environment," in *Developing New Services,* p. 35.

Delivering Financial Services

There is no area of activity in the financial services business that is being quite as radicalized as the process of delivering need-satisfying product offerings to customers on a convenient and cost-efficient basis. Delivery system changes and innovations have been coming fast and furious in recent years as bank and nonbank organizations alike have reached out on a widening geographic basis with a mix of high-tech and high-touch techniques.

"Reach out and touch someone" is as much the motto for the many players in the financial services business as it is for Ma Bell's Long Lines Division. Reach out anywhere and anytime. Reach out and sell. Reach out with the customer's ideas about time and place convenience foremost in mind. Reach out and deliver effectively through people, places, plastic, and machines. *Reach out and deliver through*

1. *People.* Not just through traditional teller types and other customer contact employees but increasingly through personal banker programs employing cadres of highly trained and highly motivated "individual and family financial quarterbacks." On the commercial side of the business, reaching out is a corporate calling officer roaming far and wide with a "computer in a briefcase" that can be used to access the bank's data base before, during and after a visit to a business customer. *And so much more.*

2. *Places.* Reaching out no longer means traditional, make-them-all-look-alike bricks-and-mortar branches but increasingly involves storefront offices; leased space for two or three bank staffers in a grocery store; leased space in a conventional branch to an insurance agent or a travel agent; mini-offices open only during high traffic hours in factories, airports, industrial parks, and larger office buildings; offices that do double duty as financial transaction centers by day and community centers by night; offices that specialize in vault storage or investment counseling; mobile offices that—like the library's bookmobile—visit one small community in the morning, another in the afternoon, and still another at night and then follow a different travel schedule the next day; and so many other approaches that have combined to obviate yesterday's 9-to-2, Monday-through-Friday financial service at the bank's convenience. Reaching out also includes a money center banking organization's scores of loan production offices and business customer offices, often spotted in key markets on a nationwide basis, that overnight could become full-service branches. *And so much more.*

3. *Plastic.* Reaching out is now credit and debit card programs workable within regional and national machine networks (i.e., PLUS, CIRRUS); it is plastic providing ever-expanding financial transaction capacities as well as nonfinancial, customer-desired amenities. It is plastic that debits an account to pay for purchases or creates a loan for that purpose. It is plastic that verifies credit. It is plastic with a toll-free number that links a customer to a card registration service and its amenities: finding lost luggage or replacing it; common carrier travel accident insurance; auto rental and motel discounts, travelers' message service, and emergency airline tickets worldwide. And tomorrow, even now waiting to explode on the financial scene, is plastic with enhanced MICR-encoding capacities or plastic with memory, accessibility, security, and transaction power in a set of microchips—no longer merely a financial transaction card but a live-work-shop-play-and-also-do-your-banking card. *And so much more.*

4. *Machines.* Reaching out first of all involves customer-driven, self-service machines such as ATMs. It also means banker-operated, customer-assisting machines such as a calling officer's "computer in a briefcase." But both self-service and customer-assisting machines must

access the bank's data center or the bank's shared time in a service center or correspondent data bank. Reaching out is ATMs and POS terminals that have trebled in number in recent years and that are being linked together in regional and national systems. It is machine banking that each day gains greater customer acceptance, that each day is being adjusted to respond to any issuer's plastic access instrument, and that each day as it stimulates increased customer use pays off at the bottom line by reducing transaction handling expenses. It is machine banking that erodes still further traditional time and space barriers impeding the delivery of financial services. And beyond ATMs, cash dispensers, POS terminals, and self-service "decision tree" terminals—today's mature machine technologies—lies the infancy (some will argue, the adolescence) of *at-home banking*. It may be at-home banking as part of a video system or only through the telephone. It may be just banking or the capacity to deliver financial services along with entertainment, education, shopping, travel planning, and household management through cable-, satellite or telephone-accessed computer-based information terminals. And it may well be banks, thrifts, brokers, and retailers selling, leasing, or renting terminals and software, not to mention *teaching* machine management. *And so much more.*

These introductory comments have focused chiefly on the retail side of the financial services business, clearly the most exciting arena in terms of delivery system change and innovation, and perhaps the most important as well since it embraces mass-market merchandising of financial products. In the 1980s and beyond, key elements in the formula for retailing success will include people, place, plastic, and machine strategies designed to "gather the maximum amount of funds at the lowest net cost, minimize operating expense," effectively mix high-touch and high-tech operating modes, satisfy the customer's demand for time and place convenience, and facilitate the expansion of both fee-based and interest-producing bank offerings.[1]

Nonetheless, vitally important changes in the business customer sector are also occurring, especially on the EFT front as the Automated Clearing House movement accelerates, as cash management capacities expand, and as wire transfer arrangements attain higher frequency levels.

FITTING IT TOGETHER

The revolution goes on. We could use all of the pages devoted to this chapter's discussion of delivering financial services to simply list and briefly explain state-of-the-art innovations in people, place, plastic, and machine techniques. We would probably only scratch the surface.

What's worse, the listing no doubt would be outdated well before this book reached the reader. *The revolution goes on, and rather rapidly at that.*

More important, listings and descriptions would not address the most critical concern facing financial institution managers today: How do we fit it all together, make it mesh, make it harmonize, make it work to satisfy bank staff member and bank customer alike?

Then, too, the change and innovation in delivery system management are not taking place in a vacuum. *The concern is how we fit it all together in light of such side-by-side developments as*

- *Geographic expansion:* interstate banking, regional reciprocity arrangements, networking, and franchising.
- *Beyond the balance sheet:* the stepped-up drive to deliver fee-based services.
- *Product line expansion:* nurtured by deregulation and continually force-fed by competitive interaction, what is desired by customers and what can be delivered by banking organizations threatens to burst the confines of long-standing delineations of banking's line of commerce and its definition of risk.
- *Structural consolidation:* thrift-to-bank conversions, mergers, holding company confederations among similar and dissimilar community-oriented institutions, and intraindustry mergers per se, not to mention the ability of many nonbank players in the financial services business to expand and consolidate retailing operations with minimal regulatory hindrance.
- *And still more players:* the still-uncertain-as-to-where-it-will-lead involvement of newspapers (Knight-Ridder), TV networks (CBS), travel and entertainment card companies (American Express), equipment manufacturers (IBM), and telecommunicators (AT&T) in the shaping and eventual management of high-tech home and place of business banking.

How do we fit it all together—people, places, plastic, and machines—while the financial services industry is concurrently writing and rewriting new rules of the road regarding locational freedom, structural alignments, and product line expansion? How do we integrate and link up within a cohesive and rational whole such extremely diverse customer service approaches as bricks-and-mortar offices, unstaffed machines, and growing numbers of personal bankers who are reaching out to where the customer lives to personally sell expanding product lines? How do we tie in a plastic card—a *Smart Card*—that functions as a debit instrument for handling financial transactions related to common consumer purchases while it could also become a library card, a driver's license, a job security identification device, an office or home door key, a telephone charge card, and quite a good deal more?[2] How do we fit it all together? It is this concern as well as the kinds of questions that follow that must be fundamentally resolved by financial industry managers as they continue to remake much of banking's delivery system.

1. Is the delivery system technology that we're developing to be viewed as a competitive product or just a utility? Are we selling something of real value to a customer or just stringing phone lines?

2. Our resources are limited. What's the best bet? Just where do we most wisely, most efficiently, and most productively, long term, allocate scarce time, effort, expertise, and dollars? People-staffed office systems that stress high-touch? ATMs and POS money machines? At-home banking? And if we have to do all of these, what's the right mix?

3. Do we try to share the cost of developing new delivery system technologies with commercial bank competitors, with thrift competitors, with the nonbank competition? Do we share the results on a pass-down basis with smaller institutions?

4. In fact, do we really even care whose electronic banking technology a customer uses, just so long as the transaction leads back to his or her account in our bank? Are we best off just becoming issuers of technology access instruments? Plastic?

5. Our people. What about them? On one hand, we're pushing hard to develop a high-tech delivery systems culture; on the other hand, we're trying to create a high-touch sales culture. Can we easily combine both cultures without confusing our people?

6. And our customers. What about them above all else? How do we convince them to accept and then frequently, even commonly, use our new cost-reducing, service-expanding technologies? How do we help them adjust to change? How do we create "perceived value" in their minds as they confront our new technologies?

7. What are we really selling? What's the distinction between a delivery system and a product offering? Personal bankers, ATMs, Smart Cards, cash management programs—each seems to be both a product and a means of delivering products. Is this important to our marketing efforts?

How do we fit it all together? The delivery system challenge confronting financial industry managers is all of the foregoing questions and many more. But the overriding concern involves fitting the answers together into a cohesive whole, and one that also reflects the revised ground rules regarding locational, structural, and product line expansion.

FIRST SOUTHEAST: A MODEL, CIRCA 1990

In the following pages, we will focus on putting it all together. We will attempt to assemble a model as a way of *speculating* about what tomorrow's overall delivery system will look like and how it will work. Tomorrow, by 1990 or thereabouts. Tomorrow, given state-of-the-art technology, given the evolving implications of interstate banking, given realistic expectations for product line expansion, given a high degree of competitive equality among the many players in the financial services business, and given the ability of bankers and customers alike to digest change. Our focus is on the primary component parts of tomorrow's delivery system and on how we believe they will fit together.[3]

For this purpose, we have created a model, a scenario that depicts the extensive delivery system of a major multistate banking organization that had evolved through a series of regional mergers and acquisitions. We postulate *First Southeast Financial Corporation* as a model competitor, a model that just happens to have been rooted in a commercial bank heritage, though it could just as easily have had its beginnings as a thrift institution, a finance company, a brokerage firm, or a retail department store chain.

First Southeast is also projected as a model that larger or smaller banks, or thrifts, or nonbank institutions, might react to competitively. It is a model of the opposition. No less, it is a model that any organization, regardless of size or marketplace characteristics, might adapt for its own use, in part or in whole. The model can be upscaled or downscaled, customized to fit an organization's operational capacities and its understanding of customer needs.

First Southeast is a speculative, suggestive model and only that. It is not exactly how it must be for a banking organization, but rather a speculation about how one regional banking organization might tie things together as it reaches out through people, places, plastic, and machines.

First Southeast will be explained through a series of figures. Much of the structure depicted in the following figures is self-explanatory. Our narrative, therefore, will be brief, focusing primarily on some of the more innovative components of tomorrow's delivery system.

We clearly realize that our modeling of First Southeast will engender considerable critical comment. It should because there is so much disagreement today within the financial services industry regarding the suitability of one or another technological approach. Some industry leaders, for example, insist that ATMs as a key delivery system technique are already obsolete and that their continued development is a waste of time, dollars, and effort. Not so, many others argue. Some industry leaders believe that at-home banking is just around the corner and that it will be the dominant delivery system by 1990. Others sharply disagree, in terms of both timing and preeminence. Smart Card techniques? Same disagreements.[4]

There should be much critical comment because the financial industry today is also divided in its thinking about high-touch banking, and especially the value of personal banker and relationship banking commitments.

And finally, we anticipate that our model—and once again, it is only a model, a suggestion, a speculation, albeit with a reasonable foundation—will entertain considerable criticism because it portrays a future that many bankers and thrift leaders don't feel comfortable with or flatly oppose. Our model, after all, is predicated on the continued evolution of interstate and nationwide banking, more intensive competition from nonbank institutions, and a marked enlargement of customer-serving product lines that pushes financial institutions inexorably toward the frontiers of financial service innovation.

A good many bankers, brokers, and thrift leaders don't want to change, let alone travel to the frontiers of financial service innovation. Neither do they have any interest in being identified as pioneers by "the arrows in their backs." They prefer the status quo, if not, in fact, "prewar" conditions. And so do their customers, many will argue. Are they right or wrong? This is not the issue at all. The issue is what they will be confronting as today's frontier quickly becomes a permanent settlement.

NECESSARY ASSUMPTIONS

Our model of First Southeast is constructed on these necessary and realistic assumptions:

1. Interstate banking is in effect, at least on a contiguous state or regional basis, a step initially brought about through state-by-state reciprocity arrangements and then rationalized by federal statute.

2. Intrastate restrictions on branching, banking machine use, and holding company activities have been removed or substantially reduced by virtually all states.

3. Intraindustry affiliations among financial service industry vendors have been encouraged by regulatory authorities within the limitations of applicable antitrust provisions.

4. Interchange with regional, national, and international EFT systems on an equitable, open-entry basis is in effect.

5. The economic and social environments continue to be favorable to broad-based advances in structural alignments, product line enhancements, and high-tech, high-touch innovations, both domestically and on a multinational basis.

6. The ongoing deregulation of restrictions on product offerings has authorized depository institutions, largely on the ground of competitive equality, to *directly* provide such key consumer banking services as brokerage, insurance, financial consulting, travel planning and travel arranging, short- and long-form tax preparation, and so much more.

7. Now-current technological experimentation with telephone banking, at-home television banking, "smart cards," POS, and related delivery modes are on-line and widely accepted by the customers of banking organizations.

Will all of this be in place for First Southeast by 1990 or thereabouts? We don't know for sure, of course. Nor are we insisting that it should be. This really is not the point. Our concern is with what reasonably might be in place and how one financial organization fits it all together in creating a customer-driven delivery system.

FIRST SOUTHEAST FINANCIAL—1990 OR THEREABOUTS

First Southeast Financial Corporation resulted from the interstate mergers involving a Washington, D.C., bank widely regarded for its commercial and international banking heritage, a Virginia bank holding company with a strong consumer orientation, a Maryland thrift corporation noted for its mortgage lending activities, and a North Carolina bank holding company well regarded for its good balance in the commercial, trust, and retail fields. This was the beginning. Afterward, a number of carefully selected thrifts, small finance companies, mortgage banks, insurance, and brokerage companies were incorporated into the First Southeast system. Today—1990 or thereabouts—it is a $35 billion organization, operating primarily from southern Pennsylvania through the Carolinas and from the coast to the Blue Ridge.

As shown in Figure 9–1, the corporate office is in Washington, the decision center for financial service industry operations. Regional administrative centers may be more or fewer than those listed; these are hub cities, with spokes reaching out to important secondary cities.

In Richmond as well as the other regional administrative centers, all of the staffed and unstaffed component offices of First Southeast are linked through the organization's Telecommunications Center and Information Collection Center. This center is a data bank, a CIF system, and much, much more. Information about customers, customer prospects, and overall organizational transaction activity continually flows in and out of the center. It can be tapped instantaneously by a teller in

FIGURE 9–1

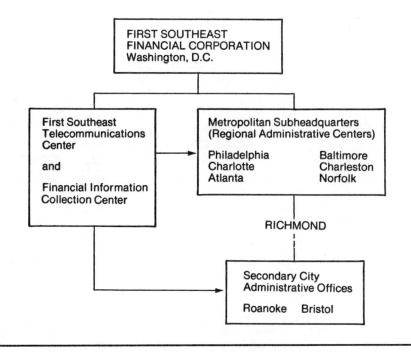

a staffed branch or by a calling officer preparing to meet with the treasurer of a small textile firm in rural South Carolina. It can be tapped by business and consumer customers through their at-work or at-home terminals. It also accesses and interacts with national and international money markets to facilitate optimal asset and liability management. It is linked to financial institution regulatory agencies to facilitate ongoing examinations. And it is the pass-through connection to national and international EFT systems.

As shown in Figure 9–2, the center is the heart of First Southeast's operations—the nerve center that permits visual as well as voice contact between bank management, employees, and customers. Cable, satellite, and telephone linkages assure flexibility.

Moreover, the center links First Southeast to its affiliated "franchisee" network. Shortly after First Interstate of California began moving eastward with its franchisee program, First Southeast began its westward expansion, largely through the south-central and southwestern tier of states targeted by demographers as key population and business activity growth areas during the 1980s and beyond. The First Southeast data bank and information collection and distribution center

FIGURE 9–2

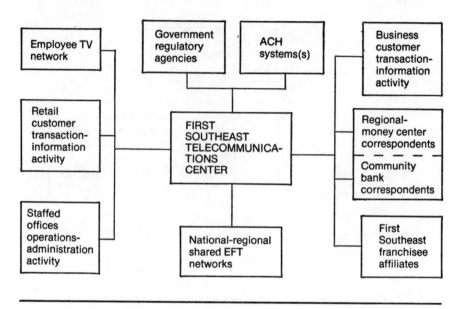

complex is also a major link in the organization's dealings with traditional upstream correspondents in national and international money
centers and its far-flung relationships with independent, community-
oriented financial service "vendors," or, more simply, "community
banks."

First Southeast serves as a data-clearing center for these community
banks. It also leases EFT "time" (at a fee, of course!) on behalf of the
community banks for their customers as well as data bank access to
these banks and their customer base. In this sense, the center is a proprietary servicing organization.

Figure 9–3 expands on this outreach approach to institutional customers. The Institutional Services Division of First Southeast manages
its traditional correspondent relationships and its franchisee program.
It also oversees "venture relationships"—that is, major participations
in the lending and securities areas with other like-sized financial service organizations, on both a national and international basis. These are
major dollar commitments that are handled on a joint-venture basis to
facilitate, for example, the development of emerging "sunrise" industries such as robotics and genetic engineering, new capital-intensive
industries that have moved to the leading edge of our society's transition from an industrial age to an information age.[5]

The Institutional Services Division, as indicated, also manages the *selling* of a wide range of *services, products,* and *advice* (consulting) to bank and nonbank institutions. The listing suggested here is just that, *suggestive.* More important is the fact that First Southeast clearly distinguishes between *services* (buying into the offerings of its data bank or utilizing what's stored in the data bank to in turn sell worldwide travel-hotel-dining tour-entertainment arrangements to an institution's customer base), *products* (tangible items such as a 1040 short-form tax preparation software package), and *consulting* (for example, designing branch offices, developing personal banker programs, or providing ad-

FIGURE 9–3

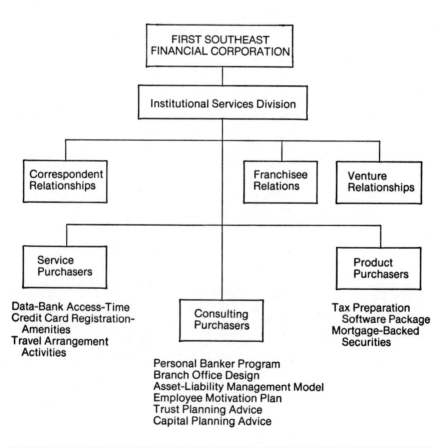

vice on establishing employee stock purchase plans and dividend rein-vestment plans as a means of "growing" banking capital).

And most of this for a fee—of course.

COMMERCE AND TRADE

First Southeast is many things to many customer groupings. As a re-tailer of financial services, it is most things—the basics—to all people and, concurrently, something very special, very unique, very personal-ized to clearly targeted groups of preferred customers. It is at once a *people bank* and a *relationships bank*. The same philosophical ap-proach to its business holds true on the corporate side of the ledger.

As shown in Figure 9–4, the Commerce and Trade Division of First Southeast administers and supports a number of domestic and interna-tional Corporate Relationship Offices. Calling officers and account ex-

FIGURE 9–4

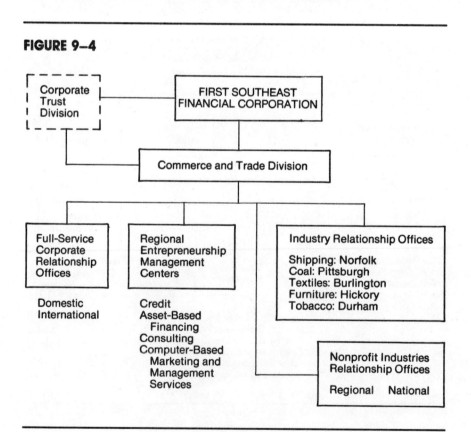

ecutives working out of these offices manage the organization's long-standing involvement with *Fortune* 1000 companies here and abroad, while also soliciting new accounts with these industrial society and information age leaders.

At the same time, however, First Southeast employs teams of credit, consulting, and marketing specialists working out of what the organization calls Entrepreneurship Management Centers, formal offices, even hotel suites, even less formally, employee homes in carefully selected business growth areas. The market is entrepreneurs, mostly small businesses, with good management, a good product, and excellent growth potential. The objective is to capture them early in their developmental stages and to help nurse them into a much larger success. The underlying philosophy is as old as economic man: "From little acorns, mighty oaks do grow."

Also, as shown in Figure 9–4, First Southeast operates a network of Industry Relationship Offices. Five industries and the key offices of First Southeast are depicted: shipping, coal, textiles, furniture, and tobacco. In time, others will no doubt be established—for example, to serve the growing wine industry of the Shenandoah Valley. But at the moment, each of the five industries is well established in First Southeast's trade zone, and each is considered vital to that area's economic infrastructure. Each, too, is a business that First Southeast and the partners that created it understand well, certainly well enough to serve it as efficiently and effectively as regional and national competitors. First Southeast fought off many of them to anchor these vital relationships; the skilled, well-trained staff in the Relationship Offices help maintain these relationships.

Finally, First Southeast has built upon and expanded its demonstrated expertise as a lender, adviser, and fund raiser for a grouping of nonprofit service industry firms: hospitals, colleges and universities, social service agencies, and the like. It advises them, handles their cash flow, manages their investments, and, utilizing the expertise of the First Southeast Corporate Trust Division, administers pension and other employee welfare programs.

Just a word or two about "people and places."

A quick glance at Figure 9–4 would seem to suggest that First Southeast has dotted its trade area with places for doing business—*with an extensive and expensive office network.* This is not exactly the case.

Some of the Commerce and Trade offices operated by First Southeast are traditional bricks-and-mortar places clearly identified by elaborate First Southeast signage and staffed by a well-balanced team of commercial account specialists. Many of these offices, however, also house retail banking units, as well as provide space for teams of Industry Relationship specialists. In fact, First Southeast has worked out *space-*

trading agreements with like-sized regional banking organizations in other parts of the country as well as overseas. First Southeast needs to be in California to closely handle its relationship with a major multinational account; likewise, a California-based regional requires representation in the Southeast. Both organizations reasoned that it was reasonable to trade space.

Other Commerce and Trade offices are rented suites in office buildings and "live-work" complexes, even hotels. These offices house a secretary or two, an administrative officer, data bank access instruments, and teleconferencing capacities that can be utilized to tap First Southeast experts in supporting commercial customer account satisfaction. Most of these specialists are, of course, First Southeast employees, though a number of them are consultants working on a retainer basis. The telecommunications "miracle" allows these specialists to be reached by verbal and visual modes—*just about anywhere in the world and at any time.*

Finally, countless First Southeast offices are the homes of calling officers—men and women, skilled, highly motivated self-starters who reach out to business customers at their convenience.

The "people and places" structure described here evolved largely in response to this question: How can we most effectively and efficiently serve existing corporate customers and also build new business? The decisions were market-driven for the most part. Surely, some decisions recognized the need to match a competitor presence, to stand out as a place for doing business. But this became the exception rather than the rule, given the continued narrowing of profit margins and the need to manage costs efficiently; the need to look good and look big in a city center building also became the exception, given the reality that the "bank" could just as easily be carried to the customer in a briefcase by an aggressive and well-trained account representative.

THE RETAIL NETWORK

A hundred miles south of corporate headquarters in Washington—and, as often said, "a hundred *years* away"—is Richmond, by 1990 a metropolitan area of about 700,000 people, a major and highly competitive financial center, a gateway to projected Sun Belt corridor growth, and the home ground for one of the initial partners that crisscrossed state lines to form First Southeast.

It will be recalled from Figure 9–1 that Richmond is one of First Southeast's major Regional Administrative Centers, the hub that oversees operations in nearby Secondary City Administrative Offices. How many and which secondary cities is not important to our scenario; nor, for that matter, are the number and location of Regional Administrative Centers. What's important is the primary function of these "lean and tough" centers—*the on-the-scene administration of local commercial and retail banking operations.* These centers direct the interaction of "people, places, plastic, and machines."

Before continuing with our chart story narration, an explanation is in order. First Southeast did not close down its trust operations. Trust activity administration remains a major department. However, First Southeast integrated the marketing of trust services "at the line." It then separated these services into commercial and retail product offerings. The Trust Department, like many other First Southeast departments (e.g., investments, asset-based financing, mortgages), is a center of managerial know-how, expertise; it is supportive rather than functional.

As shown in Figure 9–5, the Regional Administrative Center manages a number of *staffed* or people-based offices, *staffed* or machine-

FIGURE 9–5

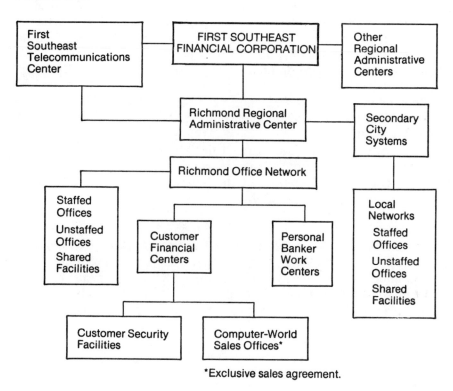

*Exclusive sales agreement.

based systems, and *shared facilities* in the Richmond area. The distinctions between these units are explained in Figure 9–6.

The largest of several Richmond-area *Customer Financial Centers* is located in a well-trafficked, midtown mall that also houses high-rise office/apartment buildings, department stores, boutiques, a supermarket, two theaters, and a bus terminal. Ample parking is provided. This First Southeast CFC is open daily from early morning to late evening to accommodate customer work schedules.

The Customer Financial Center is divided functionally into the following departments: Housing, Taxation, Financial Counseling, Investments, Trusts and Estate Management, and Travel Planning. Some of these activities are also provided at traditional branch offices. The difference is that a CFC is structured to handle a greater volume of retail customers requiring expert, in-depth assistance. Indeed, the CFC is the "hub" from which nonroutine, high-touch expertise is transmitted by phone and on-line telecommunications systems to First Southeast's branches, correspondents, even its franchises.

The Housing Department not only provides first and second mortgages and offers such options as shared appreciation and graduated mortgage plans, but also offers advice on preparing a home to be sold or restored. For a fee, the Housing Department's consulting architects will design a new home and superintend construction. Other experts provide advice on landscaping and interior decorating. In addition, the Housing Department maintains an up-to-date, computer-stored listing of home and apartment rentals, garage rentals, office space rentals, nearby vacation-area home rentals, even James River boat-docking rentals.

In sum, the Housing Department deals with every facet of placing people in homes, condominiums, apartments, and business space. The same broad approach is used by the Investments, Taxation, Financial Counseling, and Travel Planning departments.

One of the CFC's additional features is its "stock room." Actually, this is a series of comfortable meeting rooms linked to major national and international stock, money market and commodities exchanges by teleprinters and/or closed-circuit, satellite-accessed television.

Another extra is the CFC's teleshopping office. Here a customer can call up on the screen and charge his or her bank relationship account for specialty products and services not normally portrayed on home terminals.

Last, and perhaps most important of all, a Customer Financial Center houses a massive, walk-in vault storage area. Depository boxes are available in sizes ranging from a 3 × 5 × 12-inch box to a small closet and a steel-mesh enclosed bin. Numerous self-locking and self-opening inspection booths are accessed by the customer's plastic and authenticated by voiceprint. Some depository boxes are rented on an annual basis; others are available for shorter, vacation-time periods.[6]

Figure 9–5 also indicates a linkage between a Customer Financial Center and a number of local Computer-World sales offices. This independent chain store sells, rents, and leases home banking terminals and a wide range of related hardware and software packages, *including* the financial software packages developed by First Southeast for its customers and those of its correspondents and franchisees. Indeed, in its markets First Southeast has worked out an exclusive sales agreement with Computer-World. First Southeast customers, retail customers as well as business customers, are entitled to discounts at this national chain store, which competes with Sears, IBM, Ma Bell, Tandy, and others as vendors of an Information Age's mass-market electronic equipment. The arrangement with Computer-World assures that customers can easily obtain First Southeast software—for example, a household budget management program—while also benefiting from their First Southeast relationship through discounts as well as bank financing for their purchases.

PERSONAL BANKER WORK CENTERS

Very little banking is done here.

The personal banker or account relationship manager for preferred retail customers and small business firms is a concept that figures significantly in any portrayal of banking tomorrow. (See *Chapter 7: "Relationship Banking"*)

Many scenarios visualize the relationship manager working out of his or her home and making prearranged calls on individuals and small business operators. This is how First Southeast does it. Still, the process must be managed. Accordingly, First Southeast has a number of Personal Banker Work Centers in the Richmond area. In these centers, several of its relationship managers share desk space and a secretary. A conference room is available for relationship manager training and education sessions, even for seminars offered to selected customers. The work center is also linked into the First Southeast teleconferencing network, so that personal bankers and their customers can consult the banking organization's expertise on an interactive basis.

LOCAL OFFICE NETWORK

The final component of First Southeast Financial Corporation's delivery system is its local office network of staffed, unstaffed, and shared customer service facilities. Before describing this system, it should be noted that First Southeast, like many other banking organizations in the mid-1980s realized that it was administering an unnecessarily extensive structure of bricks-and-mortar places, expensive places, increasingly redundant places, given the onrush of machine technologies and, conversely, competition from nonbank institutions and their office systems. Some of First Southeast's excess physical locations over the years were turned into Customer Financial Centers and Personal Banker Work Centers, sold to Computer-World for use as sales offices, restructured as Corporate Relationship Offices and Industry Relationship Offices, and so on. Others, of course, were sold off to competitors, even sold or leased to municipal governments.

And many new ones were opened—in carefully selected markets, in areas where high-touch banking was a competitive must, and to provide needed facilities for evolving services that required optimal banker-customer interaction.

Figure 9–6 depicts the First Southeast Richmond office network of *staffed* and *unstaffed* offices. In this portrayal, the focus has been shifted, appropriately enough, from the banking organization to the *customer*. Here is how and where the retail customer, the small business customer, and even the commercial customer in his or her dual role as a corporate client and a personal banking client interface with First Southeast.

Many visions of the future projected an avalanche of ATMs and POS terminals. It was predicted that they would become as common as cigarette and soft drink vending machines, with shared rather than individual bank ownership. The rationale for sharing was cost efficiency and the commonsense view that what's most important is which banking organization issues the access card, not which owns and maintains the transaction terminal. Other visions of the future insisted that ATMs would quickly become obsolete as a primary delivery system because of at-home banking by telephone and/or through a visual mode and because of the greater efficiencies and economies associated with POS.

What happened, in fact, by 1990, as First Southeast discovered, was that this argument was still up in the air. At-home banking was moving along slower than anticipated. The same held true for point-of-sale. And finally, after so much work, so much invested effort and seed money, and so much satisfactory customer experience, well, plastic-accessed ATMs were still in vogue. The First Southeast system became a mixed system. A couple of points about its distinctive features:

- During income tax time, additional office space would be leased for tax form processing.
- What's meant by a full-service community bank depends largely on a definition of *community*. First Southeast found that community

FIGURE 9–6

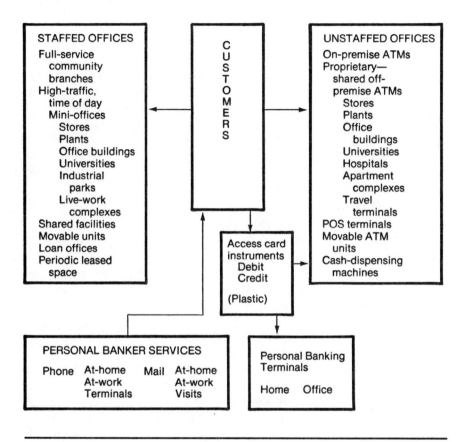

could just as easily be a rural town, a large suburban housing development, or a high-density inner-city area with strong ethnic, cultural, and racial characteristics. Its offices respond to these distinctive characteristics in management styles, in design styles, in convenience patterns, in staff selection, and in service offerings selection.

- Part of the system is portable—people-staffed offices as well as machines that can be adjusted to customer demand. First Southeast, for example, manages a fleet of mobile units that serve as temporary offices at new housing developments. One van-branch rides the circuit throughout rural sections of the Richmond marketplace, spending one day at one rented site and one day at another—much like a bookmobile route. Each spring, a truck hauls a two-section modular office to a permanent site serving James River vacationers.

- First Southeast is committed to marketing access instruments—debit cards; credit cards; for some customers, on a still experimental basis, smart cards that are debit cards and so much more; and identification cards that verify a customer relationship for check-cashing purposes. It markets access and the symbol of a First Southeast customer relationship. It markets access to the world of electronic banking—locally, regionally, nationally, and worldwide. It markets access; it assures convenience to the customer. It believes in sharing and not replicating the expense of terminal placement.
- Personal banker services are provided—are *delivered*—by telephone, by at-home and at-work terminals, by mail, and by at-home or at-work visits. The underlying philosophical approach is *outreach*, not yesterday's come-to-us-on-our-terms style of doing business.

And still, First Southeast manages many shared facilities. Sharing became rather commonplace in the mid-1980s. Branch space was leased or rented to travel agencies, legal service agencies, income tax preparation firms, personal computer sales firms, insurance brokers, and stock brokerage houses. Space was also leased to providers of community services: welfare and medicare, family crisis intervention centers, divorce counseling clinics, TB- and diabetes-check clinics, and so on. By 1990 or thereabouts, First Southeast was able to directly offer many of these services in-house so to speak; it was OK legally to engage in providing travel services, selling insurance, handling taxes, or preparing tax forms. Many of its branches did just that. Others, however, still leased space to independent vendors. Why not? A good lease created a good commercial customer. Then, too, it was more cost efficient to associate with an established insurance broker than staff up *everywhere* to provide this necessary customer service. Finally, First Southeast wisely realized that it was not always important *who* interacted with the customer—a banker who was well versed in selling insurance options or a broker who rented space from the bank. What was critical was that the service was *there*—where the customer came. What was critical was that the customer came through an entrance clearly marked *First Southeast,* that the customer perceived that he or she or the family was doing business with that bank.

Figure 9–7 portrays the shared facility that First Southeast began developing in the mid-1980s. By 1990 or thereabouts, some of these facilities continued to operate on a "sharing" basis, though others had been functionally incorporated within its local office system network. The administrative and managerial approach is secondary; *primary* is what happens at a First Southeast . . . A *People Bank* office.

Figure 9–7 takes the reader through the First Southeast door. Left-turn to a bank of ATMs, then to the office administration or personal

FIGURE 9–7

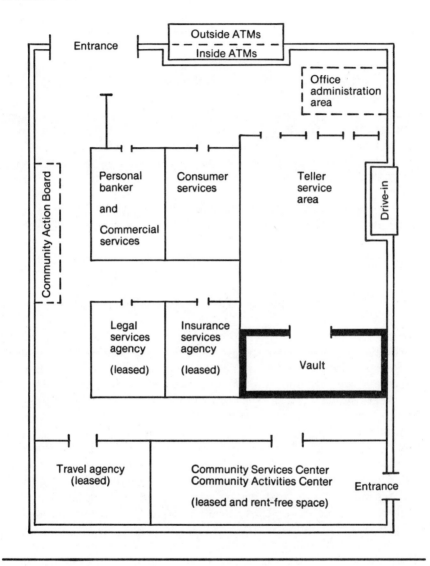

contact customer service area, to the tellers and beyond them to a vault and safe-deposit box area. That same turn takes the customer to personal banker and commercial service privacy offices and to desk space for officers specializing in such nonroutine consumer services as mortgage lending, student loan applications, car loans, and debt management counseling.

Or the customer can bypass the bank and visit offices leased to a lawyer, an insurance broker, and a travel agency. Any of those offices could just as easily be occupied by a tax preparer, a stockbroker, a personal computer sales manager, an apartment rental service, a marriage counselor—frankly, just about any provider of 1990s lifestyle services.

Or the customer can bypass all of this and visit the First Southeast Community Services Center (notice the separate entrance). Some First Southeast offices lease this space to municipal governments; it is a dispersal point for a variety of welfare services. Other First Southeast offices offer this space rent-free for senior citizens meetings, adult education programs, meeting areas for Boy Scouts and Girl Scouts, and so much, much more. Why not? The purpose of any First Southeast office is twofold: *it is to service customers, and it is to attract customer prospects.*

Note the Community Action Board. If it is happening, it is listed there. And if you need to know, you have to come to First Southeast to find out. It is a service. It is a lure.

CONCLUSION

There may be—indeed, there probably will be—other components to the delivery system of First Southeast Financial Corporation sometime tomorrow. The imperative remains: *How do we fit it all together— people, places, plastic, and machines.* It is not important that First Southeast evolve precisely as we have visualized. Nor is it important that this scenario become reality 5, 10, or 20 years from now. What is significant is the linkage, the many possibilities for interweaving the functions of bank people and the explosive dynamics of emerging technologies. The linkage employed in this model, while admittedly speculative, nonetheless appears grounded in currently discernible trends. In fact, we believe, it is conservative; we suspect that it will be radicalized as the pace of technological innovation expands in seemingly geometric proportions.

In this regard, it is not especially foolish to envision a time not far distant when a plastic access card containing a few microchips serves as a personal computer and a transaction tool—a *bank* in a pocketbook or wallet that replaces and manages money. By the same token, it is neither foolish nor shortsighted to argue that bank technologies will fail to obviate the need for bank people. As indicated earlier, as argued throughout this book, the side-by-side trends are toward high-tech accompanied by high-touch.

But a different task for bank people? We believe so, and a more rewarding and challenging task at that.

Once again, the theme of this chapter is the matching of a technology-based and people-based delivery system in a systematic manner. It is fitting them together. Our matching has been applied to a model, a multistate, large-sized banking organization whose parent today could just as easily be a bank, a thrift, a finance company, or a nonbank conglomerate. The model is offered as a delivery system structure to be pondered. It is offered as a delivery system to respond to. Is this the shape of tomorrow's competitor? If so, where does my bank, thrift, insurance company, brokerage firm, or finance company fit in? In terms of public policy goals, is this also the right direction for our banking system to be taking? Is this the desired model for an effective delivery system—*especially from a reader's perspective as a shaper or creator of tomorrow's delivery system.*

And a Caveat . . . or a Few

We believe that a few "warnings" must be attached to this portrayal of the evolving delivery system of tomorrow's financial services industry. Some things must happen between now and then if the various bits and pieces are to fall together effectively and efficiently. Not just the assumptions regarding legislative and regulatory changes but also alterations in managerial approaches, changes in the way of administering a broad-based and locationally far-flung delivery system.

First, the emerging high-tech systems so desired by financial institutions for their inherent cost efficiencies must possess *customer value.* Today automatic billpaying is perceived as valuable by the bank but not by the customer. For many years, ATM growth lagged well behind banker anticipation because the customer did not feel that he or she was getting "value" from the machine. Marketers in a high-tech environment must market or sell new systems and techniques with two fundamental and equal considerations in mind: *What's in it for the bank at the bottom line? What's in it for the customer at his or her bottom line?*

Second, EFT technology is part and parcel of a delivery system; it is not all of it. In fact, EFT may be the *least important* element in the evolving financial institution delivery system, simply because from bank to bank it will be so much alike and so much that is operated in common. People will remain important, perhaps become even more important as a means of differentiating institutional performance.

Third, the creation of an effective technology-based delivery system will involve everyone: equipment manufacturers such as IBM, Apple, and even Ma Bell; information producers such as the television, cable, and print media networks; sellers of at-home and at-work hardware and software, especially Sears and J. C. Penney, but also "Computer-World" chains; and *also* financial institutions. It will involve all of these, and it will require a necessary degree of cooperation between them. It will also involve a realistic and reasonable resolution of various *privacy* issues. High-technology delivery systems will need to serve customers and to protect customers. Otherwise, each bank-desired step forward will be challenged by a vigorous consumer-prompted objection in the form of painfully slow legislative or regulatory questioning. Banking must make its case that change benefits the customer. Banking must also understand that such new delivery system technologies as at-home banking will more than likely piggyback into place, not on their own merits, but as part of a customer-driven desire for home entertainment, home management, and home education.

Fourth, it is still up in the air whether bankers and other financial institution managers can *really* do the job of convincing staff members to believe in and then market necessary delivery system changes. And beyond this, of course, can they *really* do the job of convincing customers to believe in and buy change? Two big questions, two interwoven questions. The track record so far is not promising. ATMs are just beginning to be successful after 10 years in the marketplace. Automatic billpaying, direct deposit, and even off-premise ATMs are still lagging in terms of both staff member and customer adoption. The chip-driven Smart Card and Video-Text may be here in fact, but are they still light-years away in practice?

Fifth, will there be enough "big bank" managers available to manage the kind of "big bank" delivery systems projected in our portrayal of First Southeast—given the possibility of *scores* of like-sized institutions? The concern is not the fact of bigness—that is very easy to visualize—but rather the management of bigness, of vast regional, national and even multinational banking systems. The concern, moreover, is not with the handful of decision makers at the very top of diverse and highly complex networks, but with the customer-interfacing middle managers, *the people who make the bank real and vital to customers, who bring bigness down to the most personal, most meaningful levels.*

And sixth, lastly, where does the financial services industry obtain the dollars to pay for it all—for people, places, plastic, and machines? Housing, transportation, the health care business—all face huge capital shortfalls in their planning assessments for the next decade and beyond. Smokestack and other sunset industries are beggared today for reindustrialization capital. The sunrise industries of the Information Age will also be capital beggars. Where will we get the dollars to pay for it all? Where, especially, will the financial services industry—effectively and efficiently—find the capital to retool a people-based delivery system and simultaneously finance a complementary high-technology system?

It is a matter of sensible choices.

NOTES

1. Edward E. Furash, "Let's Be Realistic about EFT," *Bank Marketing*, May 1981, p. 13.

2. Thomas W. Thompson, "Commentary: The Smart Card—Tomorrow's Plastic," *United States Banker*, March 1983. Also see Jean Young, "What's Happening with Smart Cards," *Magazine of Bank Administration*, January 1984, pp. 28–30; and Martin Mayer, "Here Comes the Smart Card," *Fortune*, August 8, 1983, pp. 74–77, 80–81.

3. The scenario is based in part on ideas initially presented by Thomas W. Thompson in "Commentary: Branch Banking Sometime Tomorrow," *United States Banker*, April and May 1981.

4. Especially helpful was "Branch Banking in the Year 2000," the thoughtful address presented by Richard Rosenberg, vice chairman, Crocker National Bank, San Francisco, and former president of the Bank Marketing Association, at the annual meeting of the European Financial Marketing Association, Vienna, June 1979. In that address, Rosenberg predicted that "the basic branch system for personal banking business by the year 2000 [will be] a pocket calculator with a viewing screen on which we will conduct our financial transactions . . . a hand-held device [that] becomes each individual's own bank."

   Most helpful in developing this chapter were the articles contained in *Delivering Financial Services in the 1980's*, a special issue of the *Journal of Retail Banking* that appeared in June 1982.

   See also Furash, "Let's Be Realistic about EFT"; Michael P. Sullivan, "Marketing Management: Following the Road to Home Banking," *American Banker*, May 4, 1983, p. 4; David A. O'Connor, "Shared Product Systems," *Bank Marketing*, October 1982, pp. 11–19; and Charles E. Bartling, "Positioning Your Bank for In-Home Banking, *Bank Marketing*, April 1981, pp. 12–15.

5. John Naisbitt, *Megatrends: Ten New Directions Transforming Our Lives* (New York: Warner Books, 1984); see especially chap. 1, "Industrial Society—Information Society," and chap. 2, "Forced Technology—High Tech/High Touch."

6. In "Branch Banking in the Year 2000," Rosenberg noted that "sadly enough, as the world in which we live becomes more dangerous, security takes on new dimensions, and I can envision entire buildings which are merely safe deposit vaults. Indeed, we may find branching systems which are totally devoted to this function."

Promoting Financial Services

A needed service fairly priced and conveniently available is not enough. Customer prospects cannot buy the service if they are unaware of it and will not buy it if they are unpersuaded that it meets their needs. This is where promotion comes in: to *inform* and *persuade*. It is a vital element of the marketing mix.

This chapter focuses on two key elements in the promotion mix: personal selling and advertising. In the present chapter, we dwell not on promotion as it has been, but on promotion as it must be. We stress how vital personal selling has become in financial services marketing. We present in some detail the necessary steps in developing a sales program. We discuss advertising as a "partner" in the promotion mix, rather than as the "go it alone" tool it has often been. We suggest guidelines for maximizing the impact of advertising campaigns. The promotion function in the financial services industry is old. The manner by which it needs to be executed, however, is new. We offer our ideas about this in the following pages.

PROMOTING FINANCIAL SERVICES— PERSONAL SELLING

Banking and thrift institutions have traditionally been better at advertising than at personal selling. In the past, insufficiencies in personal selling were not much of a problem. Competition among different types of financial institutions was restricted, and, more often than not, the customer had to "sell" the financial institution rather than the other way around. Today many banks and thrifts are paying the piper. A modestly competitive past has not prepared them for a fiercely competitive present. The need to sell is recognized; getting it done is quite another matter.[1] Becoming good at selling—it turns out—is not something that can be accomplished overnight.

Why Selling Is So Hard

Many financial institution personnel have never before held a position in which they were asked to sell. Indeed, selling is an activity that some of them entered the financial services business to avoid. In a bank or thrift, one could be a "professional"; one would not have to "peddle." Being unfamiliar, selling conjures up images of high-pressure tactics, of canned spiels, of slick, smooth-talking hustlers. Selling also breeds fear. "Can I do it?" "Will I fall flat on my face?" Selling can be scary. It is, after all, a naked activity. One either makes the sale or doesn't make the sale. Selling performance is visible; it is *measureable!*

Richard Kendall points out several differences between what he refers to as "mainline banking" and selling:[2]

1. Mainline banking activities—loan decisions, working past-due accounts, data processing—have short deadlines. Results flow directly from efforts. Making a sale, on the other hand, may not occur until the third or fourth call on a prospect; it may not occur at all. The relationship between efforts and results is less immediate and less direct.
2. Mainline banking has traditionally been reactive. The institution opens its doors; customers come through them with problems or needs; and then the institution acts. The customer assumes the initiative. In selling, it is the banker who must assume the initiative— to solve the customer's problem (which may be different from what the customer thinks it is), to cross-sell, to target accounts, to seek out prospects.

Developing an effective selling program on an ongoing basis presents a formidable task. People are the medium of information transfer, problem solving, and persuasion. People are the sellers. Not machines. Not advertisements. Accordingly, all of the challenges normally associated with managing people—selection, motivation, training, supervision, and so forth—come into play when a sales program is being developed. That personnel are perhaps being asked to do something they have never before done—and do not want to do—makes the challenge all the more imposing.

Why Selling Is So Important

Why selling? The answer lies in a shifting product line and shifting financial institution objectives. Financial services are becoming more complex, and there are more of them from which to choose. Financial institutions can market checking or savings accounts without salespeople. Newspaper advertising would be sufficient. Contact personnel could be order takers. Not so with cash management accounts, retirement accounts, variable-rate mortgages, consumer and commercial loans, financial planning, insurance, and personal trusts. Marketing complex services requires addressing confusion, answering questions, and discussing alternative courses of action. It requires the *interactive dialogue* that is provided by salespeople, not advertising. The more complex the service line, the more "teaching" financial institutions must do. Advertising can build awareness and interest for complex services, but normally a salesperson will be required to secure conviction to buy, to "close the sale."

To think of advertising and selling as substitutes for each other is a mistake. IBM discovered years ago that advertising was more effective in the earlier stages of the buying process and selling was more effective in the later, decision-making stages. Said more precisely, advertising was most effective in creating *awareness* and stimulating *interest* and product *evaluation*. Selling by people accomplished *trial usage* or *product adoption*. IBM learned to *coordinate* advertising and selling to market complex products. Financial institutions must learn the same thing.

The objective of relationship banking presents another powerful argument in favor of building a sales program. Electronic banking machines cannot produce client relationships. Nor can advertising. Turning customers into clients requires a *real person*—someone who will become familiar with the client's needs, someone who will take a genuine interest in the client's welfare, someone who will be available *after* the sale, not just before. Relationship banking requires high-touch promotion; selling is high-touch. In relationship banking, the prospective client is buying a banker, not just a product. The potential for relationship banking is nonexistent if there is no banker to buy.

Improving Selling Effectiveness

Developing an ongoing, professional, and proactive sales program in a banking or thrift institution is tough. The odds are stacked against such a program for reasons already enumerated. Under the best of circumstances, the task is tenuous and drawn out. It requires deep-down commitment and a realistic understanding of the obstacles to be overcome by top management. It also requires the persistence and energy of one or more "sales champions," the vital coordinators who plan, steer, nurse, and protect the process by which a sales program is implemented, who execute the most difficult sale of them all, namely, the sale of selling. In a large institution, a different sales champion may be needed for each major division. In smaller institutions, the CEO and the sales champion may be the same person. The central challenge is installing a *sales culture* which necessitates the performance of two functions: (1) visible, aggressive support for selling at the top of the organization; and (2) coordination and implementation of the program itself. The sales program has no chance if either of these components is missing.

Organizational culture defines what is important in an organization. It is the chemistry of organizational history right up to yesterday: management deeds not just management words; behavior that is rewarded; projects that win approval and funding. The possibilities for building a true sales culture rise when sales is a key results area for senior line officers, when those who sell get ahead and those who don't stay behind, when senior managers set a sales example through their own behavior, and when management moves beyond the "interest in selling" stage to the "investment in selling" stage.

Neither quick-fix formulas nor coercion will result in an effective sales program. Pieces of a puzzle must be melded together. If properly put together, the puzzle leads to the sales culture that leads to sales behavior. We now turn to the puzzle's pieces.

1. Staffing to Sell. Training, incentives, and other critical factors in developing a sales program are of limited value if the wrong people are placed in sales positions. One key to building a sales program is factoring criteria relating to selling potential into hiring decisions. Financial institutions that give short shrift to hiring decisions involving entry-level positions, that entrust these decisions exclusively to the personnel department, that hire just about anyone to fill open positions— these institutions inhibit from the start their ability to become successful in selling. Holding out for the best people is one of the most important things to do in developing a sales program. Input shapes output.

We recall an experience that helps emphasize this point, though with a touch of reverse spin. Some years back, a large southeastern bank involved employees in a credit card sales program. All employees could participate, and ,they earned a dollar on every accepted credit card application. The winner was a janitor, a fellow who cleaned the office after the 9-to-5 managers and clerical staff went home. The winner earned a nice trophy and a bonus in addition to his "dollar a card." He then went back to being—yes, that's right, a *janitor*. Lost was very probably a very good salesman who just didn't fit that bank's idea of what selling and being a salesperson was all about.

A second key in staffing to sell is identifying existing customer contact staff who are not good candidates for selling positions and reassigning them to nonselling jobs or letting them go. Recognize that this process of identifying who should stay in selling jobs and who should leave them should occur over time, be based on performance, dig beneath the superficial, and be fair.

The tendency to look for glibness, or extroverted behavior, and to assume that this is what it takes for sales, should be avoided at all costs. The best salespeople tend to be *assertive* and *empathetic*. They have the drive to take control in selling situations and yet are sensitive to the prospect's needs. They are *enthusiastic* about the sales role, exhibit a high degree of *professionalism* and *concern for the customer's well-being*, have good *interpersonal skills*, are *self-motivated*, *goal-oriented* people, are *entrepreneurial*, and are *team players* inside their own organizations.[3] These should be among the attributes considered when interviewing candidates for contact positions and when assessing whether existing personnel are in the right jobs or not.

2. Defining Selling Behaviors. Determining just what it is that contact personnel should do in selling—defining their specific selling tasks—is an important step in building a sales program. *Sales task clarity* is a crucial element in salesperson motivation.[4] Precisely defined sales behaviors should be reflected in the job descriptions of every contact position in the institution. Personnel holding these should clearly understand what selling behaviors are expected.

Figure 10–1 provides examples of specific selling behaviors for three customer-contact positions: teller, new accounts representative, and calling officer. Limiting the desired selling behaviors to a few critical ones allows salespeople to focus their efforts, to understand exactly what they are supposed to do, and to keep score themselves.

The task of defining job category selling behaviors is not to be confused with goal setting or performance measurement, though they are all closely related. Selling behaviors concern ongoing efforts, that is, the critical tasks. Goals are statements—usually quantitative in nature—

FIGURE 10-1

Defining Selling Behaviors

position	*selling behavior*
Teller	1. Give each customer a pleasant greeting. 2. Perform "clue" selling, and refer customers to the new accounts desk. 3. Thank the customer by name.
New accounts representative	1. Determine the nature and extent of each customer's financial service needs. 2. Make the customer aware of the benefits of at least one service in addition to the one that the customer requested. 3. Give every customer the best possible service, regardless of the size of the account being opened, and the customer's appearance. 4. Use the customer's name, and thank the customer for the business.
Calling officer	1. Call on every existing account at least once a year. 2. Present a need-meeting bank service to every existing account at least once a year. 3. Assure that at least 25 percent of each year's calls are on noncustomer prospects. 4. Sell a full range of financial services. Be a good lender, but be more than a lender.

concerning results to be achieved within these task areas during a certain time span. Measurement is a process to determine what results are achieved. Sales task clarity is greatest when selling behaviors are limited in number, specific in nature, and well understood; when selling goals are clear-cut, precise, measurable, and within the control of the salesperson; and when sales performance measurement is timely, accurate, and consistent with defined selling behaviors and goals.[5] More will be said about goals and measurement shortly.

3. Preparing People to Sell. Sales performance is a function of the capabilities that individuals bring to the job, the capabilities that they develop or improve once in the job, and their motivation in performing the job.[6] Figure 10-2 presents this relationship. Preparing personnel for selling responsibilities directly contributes to development and improvement of capabilities and to motivation.

The task is larger than so-called sales training. Rather, the task is *sales knowledge and skill development*(SK/SD) for those personnel charged with the responsibility of selling the institution's services. The

FIGURE 10-2

The Sales Results Equation

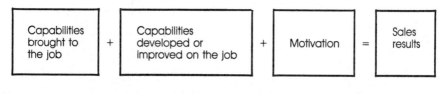

goals for the SK/SD program should relate to the goals for the sales program itself. To design an SK/SD program in a vacuum, without regard to the overall objectives of the institution's sales and marketing strategy, is utter nonsense. For example, if relationship management is one of the institution's marketing objectives, then relationship management skills development ought to be incorporated into the SK/SD program.

A strong SK/SD program is an imperative in building an effective sales program. Sales results are a function of three factors, as noted in Figure 10-2, and SK/SD affects two of them. Preparation to sell is integral to self-confidence, and self-confidence is integral to motivation. The costs involved in installing an SK/SD program may be burdensome. The costs involved in *not* installing an SK/SD program are prohibitive: employee turnover, employee ineffectiveness, poor customer service, lost business.[7]

Figure 10-3 presents important sales knowledge and skill development areas. The contents of Figure 10-3 are influenced by the Forum Corporation's research concerning the characteristics of high-and moderate-performing salespeople in six different industries. A principal conclusion of this research: sales skills normally taught in the better training programs—probing, selling product features and benefits, closing—have been mastered by both high and moderate performers. High-performers, however, go beyond these basic skills.[8]

Product knowledge is the foundation—the bedrock—of sales knowledge development. Superficial knowledge is not enough. Sales personnel need in-depth understanding of the features and benefits of the services they are asked to sell. They cannot sell the service if they do not understand its features; they won't want to if they don't understand its benefits.

Understanding the sales role is also important. Is the salesperson's function simply to "hawk the wares"? Or is it something else? Salespeople should understand the *customer-serving* characteristic of pro-

---

FIGURE 10–3

Components of an SK/SD Program

sales knowledge development

1. Product knowledge.
2. Sales role.
3. Institutional values, objectives, strategies, and policies.
4. Competitor analysis.
5. Industry analysis.

sales skills development

1. Selling to prospects.
2. Managing account relationships.
3. Communications skills.

---

fessional selling. They should understand how the sales role relates to the institution's mission, values, objectives, and strategy. They should understand the institution's "fit" in the bigger competitive and industry picture. To be of maximum service to their own customers, and for purposes of their own motivation, salespeople need to know what professional selling means, how it relates to the institution, and what's going on in the bigger competitive arena in which they and the institution function.

Sales skill development is just as important as sales knowledge development. It is a fatal mistake to develop product knowledge in contact personnel but not the skills to transmit it to prospects. Sales knowledge absent sales skills is insufficient. Here it is important to bear in mind that sales skills critical to making the initial sale are in some respects different from those required to service existing accounts. Sales personnel need to develop skills in both areas. Prospecting, call planning, probing, making a good first impression, following up—all are essential components of an SK/SD program for calling officers. But so are "after-the-sale" areas such as staying-in-touch and time-management skills.

The development of better communications skills—persuasive communications, nonverbal communications, speaking, writing, and listening—is also essential. Why listening? Because the best salespeople are problem solvers; they creatively match up customer needs with just the right services to satisfy those needs. The best salespeople serve the customer, not just the institution.

Three additional points should be made about SK/SD programs. First, SK/SD should be *ongoing*. Salespeople, like other professionals, need to continue growing in their work.

Second, salespeople should be encouraged to develop their own selling style, one that is comfortable and natural and plays to their strengths. Exposing sales personnel to selling approaches, techniques, and ideas is—as noted—necessary. Allowing them the freedom to use this input in their own way is also necessary. As George Rieder, a human resources specialist, once put it in a speech: "Give me the game plan and the plays you think will work. I expect your leadership and ideas. But let me execute."[9]

Third, remember that SK/SD is done with people rather than to people. Stress a mix of educational approaches. *Involvement, interaction, sharing, mentoring,* and *doing* are the key concepts.

4. Making It Easier to Sell. The best financial institution marketing departments are not those that are exceptionally clever in practicing marketing; they are those that are exceptionally clever in getting everyone else in the organization to practice marketing. A central strategy in this regard is making it easier for employees to sell.

It is easier to sell when:

- The product line is superior.
- The product line is simple, straightforward, and not beset with redundancies.
- An up-to-date product manual is in the possession of every salesperson.
- Multiple accounts can be opened with one common form.
- The paperwork associated with creating new business is minimized and clerical personnel are available to assist with the paperwork that must be completed.
- Point-of-sale materials are available to assist contact personnel in communicating service features and benefits.
- Senior executives are willing to help out in closing a big sale.

Regularly asking contact personnel what needs to be done for them so that they will be most successful in selling is one of the most useful things that marketing department personnel can do in building a selling program. But only if they are prepared to follow-up on the suggestions made.

5. Measuring Sales Performance. Measuring sales performance is essential. One cannot realistically hope to build a sales program without keeping score. The absence of an effective monitoring system demotivates those who want to sell and plays right into the hands of those who don't. Quite simply, sales measurement is a must. Expecting selling behavior without *inspecting* it inevitably results in disappointment. Personnel asked to sell need to know *that others will know* how they are performing.

The ideal sales measurement system will:

1. Measure the sales performance of each individual salesperson in addition to providing aggregated data, (e.g., sales by branches and regions).
2. Provide frequent and timely feedback.
3. Be accurate.
4. Be easy to understand and use.
5. Be fair.
6. Emphasize results rather than efforts.
7. Contribute to sales task clarity by focusing on the key expected selling behaviors.
8. Report names next to results to unleash the most powerful of all motivators, which is peer pressure.

Designing and implementing a sales measurement system incorporating the above qualities present no small challenge. We suggest testing and retesting system components before installation, testing the completed system in a specific unit or location before a full-scale roll-out, soliciting input from those who will be affected by the system during the design phase, and, in general, allocating the resources and taking the time to do the job right.

6. Rewarding Sales Performance.   Installing an effective sales measurement system puts a financial institution in position to reward selling performance. Few actions have a more telling impact on organizational culture than the rewarding of behaviors. Senior executives wishing to build sales cultures in their organizations must be prepared to *visibly, tangibly,* and *continually* reward selling performance. One does not build a sales culture by giving the new accounts representative with a 2.6 cross-sell average the same merit raise as is given to the new accounts representative with a 1.4 average. A sales program must have *teeth* if the players are to perceive it as legitimate!

Sales performance can be rewarded in three ways. All are important. *Direct financial rewards* involve merit raises, commissions, bonuses, and prizes. We believe that sustained selling effectiveness is more likely to occur when selling is viewed as part of the everyday job. Accordingly, we advocate sales performance as a central criterion in the performance appraisal/merit raise cycle. Incentive programs can also be valuable, especially if they are used as an adjunct to merit salary increases rather than as a substitute for them. Commission systems can easily backfire, given the cultural heritage of most banks and thrifts, and, in any case, are not necessary if other rewards are properly used.

Indirect financial rewards concern the career progression opportunities available to high-performing salespeople. Management gives one signal when the best salespeople move ahead in the organization and another signal when they don't. Career progression is tricky business since a good salesperson will not necessarily make a good manager. The answer lies in a dual-track system providing promotion opportunities both *outside* and *within* a selling position.

Nonfinancial rewards center on *recognition*—receiving a handwritten note of congratulations from the CEO, being given membership in the "top 20" club, receiving a plaque at an awards banquet, being written up in the company newspaper. The motivational impact of these forms of recognition—if they are reserved for special performances and performers rather than overused and cheapened—boggles the mind. Those who assume that good salespeople are driven only by money are wrong. As Kent Stickler, a sales consultant, likes to put it: "Money is good as long as it is accompanied by a pat on the back."

Three additional points about reward systems. First, accentuate the positive. The bias should be toward rewarding good sales performance rather than toward punishing poor performance. Second, give personnel time to develop their skills and confidence. Establish initial goals at modest levels, and raise them over time. Create a system in which good people who make a good effort win instead of lose. Third, take advantage of team-building opportunities. Instead of pitting individual against individual in a sales contest, pit branch against branch or region against region. Most people enjoy the sense of "team," of pulling and striving together. Create sales offices or sales units, not just salespeople.

7. Turning Supervisors into Sales Managers. Quite naturally, employee behavior is influenced by what managers emphasize . . . and don't emphasize. Employee role conflict and job stress are the inevitable consequences of more distant parts of the organization emphasizing selling and more immediate parts (e.g., the supervisor) emphasizing other behaviors. Clearly, reaching the supervisor with the sales message is critical.

Each of the preceding steps involving the *salesperson* also applies to the *sales manager*. A sales orientation should be a primary criterion in selecting contact personnel supervisors, for example, branch managers. Specific sales management behaviors require definition, just as specific selling behaviors require definition. Sales managers need to develop knowledge of the sales process and buyer behavior as well as skills in the areas of motivation, leadership, and administration.[10] Finally, the selling effectiveness of subordinates should figure in the appraisal/reward system involving supervisors. Rewarding supervisors when the sales performance of those they supervise is good is an effective way to reach supervisors with the "sales message."

Time to Bite the Bullet

Increasingly complex services and relationship-building institutional objectives require the company/prospect dialogue that personal selling provides. Advertising has key promotional roles to play, as the next section suggests, but advertising alone is not enough. Financial institutions need to sell. The absence of a sales tradition makes the task harder, but it does not remove the need.

Building an effective sales program presents a *multifaceted* challenge, as the previous sections point out. Magical, overnight solutions do not exist. Attempts at quick fixes will fail. To prepare people to sell but not measure their sales performance is wasteful. To measure their sales performance but not prepare them to sell is unproductive and unfair. To speak of sales but pay no attention to sales when appraising performance destroys credibility. All the pieces of the sales puzzle must be in place.

FINANCIAL SERVICES PROMOTION—ADVERTISING

The growing importance of personal selling in financial institutions does not mean that advertising will become unimportant. It does mean, however, that the role of advertising will change. We have already implied that the tendency within financial institutions is to view advertising as a substitute for personal selling rather than as a complement to it. The net effect is to shoulder advertising with the entire burden of promotion: creating awareness, informing, persuading, closing the sale. However, the complexity of today's financial services and the institutional desire to build client relationships make an *advertising/selling partnership* essential. Increasingly, advertising's job will be to create awareness and selling's job will be to inform, persuade, and close the sale. Advertising's job will be to *pave the way* for the salesperson, to provide more opportunities for salespeople to communicate with prospects. This is a vital role, given the time, effort, expense, and commitment required to mount a professional sales program. It makes little sense to work through the steps in building a sales program that we have enumerated but then to couple this program with bland or uninteresting or aimless advertising.

Paving the Way

The best financial services advertisers will attempt to pave the way for salespeople in three ways. First, they will use advertising to promote the institution, not just individual services. They will recognize the need to break through the clutter of financial institutions and will view advertising as a vehicle to establish the *institution's distinctiveness, the institution's reason for being.* They will attempt to make the institution stand apart so as to help the salesperson stand apart.

Second, financial advertisers will use advertising to *educate, to add value.* They will see the opportunity to use advertising in such a way that the institution becomes more believable, more credible. They will insist on advertising that is *on the customer's side.*

Third, financial advertisers will advertise to *market segments* rather than to markets. They will tailor messages, hone messages, to specific groups. They will be skilled users of segmented media, such as cable television, direct mail, in-house magazines, and newsletters. They will seek a *dominant presence* within chosen segments.

Eight Guidelines for Better Financial Advertising[11]

1. Have Something to Say. Advertising dollars should be spent in bunches when there is something important to say. Advertising for any other reason is foolish. Advertising need not be an ongoing process, devoid of interruption. The consumer will not miss the Acme Bank ad that doesn't appear in Sunday's newspaper. Advertising expenditures should be made only on campaigns that have a *purpose.* Advertising just to advertise is a mistake.

2. Make Special Efforts to Attract Attention. Advertising absent the target audience's attention is a waste of money. Gaining attention for advertising is both difficult and imperative. It is difficult because people are bombarded with advertising in their everyday lives. They have no choice but to be highly selective concerning the advertisements to which they pay attention. It is imperative because communicating with people requires that they be paying attention.

The challenge is to create advertising that is difficult to ignore. Doing this requires special efforts. All great advertising campaigns use special devices to attract a "more than fair share" of attention. Philip Morris used humor with Miller Lite Beer. The great Volkswagen campaigns of the 1960s incorporated humor, unusual headlines, and excessive white space in various ads. Jockey turned men's underwear into a fashion item by picturing baseball pitcher Jim Palmer wearing colored, patterned briefs and little else.

The trick is to use special, attention-getting devices in such a way that they contribute to the overall purposes of the advertisement. As advertising pioneer Leo Burnett was fond of saying: "We want people to say 'what a great product' not 'what a great ad.'"[12]

3. Create Distinctive Advertising. Distinctive advertising is more likely to be attention-getting and memorable than "look-alike" advertising. In many communities, competing financial institutions tend to blend together into a big "glob." The names are similar, the services are similar, the rates are similar, the facilities are similar, the machines are similar (or the same), and the ads are similar. This need not be the case. A financial institution's advertising can—and should—stand apart from competitive advertising. Although me-too services are to some extent inevitable in financial marketing, me-too advertising is not inevitable and should be avoided. What is required is an insistence on originality, an intolerance for bland, punchless ads. Leo Burnett also believed that one of the greatest dangers in advertising was boring people to death. He felt that an advertising audience deserved to be rewarded for its time and attention.[13]

4. Seek Advertising Continuity. To develop a distinctive advertising campaign is one thing; to remain a distinctive advertiser over time is quite another. The key is *advertising continuity*, the relentless use of certain symbols, styles, or themes even though specific campaigns continue to change.

The idea of advertising continuity is to give an institution's advertising a *recognizability* that communicates and reinforces its "reason for being." Merrill Lynch's continual use of a bull and Marlboro's continual use of a rugged cowboy are classic examples of advertising continuity *well executed*. Merrill Lynch and Marlboro advertising would be recognizable even if the Merrill Lynch and Marlboro names were left out.

Financial advertisers that move from one advertising approach to a completely new approach with each new campaign make a mistake. Campaigns should "bridge" one another; they should tie the present to the past because the past or the present alone may not be enough to establish an institution's *distinctiveness*. The "glob" problem awaits any financial institution that fails to capitalize on every available tool to create and sustain a specific, meaningful identity.

5. Repromote Key Services. Financial services need to be periodically "readvertised." Introducing new services with an intensive kickoff campaign but not following up with additional advertising at later intervals fails to establish product awareness among those who were unready to buy when a service was first introduced but who nevertheless could be legitimate prospects for the service. Service-specific advertising is likely to be most effective in creating awareness and prompting buying interest if it runs when prospects are deciding to take some action concerning the management of their financial affairs.

One way to repromote key services is to run periodic "umbrella" campaigns that simultaneously present a number of services. A savings and loan association, for instance, that introduced a discount brokerage service in the first quarter, a new adjustable-rate mortgage instrument in the second quarter, and a modified individual retirement account in the fourth quarter is probably ready for an umbrella campaign tying all of these services, and perhaps others, together.

6. Provide Tangible Clues. Financial advertisers should seek out opportunities to incorporate into advertising tangibles associated with a service that provide evidence of the service's nature and quality. This is necessary to compensate for the reality that advertising media (except for radio) are visual in nature, whereas services are essentially invisible. Whereas goods can be shown and pointed to and demonstrated in advertising, services, which are intangible, cannot be. The beer advertiser can use television to picture a tub of iced beer that is to be consumed at a beach party. For purposes of attention-getting, the participants at the beach party might be glorious physical specimens wearing skimpy bathing suits. What to "picture" when advertising cash management accounts is quite another matter.

Using relevant objects that either signify the service or make a visual statement about the service can help customer prospects to better understand and evaluate what they are being asked to buy. The Trans-America Corporation, a service conglomerate, effectively features its unique, pyramid-like headquarters building in its advertising to portray progressiveness and financial strength. Insurance companies such as State Farm feature insurance agents in their advertising and stress the relationship that these agents have with their clients. Great Western Savings and Loan Association for many years used John Wayne in its advertising to associate Wayne's film characterizations as a rugged and honest cowboy with the qualities of the company.

A unique headquarters building, insurance agents, a movie star known for a certain type of role—what these examples have in common is a visual concreteness that is frequently missing from services advertising. They are tangibles that offer evidence about the service that the service itself cannot offer.

7. Think Simplicity. However complex the research and planning process that leads to the development of an advertising campaign, ideally the campaign itself will revolve around a powerful—but *simple*—idea. Stark, basic, understandable communications are especially important in financial services advertising as an antidote to the growing complexity of these services.

The great advertising campaigns are almost always characterized by a fundamentally simple message: "Our L'eggs Fit Your L'eggs"; "We're Number Two, We Try Harder"; "It's the Real Thing. Coke." In 1984, the Wendy's hamburger chain provoked much national interest and sparked sales with a television commercial showing an elderly lady in a competitor establishment confronting a tiny hamburger patty on a huge bun and demanding to know: "Where's the Beef?" One cannot see this commercial and fail to grasp the message. It is powerful but simple.

Financial services advertisers should strive to communicate in the customer's language rather than in the industry's language. As a bank customer once asked one of us in the course of a research project: "What is this mysterious thing called average daily balance?" Financial institution advertising copy is normally written by people who themselves use "industry" language every day; such language becomes ingrained; it becomes increasingly difficult to remember that most people don't talk this way. Major campaigns should be pretested to assess the communications effectiveness of the intended message, including the understandability of the key phrases and words used. To spend money on advertising that customer prospects do not understand makes no sense whatsoever.

8. Make Keepable Promises. Customer perceptions of the quality of a service are a function of the expectations that customers bring to the service situation and of their experiences in buying and using the service.[14] It is especially important that financial service advertisers foster realistic expectations to minimize the dissatisfaction that occurs when expectations are violated.

As discussed in Chapter 8, labor-intensive services are prone to variability. It is difficult to *always* be the "friendly bank" in a 200-branch network in which the labors of perhaps 1,200 people are involved.

Several years ago, when Holiday Inns' advertising agency used consumer research as the basis for a television campaign promising "no surprises," top management accepted the campaign theme, whereas operations executives opposed it. The operations executives knew that "surprises" frequently occur in a complex company such as Holiday Inns in which thousands of people operate facilities throughout the world. When the campaign was aired, it raised consumer expectations and provided dissatisfied customers with additional grounds for venting frustrations. The "no surprises" advertising had to be discontinued, which is no surprise.

In financial services advertising, it is better to promise only what can be delivered a high percentage of the time. It is wiser to make keepable promises that result in customer satisfaction than to make unrealistic promises that result in customer dissatisfaction.

Summing Up

The eight guidelines just presented are based on our assessment of the areas in which financial services advertising as a whole has traditionally been weak. The guidelines will not apply to every circumstance, and in any case they do not represent an exhaustive listing of everything that should be considered in developing an advertising campaign. What these guidelines do provide are eight questions to raise when designing and evaluating an advertising campaign. In this sense, they should prove helpful. The questions to raise:

- Are we advertising with a *purpose*? Do we have something important to say?
- Are we making special efforts to attract attention? Are we making our advertising *difficult to ignore*?
- Are we delivering *distinctive* advertising? Does our advertising stand apart?
- Are we achieving advertising *continuity*? Is our advertising recognizable?
- Are we sufficiently *repromoting* key services?
- Are we using relevant *tangibles* to convey the nature and quality of our services? Is our advertising visually concrete?
- Are we communicating? Is the message understandable? Is it clear cut? Is it *simple*?
- Are we making *keepable* promises? Can we back up our promises?

CONCLUSION

The best-managed financial services marketing departments will seek to develop a strong advertising/personal selling *partnership* in the years ahead. The prevailing objective will be to *meld* advertising and selling strategies, to focus the advertising and selling tools on the uses for which they are best suited, and to coordinate them to achieve a maximum impact. More and more, advertising's tasks will revolve around image-making, education, creating service awareness, and "opening the door" for the salesperson. Selling's tasks will revolve around taking advantage of the opportunities that advertising presents: informing, building credibility, securing conviction to buy, establishing client relationships, and being of service after the sale.

Installing a professional, proactive, ongoing personal selling program is one of the toughest marketing challenges facing financial services marketers. Most financial institutions have yet to "bite the bullet" in terms of making the commitments necessary to get the job done (e.g., measuring sales performance, rewarding sales performance, taking greater care in selecting the people who are put in front of the customer). Until those commitments are made, the idea of building a selling institution is just so much talk. Rhetoric about the importance of selling may flow, but employee behavior remains essentially unchanged. Periodic quick fixes are tried; they all fail. Meanwhile, the institution loses precious time that could be used to install the essential components of a sales culture.

Rethinking advertising along the lines that we have discussed is also difficult. Our habit in financial services is not only to lead with advertising but to close with advertising. Advertising has been more an "independent player" than a "partner." Moreover, the creative challenge facing financial advertisers is not to be sneezed at. It is no small matter to attract attention with advertising when so many competing financial institutions are active in the media. Nor is it easy to create distinctive advertising when there is so much pressure to advertise interest rates. After all, it's hard to be different with a big "12%" (or whatever) in the headline. Creating visually exciting advertising for an invisible product is not easy either. And so on.

Building a genuine sales program, rethinking the roles and creative requirements of advertising, and establishing a strong advertising/selling partnership offer fundamentally important marketing challenges. These challenges will test those of us who think that we are pretty good marketers.

Notes

1. See Leonard L. Berry, Michael Bowers, and Charles Futrell, "The Current Status of Personal Selling in Wholesale Banking," *Bankers Magazine*, March–April 1984, pp. 39–43; and Leonard L. Berry, Charles Futrell, and Michael Bowers, "The State of Personal Selling in Retail Banking," *Journal of Retail Banking*, Fall 1983, pp. 1–7.

2. Richard L. Kendall, "What's Missing in Officer Call Programs That Fail," *Bank Marketing*, January 1984, p. 14.

3. David Mayer and Herbert M. Greenberg, "What Makes a Good Salesman?" *Harvard Business Review*, July–August 1964, pp. 119–25; and William M. DeMarco and Michael D. Maginn, *Sales Competency Research Report* (Forum Corporation, 1982).

4. Benson P. Shapiro and Stephen X. Doyle, "Make the Sales Task Clear," *Harvard Business Review*, November–December 1983, pp. 72–76.

5. Ibid., p. 76.

6. Adapted from M. Marshall Weems, "A System for Improving Customer Contact Performance," *Bank Marketing*, December 1978, pp. 26–33.

7. Robert Negri, "A Sales Training Program for Affliates," *Bank Marketing*, December 1973, pp. 25–28.

8. DeMarco and Maginn, Sales Competency Research Report, pp. 25–26.

9. George Rieder, "Nobody Will Buy if You Don't Ask Them—Building a Professional Sales Force," Bank Marketing Association National Convention, Phoenix, Arizona, October 25, 1982.

10. Bert Rosenbloom and Rolph E. Anderson, "The Sales Manager: Tomorrow's Super Marketer," *Business Horizons*, March–April 1984, pp. 50–56.

11. Some of the material in this section is based on two earlier works: Leonard L. Berry, "Guidelines for Better Bank Advertising," *Bankers Magazine*, Summer 1977, pp. 65–68; and William R. George and Leonard L. Berry, "Guidelines for the Advertising of Services," *Business Horizons*, May–June 1981, pp. 52–55.

12. As quoted in Carl Hixon, "Leo," *Advertising Age*, February 9, 1982, p. M–8.

13. Ibid.

14. A. Parasuraman, Valarie Zeithaml, and Leonard L. Berry, "A Conceptual Model of Service Quality and Its Implications for Future Research," *Marketing Science Institute*, 1984.

The New PR: Communications

"Let me give you my golden rules about PR," Mr. Hack said to the young J-school graduate joining his staff.

"Tell them nothing unless you absolutely have to. Never volunteer any ideas about us and our business."

"The only good news about our bank is no news."

"The press . . . those flaky consumerists . . . the politicians . . . they're all out to get us. They're the enemy. The less they know about us, the less likely they are to pick on us.

"What do we want to see in the newspaper? I'll tell you. We want to see only the words we write in our press releases. No more, no less. We want them to come to our branch openings and take a picture of the boss and the mayor cutting a ribbon. We want them to do a nice story about our softball team; good bunch of guys and gals, and they've got a good chance to win the business league tournament this year.

"And what's this about you wanting to enroll in some AIB courses? You don't need to know anything about banking in this job."

INTRODUCTION

We couldn't disagree more, and that is what this chapter is all about. It deals with *managing communications through planning.* Let's begin by breaking down this theme into its component elements.

First, communications must be managed: structured, organized, given purpose, and administered with measurable results in mind. Communications is part of an organization's reaction to marketplace events: to changes in the prime rate, or a lull in housing starts, or a city council's decision to build a much-needed local hospital by floating a bond issue. At the same time, communications is an offensive weapon for developing new business, motivating bank people to sell, and creating positive organizational identity or "image" with customers, community opinion makers, and the financial organization's staff. None of this happens; it must be made to happen. It must be managed on a continuing basis.

Second, good communications management is effected through soundly conceived and structured planning techniques. Communications management involves translating corporate objectives into results-producing communications programs. The organization, for example, may desire to be regarded as as a progressive, innovative, caring, and community-oriented financial institution. Communications involves giving this idea feet, pointing out the right direction, and helping it run.

Third, "communications" is a more realistic label than "PR"—public relations—or "public affairs." Unfortunately, PR connotes dealing almost exclusively with the media, and particularly the print media. PR also has a negative ring to it. Too many Mr. Hacks employed in this sensitive position for too many years have fostered the notion that "bank PR" is passive if not reactive, cosmetic if not of questionable purpose, protective if not barrier creating, and selective in the sense that its major intention is to proclaim the good news loud and clear and to stonewall the bad news.

Fourth, communications recognizes the massive growth of a financial institution's *publics*—the individuals, the groups, the causes, the decision makers in society that the financial institution absolutely must deal with on a day to day basis.

The media remain important. But they are no more important to a financial institution in this day and age than consumer advocates, regulatory authorities, academics, financial analysts, community leadership groups, and so many others that are part of a growing army of "publics" involved in making decisions that affect the performance of financial institutions.

A Business in Transition

Whether or not the reader accepts *communications* as a better descriptive term than either *public relations* or *public affairs* is secondary. Of far greater consequence is the importance of the communications task ın today's operating environment. There is no more important organızational task than explaining the transition from the banking business, the thrift business, or the brokerage business to the financial services business. There is no more important organizational task than explaining an organization's transition from local or statewide operations to an interstate posture. There is no more important organizational task than explaining why personal banker programs are being offered to some customers and not to others. There is no more important organizational task than explaining why a community branch office is being closed down and replaced by an ATM. Or why a high balance is needed for a NOW account or a still higher balance is needed for a money market checking account. There is no more important organizational task facıng management today than explaining why First National wants to sell stocks and bonds, sell insurance, offer travel services, and so much more.

Communications is not limited to what the public relations practitioner does. It has become a *primary management responsibility* as the modern financial services institution reaches out to its many publics in an understandable, believable, and action-producing fashion to state its case in our rapidly changing environment.

COMMUNICATIONS PRINCIPLES

At the Edge of Change

Communications is at the leading edge of a top-performing financial institution's response to change. The concern of this chapter is with managing that response through effective planning procedures. Before we go further with our evaluation of this task-oriented approach, four guiding principles must be spelled out. Change has created new rules of the road for directing communications traffic. Understanding them is easy. The difficult assignment is abiding by them in developing communications programs. The even harder task is convincing management, especially middle management, that it is part of the communications team and must abide by the new rules.

The *first* guiding principle of the New PR is the need to turn Mr. Hack into a financial institution executive, a professional communicator who understands banking and finance, the consequences of intensified competition, and the implications of new technologies. It may be necessary to staff his department with the required expertise. Or to make sure that Mr. Hack functions as a responsible *intermediary* between the editor or consumerist or financial analyst and the organization's *real bankers*. And to prepare them in turn to be candid, authoritative, and fair-minded communicatıons brokers.

You see, our publics have also changed. The business writer for a local paper and the editor of an industry trade journal know just a bit more about the financial services business and its mysteries than they did yesterday. They possess enough smarts to ask tougher questions, and they know just enough more to be turned off by less than satisfactory answers.

In leafing through a file of yellowing newspaper clips on the public relations function, we ran across a 1978 *Wall Street Journal* article discussing the "ethical dilemmas" encountered in the PR business. It cited the recent firing of a southeastern bank holding company press officer for complaining publicly about distributing releases containing false or misleading information. The holding company's lawyer told the *WSJ* writer that the fired press officer's job was to serve "as a ministerial disseminator of information provided by such employees as accountants and lawyers." Accordingly, the financial institution's legal counsel insisted that the press officer "wasn't authorized to comment on [this information] because of the possibility of errors" stemming from his inability to fully understand the information.[1]

Assuming that the stated facts are correct, the essential ideas embraced in this story still rankle. A "ministerial disseminator"! This is not what the New PR is all about. This may have been Mr. Hack's vision of his job, but it no longer stands up. "Wasn't authorized to comment . . . because of the possibility of errors," because he didn't understand! If so, he never should have been authorized to deal with any of that organization's publics. He never should have been employed as a bank officer. If he didn't understand, moreover, the fault rests with the bank.

Lee Silberman, former banking editor of *The Wall Street Journal* and one-time editor of *Finance Magazine*, argues the need for a "new breed of communicator" by insisting that "dealings with the media are too fragile and potentially adverse to be handled on anything but the surest footing." The same point applies to other communications publics. Silberman adds:

> Banks today not only must be responsive to a growing galaxy of social issues . . . but also must be able to articulate their positions clearly, crisply, and convincingly. Banks today, for example, must be ready to respond to press queries on equal employment practices, truth-in-lending and fair credit procedures, computer privacy, compliance with CRA guidelines, and the like. They also have the opportunity to capitalize on these activities as a means of enhancing their image.
>
> Increasingly, elements of the public are looking to the banks to serve as an instrument of social change . . . It's when public expectations outrun reality that a bank's public relations skills are put to their severest test.[2]

What this all means "for communicators of the eighties," Siberman believes, is that they will be challenged to grow professionally and personally '

We Have ı/let the Enemy

This discussion points up a *second* guiding principle for effective communications management. To quote cartoon philosopher Pogo, "We have met the enemy . . . and he is us." Yesterday financial institution managers resided in marble mausoleums well hidden from the public. Their day-to-day business was arcane, mysterious, surrounded by myth and mystique, inpenetrable. What the public didn't know, we conjectured, really didn't hurt it. The public trusted us. The public had confidence in financial institutions to wisely manage society's financial affairs. The public listened to and accepted with little doubt our explanations of marketplace gyrations.

Today our house is made of glass. Financial institution managers operate under ever-closer scrutiny.

There are many reasons why this is so; among them—the radicalizing kinds and degrees of change that have been nourished and then hurried along by deregulation and the technology explosion; the recent two-year long roller-coaster ride that saw the prime soar from 6 percent to 20 percent, down by half as much, then back across the 20 percent line only to drop sharply once again; mortgage rates and home prices that went out of sight—and for many younger families still remain there; Sears and Merrill Lynch somehow talking and acting like financial institutions; large institutions as well as small ones closing their doors in unprecedented numbers or being merged just short of insolvency; the entire savings and loan industry, not just a handful of thrifts, portrayed in the media as "just hanging on" by the slimmest of lifelines; and, perhaps above all else, the international lending spree to less developed countries (LDCs) that seems to have brought the American banking system to the edge of a yawning chasm.

Banking—the financial services business—lives in a house made of glass because of discontinuity and disruption. For these same reasons and also because their many publics are more questing, more discerning, more demanding and less trustful—more insistent, moreover, that financial institutions commit greater resources to satisfying broader societal objectives—bankers have become the "black hat boys."

Many financial industry leaders try to pass this off as "ambush journalism." There is some truth to this charge. After all, the financial industry is the citadel of "establishment conservatism" and presumed "capitalistic uncaring." And the media in this day and age comfortably acknowledge their higher responsibility as public interest advocates. If "ambush journalism" is too strong a charge, confrontation journalism is not. Moreover, if journalists are wary, cynical, their attitudes are not entirely without justification. The past decade in particular presented the media and the public with many moments of financial institution "excesses and abuses." Tick them off: Lance and Sindona; Penn Square and Continental Illinois; Poland and Brazil. The evidence of misconduct and questionable judgment is there, and it overwhelms by far the abundant evidence of the financial industry's positive contributions to economic growth and public well-being. However, you seldom read the good news on page one.[3]

"We have met the enemy . . . and he is us." The decline in public confidence and the shift in media attitudes is no one's fault. It is the times. It is change and discontinuity. It is the cynicism nurtured by Vietnam and Watergate. It is Toffler's "Future Shock" world. It is corporate bigness that overwhelms and frightens. It is the liberating forces of new technologies that also threaten to enslave: computers and personal privacy; robots and job security.

The *reality* is that the savings bank industry did not get into trouble several years back because of poor management, insensitivity to public needs, or lack or foresight. More at fault was long-standing governmental policy confining savings banks to mortgage lending and forcing them to lend long and borrow short in a volatile, unstable economic environment. The *reality* is that the nation's major financial organizations did not lend heavily to LDCs without a large dose of governmental encouragement. And the *reality* is that financial institutions did not create inflation and push-pull the prime into double-digit figures and beyond; 20 years of governmental "guns and butter" spending is a truer villain.

The guiding principle applicable to contemporary financial communications management is that little can be taken for granted. A financial institution must continually prove itself. It must continually demonstrate and reinforce commitment to a community's well-being, to equal credit and employment opportunities, and to effective disclosure standards. The industry's word, traditions, and past performance are no longer its bond. The new guiding principle is that an institution's continuing conduct—its deeds and not its PR cosmetics and semantic shufflings—must ever plead its case in the public mind and in the mind-set of media or consumerist advocates.

Defensive strategies just won't work anymore. The "credibility gap" that is at the heart of the financial industry's image problem came about largely because of a *passive* PR posture. The gap can be bridged and credibility substantially restored, but only through *activist* communications anchored in candor and outreach.[4]

There is another and very well understood side to this coin. It is what people think about *bankers* individually, not the organizations that financial managers work for, but the managers as a class grouping. What people perceive about bankers affects their perceptions of the organization itself.

Norwood W. "Red" Pope raised this issue and nicely interred it for the thoughtful reader in one of his periodic *American Banker* columns. Pope wrote:

> Bankers are pictured in stereotypes as being rather tough, glass-eyed, insensitive, calculating sorts who wear pinstripe suits, sit at great mahogany desks, and relish evicting widows. To tell the truth, I'd be hard-pressed to find many of my associates who fit that description or come close.
>
> Instead, I can point out quickly a great many bankers who are outgoing, understanding, warm, generous with their time and the bank's support of local activities, who wear sports jackets to work, operate from landscaped furnishings in contemporary surroundings, and haven't evicted a widow in days.[5]

Still, perceived images remain part of the "we are the enemy" syndrome complicating financial institution communications activities. There is the perception of what a banker is and a more mundane reality. The challenge that must always confront a communications manager is dealing with *both* the perceptions surrounding an organization's image and the perceptions surrounding the people who manage it. If the manager must work to debunk financial institution stereotypes as part of improving communications flows between the organization and its many publics, the concurrent task is to humanize management.

The Age of the People

The *third* guiding principle for effective communications management is rooted in the thesis that the underlying social, political, and economic values of, first, an agricultural society and then our industrial society began giving way in the 1970s to values associated with a "people first, things second culture." This theme belongs to the breed of ideas embraced by futurist commentators Herman Kahn and Alvin Toffler and by Megatrender John Naisbitt.

Many social commentators dispute this contention and claim that American society is slipping back to "comforting materialism." This is simply too heady a discussion to moderate in this chapter. Yet we believe that there is considerable evidence of new yearnings in our culture for heightened levels of individualism—a me-oriented value system; for greater quality in the acts of living and dying—the hospice movement, for example; for social justice—the women's movement, the Indian movement, movement for the the rights of homosexuals; and for ecological constraints—the environmental issues, the concern over nuclear energy, and the concern over arms buildups.

Call it consumerism or the Age of the People, the New Capitalism or the coming of Toffler's "third wave," the critically important implication for communications practitioners is that these new yearnings are broadly shared. Consumerism is not a fringe issue pushed by the young and discontented only. Consumerism is not just the tinkering of special interest groups with the political and economic process. It is a feeling, now deeply implanted in society, about the rights of individuals in relationship to government, social institutions, and business and financial institutions. The Age of the People is about rights, relationships, opportunities, privacy, security, and human worth in an increasingly impersonal world.

The inherent task of financial institution executives, marketers, and communicators is to recognize and respond to the value changes embraced by the Age of the People.

This point identifies our third guiding principle. The financial institution communicator is the organization's "eyes and ears" for "testing and sensing" the environment, for understanding the new values of the Age of the People and transmitting them judiciously to management. More than this, the guiding principle is the communicator's responsibility for assuring and actualizing management's response.

We would take this concept a step further. In an era of change, deregulation, and consumerism, the public relations professional must necessarily be a thorn in management's side. The communicator has the specific job of being an irritant, provoking honest, out-in-the-open interaction between a bank and its public. He or she serves two masters: the communicator is an advocate of the institution clearly; but no less, the communicator is a customer advocate. He or she is the corporate hair-shirt, an ever nagging organizational conscience.

In this capacity, the public relations or communications professional cannot be, cannot be allowed to be, an infrequent visitor to the executive suite. The assignment, by implication, involves speaking up, informing, and counseling, and this involves as much a knowledge of the industry and the customers' new yearnings as it does skill in the communications arts. The rationale, the why of it all, is the visible evidence that in the emerging future a financial institution's real or perceived public image will have a bottom line to it, *a measureable dollar and cents bottom line.*

Beyond Informing

The *fourth* financial communications guideline can be called the *multiplicity of the communications assignment.* Traditionally, public relations meant the *dissemination of information.* The basic task was to inform the media, community leaders, customers, staff members, and a financial institution's other publics. Inform, and some practitioners would insist, but not too much since they won't understand; not too much because it will generate confusion; not too much because they don't have the right to know about the ins and outs of our business.

As we have seen, communicator perspectives on this information-providing task are greatly changing. The media, for example, do understand, are vitally interested in banking and finance, and do have a right to know a good deal about the financial services industry. And the same holds true for the industry's countless other publics.

It is also becoming clear that informing is only one element of the communications assignment. Five other elements are achieving equal status: *education, selling, crisis management, image creation, and representation or spokesmanship.*

1. If the job of marketing within a financial organization is to *teach* marketing, to make tellers understand, for example, that they are truly engaged in marketing when they courteously respond to customer complaints or when they suggest that an old customer might like to chat with a loan officer about an equity credit line, then effective communications similarly embraces educational activities. Educating customers to comprehend the value of ATMs and other technologies as well as how to use them efficiently is a communications task. Educating staff members to comprehend why a bank is closing down branch offices while increasing the number of ATMs in its network is a communications task of no small magnitude. Educating shareholders about such mysteries as foreign earnings translation expenses (or hedges) and their impact on corporate earnings is a communications task. And so, too, is explaining the rhyme and reason of mergers between major holding companies in order to position the consolidated organization for interstate banking.

2. Communications also embraces *selling*—direct selling of both the financial organization and its product lines. One regional holding company, for example, each year prints 40,000 annual reports at a production cost of approximately $8.50 per copy—$340,000, and this does not include staff time or mailing and other distribution expenses. This organization has approximately 4,000 shareholders and nearly as many employees, many of whom are shareholders themselves. Satisfying regulatory compliance requirements and the needs of financial analysts chews up another 1,000 copies at most. The remaining 31,000 copies of its 40-page, four-color annual report is employed as a business development tool. Some copies are mailed or hand-carried to municipal financial officers, small business owners, corporation executives, hospital managers, multimember law firms, multimember accounting firms, academics, real estate agents, home builders, and on and on through a very long and well-thought-through list. What's the underlying pur-

pose? Information, yes. Helping create and support a desired image, certainly. But the purpose also is *selling*: selling people and expertise, product lines and how efficiently they appear to be managed, and above all, the wisdom of purchasing or reinvesting in this organization's debt and equity offerings.

3. The communications task is *crisis management*. On one hand, it is dealing with the rising incidence of often violent robbery and often pitiful white-color crime. But also consider that Penn Square was not one institution's problem but a crisis affecting many financial institutions. The thrift industry's "years of trouble" was a different type of crisis, yet it begged for no less adroit handling by communications practitioners. Poland may default on its loans. Mexico. Brazil. Zaire. Is my bank involved with this? Is my bank safe? Crisis. Explaining and giving assurances are at the heart of crisis management. Crisis management is also soothing community leaders, customers, staff members, and others over an office closing or an institutional takeover. It is dealing both with anticipated problems (a merger or branch office closing) and with unexpected events (a consumer group's recommendation that people withdraw deposits because the bank is "suspected" of extending credit to racist South Africa).

Crisis management differs from the dissemination of information largely because of the "glass house" syndrome discussed earlier. It differs, too, because of the dexterity required in coping with crisis.

4. Communications is all about *creating and managing the organization's image or identity* in the marketplace. This key point can be approached from several different directions, including, as discussed in Chapter 6, its integral place in an organization's positioning strategy. The point can be underscored, however, by once again raising the obvious. Yesterday, when banks were in the banking business and thrifts were neatly positioned in the deposit-gathering and home lending business and Sears was a place where Middle America shopped, a bank's "identity" concern was chiefly to differentiate itself from other banks. Since then, such demarcations have blurred. Today's image issue involves differentiating ourselves by what we stand for and by how we perform in a setting where, one and all, *we all are banks*. Image and identity also involve standing apart distinctively as traditional geographic boundaries are breached.

5. Finally, the expanded communications task embraces *representation or spokesmanship*. Being an institution's chief observer in the marketplace, its "eyes and ears," should entail active membership in the institution's managerial process. The same holds true, we believe, if the heart of the communications task is the translation of corporate positioning objectives into workable, concrete action programs. It may have been appropriate for the passive, organization-protecting PR practi-

tioner to be an outsider or an occasional visitor to the executive suite. It is not appropriate, however, for the communications officer of a financial institution that is determined to succeed as a marketplace leader.

Representation must be earned. This requires demonstrating both communications skills and financial skills. You don't need experience in making loans to understand credit functions and the essence of modern asset-liability management; you don't need experience in running a branch to comprehend "hub and spoke" branch network strategies. You must, however, be able to *think* as a financial institution executive in order to more effectively utilize communications skills.

Once the right of representation has been earned, the responsibility of spokesmanship should fall in place. The activist communicator should be in the marketplace informing, teaching, selling, and fostering the organization's image among its many publics.

Figure 11–1 summarizes our thinking about the role and relationship of communications management within the modern financial institution. The structure shown in Figure 11–1 is responsive to the four guiding principles of successful program planning and implementation:

1. Understanding banking and finance as well as the communications art.
2. Taking little for granted; realizing that the institution must ever prove itself by words, deeds, and its continuing conduct in the marketplace.
3. Recognizing and helping the organization respond to the value changes in society, consumerism, and the Age of the People.
4. Understanding the multiplicity of the communications assignment.

These principles—and, there are no doubt others that tie in distinctively with the character of an individual financial institution and the nature of its primary business and traditions—play a vital role in the design of an organization's *communications management matrix.* They represent the fundamental assumptions, the *givens.* The communications manager builds on them.

We must address one additional point briefly before we present our model. Simply said, the arsenal of available communications tools has been greatly expanded in recent years. Not so long ago, communications was virtually confined to the printed word: press releases, annual reports, management newsletters, speeches, the employee house organ. Communications today embraces the visual age: films, employee television networks, audiovisual cassettes for calling officers, and so much more. The tools of yesterday, moreover, tended to be defensive and

FIGURE 11–1

Communications Management

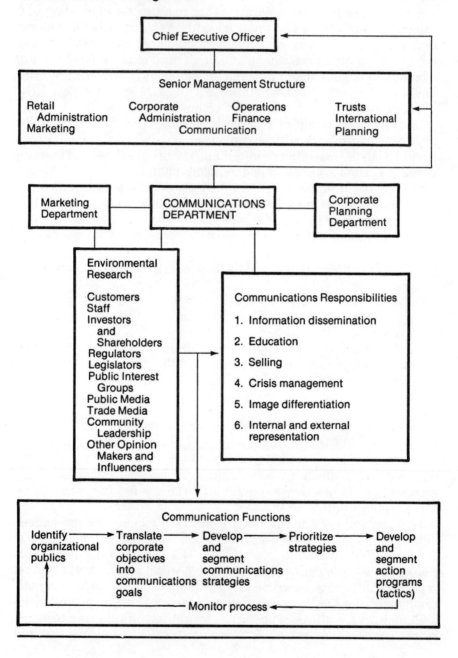

largely explanatory. Many new communications tools are designed to help the financial institution reach out in an active, competitive manner to its growing legion of publics. And finally, today's communications tools reflect the same heightened degree of segmentation that is applicable to other areas of an institution's operations.[6]

Communications planning begins with identifying the needs and wants of a particular communications public or audience.. It continues with strategies for *handcrafting* appropriate response mechanisms. One idea will help get this point across. Routinely, most financial institutions submit a *written* press release on quarterly earnings or the year-end statement (or, for that matter, the appointment of a new chief executive) to the newspapers, radio, and television. More often than not, the print media run the one- or two-page release as received or with only minor changes. Radio and television must commonly redo the release to satisfy the special requirements of those media. The revisions are not always effective, never mind "fair," because radio and television is "now"newscasting and because business analysis expertise is less prevalent in radio and television than in the print media.

The financial organization can adapt to differences between the print media and radio or television by moving beyond total reliance on the printed word release. *Tape* two minutes on quarterly earnings; include a chart depicting changes in earnings; employ the chairman or president to briefly and candidly explain these changes. Let the managers of *visual* media *see* as well as read what your organization is trying to get across.[7]

COMMUNICATIONS MANAGEMENT[8]

Identify Communications Publics

Figure 11–2 portrays the initial step in developing a communications management program. The organization's range of publics must be identified, and especially those publics that it must deal with on a continuing basis. The descriptive labels employed in Figure 11–2 appear obvious enough. The *general media*, for example, embrace national newspapers such as the *New York Times* and *The Wall Street Journal*, local newspapers, national magazines such as *Time* and *Business Week*, local radio stations, network and independent television channels, and local or regional magazines such as *New York*.

The *independent financial industry media* would include such publications as the *American Banker*, the *United States Banker*, and *Institutional Investor*. *Association media*, by comparison, are such publications as *Bank Marketing*, *Bank Administration*, and *Banking* and, for

FIGURE 11-2

Communications Publics

management	staff	shareholders	regulatory authorities	community leadership	media	customer groupings	
						corporate	retail
Executive officers	Managerial, supervisory personnel	Equity investors	State and federal regulatory agencies	Business leadership	General media	Corporations	Customers segmented by functional activities (DDA, loans, etc.)
Directors	All other staff members	Debtholders	State and federal legislative groups	Civic leadership	Financial industry independent media	Middle-market firms	
Area board members	Retired staff members	Financial analysts	Industry trade associations	Political leadership	Financial industry association media	Small business concerns	Customers segmented by demographic factors (income, age, etc.)
Affiliate board members		Brokerage firms	Consumer advocacy organizations	Local consumer organizations	Non-financial industry specialized media	Correspondents	
		SEC, FASB, and other disclosure control agencies		Academics	Advertising, public relations agencies	Affiliate customers	Customers segmented by geographic factors
	Spouses	Accounting firms		Labor unions		Financial services clients	New product or new service customers (e.g., ATM users, discount brokerage users,
						Trust clients	

Local	Regional	National	International

Geographic Dimensions

that matter, such well-regarded refereed journals as the *Journal of Bank Research* and the *Journal of Retail Banking*. Finally, *specialized media* might include such publications as *House Beautiful, Southern Living,* and *Women's Wear Daily,* depending on the financial organization's involvement in certain lines of specialized business activity.

It will be noted that these groupings of *communications publics* have been "tracked" in terms of their normative relationship to the financial institution. Each "track" possesses certain similarities of need, interest, and perspective or mind-set about the organization.

This chart is already quite "busy." Otherwise, a number of the blocks portrayed would be segmented further. Quite probably, moreover, an individual banking organization would delete some of these publics and add others—*depending on size, location, operational characteristics, expansion strategies, and so on.* Then, too, and again depending on the structure and goals of the organization, each of these publics might possess a local, regional, national, and even international dimension.

These determinations rest with the financial institution as it engages in communications planning. The singular concern stressed in Figure 11–2 is the need to define important communications publics and then to research their distinctive needs and wants. *Objectives, strategies, and tactics evolve from this knowledge.*

Figure 11–3 is essentially a restatement of our listing of communications publics, but with an additional dimension. It suggests that some groupings must be viewed as *internal* customers and others as *external* customers for an organization's communications activities.

This distinction implies a markedly different communications approach. An insider perspective will understandably reflect higher degrees of loyalty and trust for an institution's messages. The higher a communications manager targets a message within the organizational hierarchy, moreover, the greater are the levels of discernment. The upper levels of management trust more, but by the same token they see through window dressing and padding more easily. Candor (or its absence) goes a very long way in satisfying (or frustrating) internal publics.

Figure 11–3 also expands on a critical point raised in *Figure 11–1.* For each of an institution's numerous publics, a communications manager most often will need to fulfill separate responsibilities: the dissemination of information, education and training, selling, crisis management, image differentiation, and representation or spokesmanship. Figure 11–3 singles out only the necessary *education and training* responsibilities applicable to certain *internal* customers.

Among these *internal publics,* a dual need has to be satisfied through the communications task, especially for an institution's managerial staff

FIGURE 11–3

Education and Training Responsibilities

external publics

The media

Government relations
Legislators
Regulators
Consumer groups
Industry trade groups

Community leadership
Business groups
Political leadership
Civic and philanthropic
    groups

Corporate relationships
National corporations
Middle-market firms
Small business firms
Upstream and downstream
    correspondents
Financial service vendors

**Retail relationships and
    special retail market
    segments**
Professionals
Retireds
Women
Students
Minorities
Electronic banking
    Early user prospects

Trust customer relationships

**Major opinion makers
    and influencers**
Financial analysts
Accounting firms
Advertising agency
    executives
Academics
Consulting firms

Others: Locally, regionally,
    nationally,
    internationally

internal publics

Senior management   Directors
Shareholders   Debtholders
Area boards/councils   Affiliate boards

employees

Officers   Retired personnel
Managers   Spouses and families
Staff

education responsibilities	*training responsibilities*

Industry awareness
  Competition
  Technology
  Regulation
Economic conditions
  and impacts
Affirmative action
  implications
Consumerist and social
  responsibility criteria
Organizational objectives
  and strategies
  Expansion plans
  Earnings goals
  Asset-liability
    management
    perspectives
Industry objectives
  and strategies
	Specific job skills
	Sales motivation
	Compliance requirement
	  satisfaction
	New products explanation
	  and implementation
	  procedures
	New service delivery
	  explanation and
	  implementation
	  procedures
	Job retraining

and employees (and also their spouses and families). First, there is the need for "nuts and bolts" *training* to accompany such developments as the organization's introduction of major new product lines (money market checking and savings accounts or an equity credit line) and simply to stimulate product sales activity. Second, there is the need for issues-oriented *education* designed to enhance the employee's understanding of industry developments and, within that broad sphere of awareness, his or her understanding of the desired organizational response.

While Figure 11–3 details only *internal* customers and applicable *education and training* responsibilities, it follows that similar approaches must be developed for *external* customers. In the area of *education and training*, for example, we would identify a fundamental *media need* for an enhanced understanding of industry dynamics: the structure of the financial industry, the regulatory rules of the road, the causes and consequences of the drive toward interstate banking or the relaxation of Glass-Steagall constraints, the concern for initiating cost-reducing technologies, and so on. Middle-market and small business customers, on the other hand, might view their major need as improved levels of economic understanding or the operational benefits that they can expect from new bank-managed technologies.

Yes, it does seem like a great deal of work. Yes, in fact, considerable planning and follow-through are required. But perhaps not quite as much as may seem to be the case. For one thing, a high level of duplication is implied. Strategies and tactical programs that are designed for one group might need to be modified only slightly to fit another group equally well.

More important, the primary consideration at this point in the communications management process is with *customer needs identification:* Who are your key publics, and what—distinctively, individually—are their needs? You are designing a format listing what optimally needs to be done. In developing specific action programs, however, a communications department will respond to these needs based on available people, time, and dollar resources. And where possible, where practicable, the communications department works to make action programs perform double or triple duty. This point is clarified further in considering the next step in communications management.

Segment and Prioritize

Figure 11–4 reflects the necessity to *translate fundamental corporate objectives*—what the organization wants to achieve over a reasonable period of time—*into communications objectives* and then to prioritize these objectives for various communications publics. The creation of priorities, once again, must recognize this customer equally in terms of what the organization is trying to communicate and what this customer especially wants to hear. *Communications is always a two-way street.*

In the upper part of Figure 11–4, six common corporate and communications objectives have been arbitrarily selected. These are ours. Each

FIGURE 11–4

Communications Priorities

corporation objectives ⟷ *communications objectives*

1. Progressive financial institution.
2. High-quality product-service provider.
3. Profitable and stable performer.
4. Growth-oriented financial institution.
5. Candid, responsive leadership.
6. Good corporate citizen.

Rank-order

customer priorities	employees	financial analysts	media	shareholders
First	4	3	5	3
Second	2	5	6	4
Third	1	4	1	6
Special customer priorities	Job training programs	Capital adequacy	Easy, continuing contact	Dynamic management
	Advancement opportunities	Management strength	Access to leadership	Management that "personally" cares

financial organization must determine its own. The objectives on our list include:

1. Recognition as a *progressive* firm—for example, as an innovator in technology or in the development of new products and new service delivery procedures; as a leader in interstate banking moves; as a pacesetter in devising fee-income programs.
2. Recognition for the overall *quality* of the institution and the expertise of its people, its product lines, and its delivery systems.
3. Recognition of the institution's track record as a good *earner* but also as an earner that performs well at the bottom line *consistently*.
4. Recognition as an institution that has a good handle on *where it is going and how it plans to get there*, an organization that practices and actualizes *planning*.
5. Recognition as an institution with well-regarded *leadership*, people at the helm who are innovators but who are also *responsive* to customer concerns and societal issues.
6. Recognition as an institution that has created and maintained a reputation as a good corporate citizen, as a *socially responsible institution*.

The middle portion of Figure 11–4 argues the concept that each of tnese six corporate and communications objectives is more or less important to one or another communications public. The priority from that customer's perspective is different. Four publics have been singled cut: *employees; financial analysts*, those ever-important makers and shapers of the market for an organization's growth and expansion capital; the *media*; and *shareholders*, the buyers of debt and equity instruments, including those who are willing to reinvest dividends or purchase additional shares.

The institution's employees, we believe (and again, this is an "educated" though arbitrary decision on our part—you make your own), would probably feel that their three most important priorities are 4 (growth orientation); 2 (high-quality service provider), and 1 (progressive firm). There are understandable reasons for this rank-ordering. A growth orientation would be their highest priority because growth holds out the promise of reward: salary, bonus, promotion, job mobility, and so forth. High-quality service is a priority because providing it is the bank employee's basic function and personal achievement measurement.

The financial analysts, the media, and the organization's shareholders, as indicated, would *prioritize* these corporate and communications objectives somewhat differently. Again, these are our rank-orderings, and we believe that our choices are reasonably and realistically justifiable—*though admittedly, on an institution-by-institution basis, arguable.*

The bottom portion of Figure 11–4 maintains that one or another communications public will have certain *special priorities* recognizing its particular interests and concerns. The financial analyst, for example, may be most interested in the organization's capital structure, its leverage, and in the strength of its managment team.

Before we move on to the next step in the communications management process—from determining objectives to developing action programs and making them happen—several critical planning concepts merit restatement.

- *First*, action programs oriented toward a particular communications public build on the foregoing priorities.
- *Second*, these priorities recognize both the concerns the that financial institution wants to get across and the concerns that a distinctive public insists must be addressed.
- *Third*, our model reflects the activities of a larger money center or regional financial organization that necessarily deals with a wide array of publics. The model must be whittled down to fit the realities of your organization's marketplace position, or in the case of a larger organization, expanded.

- *Fourth*, the resulting action programs, while designed with appropriate priorities in mind, should nonetheless be conceived so as to optimally utilize people, budget dollars, and creative as well as managerial time. Make the most of what's available.

The Media as Market

Our book is concerned primarily with marketing management theory. In this instance, however, some ideas about application are in order as a way of better explaining our conceptual approach.

Figure 11–5 suggests the need to perceive the media as a customer. The media are a market for a financial institution's products and services. To be sure, editors, writers, and radio-TV commentators in those capacities are not depositors or borrowers. What they write or say, however, can markedly influence management activities. Media interpretors of a financial institution's performance characteristics can and do affect customer behavior. In this vital sense, the media—the general press, radio, and television chiefly—are a customer whose concerns must be well researched, well understood, and well satisfied. The smart communications manager, moreover, does not wait for the media to came knocking. *This manager plans, anticipates, and reaches out.*

The left-hand column of figure 11–5 identifies four high-level *media objectives*—priorities from the institution's point of view, priorities as the media see it. These priorities, once again, have been selected arbitrarily.

The "blocks" in the middle column identify sample or *exemplifying media strategies* through which the financial organization can actualize media objectives. Bear in mind that these are only sample strategies. Any number of others could be listed. Far more important, this simplified approach sets out only one media objective, one matching strategy, and one matching set of tactics. *In fact, the media objective of demonstrating the organization's desire to achieve recognition for "candid, responsive leadership" can and hopefully would be evidenced in each of the other listed strategies and their matching sets of tactics.*

The same point applies to the other listed media objectives. Corporate citizenship, progressiveness, and leadership access should be satisfied *commonly* through just about any specific media strategies and their implementation programs.

The right-hand column of *Figure 11–5* delineates an ordering of sample or *exemplifying media tactics* designed to actualize the strategic approach, to make it happen, to make it come out the way the financial organization wants it to while also satisfying the media or *mediaperson*. We have employed the latter term only to imply a need to *personalize* media relationships. Most often, the communicator is dealing

FIGURE 11–5

The Media As Market

Media objectives and priorities	exemplifying media strategies	exemplifying media tactics
1. Candid, responsive leadership	Prepublication annual report briefing	Provide advance copy Review with respective media-person Arrange leadership briefing Supply appropriate charts/visuals Make release-time check on media questions
2. Good corporate citizen	Involvement in urban renewal housing program	Supply project background data Arrange leadership briefing Facilitate on-site visitation Facilitate project leadership meetings Suggest community-impact interviews Arrange credit officer briefing to demonstrate longer-term housing aid
3. Progressive financial organization	Introduction of home banking experimental program	Supply project background data Arrange "neutral" technology briefing with systems vendors Arrange organizational leadersnip briefing Facilitate possible media-person "hands-on" trial and use critique Arrange interviews on customer-user impact Supply "product in use" explanatory visual aids
4. Access to leadership	Major loan loss crisis	Provide advance copy of detailed press release with appropriate background data, including earnings impact data Follow up with personal communications officer briefing Assure interview access with organizational leadership Assure continuing availability of leadership access Provide frequent status reports to media-person

with a specific writer or editor. Understandably, the communicator will realize how and why to "slant" a relationship based on differing media characteristics.

The tactics suggested are exemplifying, illustrative. The listing is not intended to be all-inclusive. Nor does it go much beyond basics— simple, sound fundamentals. But that's where a communications officer starts, with the fundamentals, and then building on them.

This listing of fundamental tactics provides an opportunity to summarize our thinking about effective communications management. The organization must *reach out* to communications publics, employing where possible an activist posture. You reach out, and you make it easy for the media or another communications customer to *understand* exactly what the organization is trying to "show and tell." You provide the necessary background and then *open the door* for a *candid discussion* with communications department representatives and *organizational leadership*. You keep the door open, and you *follow through*. As we argued earlier in this chapter, *words count, deeds count more, and continuing conduct counts most of all.*

Communications management, or the New PR, is the task—a bottom-line task that is just as important as landing a major corporate account—of turning desired ambitions into understood and accepted perceptions. *Done especially well, it turns perceptions into unchallenged re-alities.*

"Let me give you a few of my guiding principles about communications," the department executive said to the young J-school graduate with a business minor who was joining the bank's staff.

"Never play games with the media. They'll forgive you once, maybe twice, never a third time. The same is true for consumerists and financial analysts. And in our business, if we lose our credibility, we have lost the game.

"Besides, they're too smart to play games with. Forget what you've heard about dealing with an *enemy*. Sure, some of our communications customers are biased. Many are pushing a special interest. We can deal with that by being fair . . . reaching out . . . trying to understand them and being reasonable about their objectives. Don't fight them. But don't run from them either. *Get their respect*. Do that, and we've done our job.

"What do we want to see in the newspaper or on television? Just fair and intelligent reporting about our achievements or our shortcomings. We can't always assure that the reporting will be fair. After all, 'beauty is in the eyes of the beholder' and our ideas about fairness won't always be the same. But making sure it is intelligent reporting—that the editor really understands our business—is something we can make happen.

"The kind of news we want to see about our bank? We want people to know we're doing something and doing it well. We want them to understand we're not isolated from their day-to-day concerns. We're involved in the communities where we're located. We care. We want them to understand how and why our business is changing and how much of this change is in their best interests. We're leaders. We want them to know that. We're also bankers in the broadest and truest sense of the word. Satisfying customers is what our business is all about. It is also about trust and ethics. It is about making sound loans to good customers and keeping them that way.

"Last rule. We have two sets of bosses. And we have to be brutally honest with each of them. One set is the people who run our bank. The other is our customers. We're not doing our job unless we represent the customer in the executive suite . . . or in our branches. Frankly, management either understands this or it doesn't really need people like you."

"Glad you're with us. Your first assignment is to work with Mary in our department and with Tom Smith in the corporate treasurer's office. The annual report is coming out late next month. All of the financial data are in. We need to get together a slide presentation that we can use at media briefings . . . show at the shareholders meetings . . . show our employees . . . and show to our area board members. Let me have your ideas on what the scripting should include. Yes, I like your idea about including a segment with a group of media people interviewing the chairman about the impact of branch office closing on earnings and customer relations."

CONCLUSION

Communications management—the New PR—first of all recognizes that financial institutions are dealing with a growing number of customers or communications publics that are vitally concerned with institutional performance. It recognizes the need for soundly conceived and structured planning techniques in the task of translating corporate objectives into results-producing communications programs.

In arguing that communications must be at the leading edge of a top-performing financial organization's response to change in a deregulated and increasingly high-technology environment, we cited four guiding principles for directing communications traffic: (1) the need on the part of communications practitioners to understand banking and finance as well as the public relations art; (2) the newfound reality that financial institutions must prove themselves again and again by candid words, proven deeds, and their continuing conduct in the marketplace; (3) the need for an awareness of value changes in society; and (4) the need to understand the multiplicity of the communications assignment.

The communications assignment today must embrace not only the dissemination of information but also *education, selling, crisis management, image differentiation*, and *spokesmanship*.

With these guiding principles in mind, we offered an illustrative model for managing communications with a widening range of diverse but vitally important publics. The difference between yesterday's PR and today and tomorrow's communications commitment, we argued, involves no less than a shift away from reactive and often negative responses to concerns over institutional performance *and* toward a proactive, positive, outreach posture embracing the notion that the communications manager is the "eyes and ears" of the organization, forever "testing and sensing" the environment. That manager also serves two masters in this unique capacity: the financial institution *and*, in an advocacy role, its many publics.

NOTES

1. Jim Montgomery, "The Image Makers: In Public Relations, Ethical Conflicts Pose Continuing Problems," *The Wall Street Journal*, May 25, 1978, p. 1.

2. Lee Silberman, "Needed: A New Breed of Communicator," *Bank Marketing*, November 1980, p. 28.

3. A noteworthy discussion of "ambush journalism" and its impact on the communications practices of financial institutions is found in a two-part series by *American Banker* staff writer Geof Brouillette. See "How Not to Look Bad on the 6 O'clock News," March 31, 1982 and "Ambush Journalism: Only Useful Advice Is Stay Cool," April 7, 1982.

4. An excellent evaluation of realistic procedures for closing the "credibility gap" between the corporation and the media can be found in Stephen Berg, "Media Relations Needn't Be Strained," *Amex Journal*, June 1982, p. 1. Berg argues that underlying corporation-media problems are (1) the corporation's "inherent fear of disclosing too much information or being misquoted," (2) "a natural inclination to remain private—like the good old days before [financial institutions] went public," and (3) a fundamental "misunderstanding of how the media work."

5. Norwood W. "Red" Pope, "Marketing Management: Use Good Public Relations to Keep the Public with You," *American Banker*, August 17, 1983, p. 2.

6. Especially helpful as guides to the communications thinking and technique of the financial industry are *Issues in Communications—I* (1978) and *Issues in Communications—II* (1981). These two compilations of articles prepared by leading industry practitioners were published by the Bank Marketing Association.

7. One of the best current "how to" books on communications management is Robert S. Cole, *The Practical Handbook of Public Relations* (Engle-

wood Cliffs, N.J.: Prentice-Hall, 1981). Cole is vice president—communications, New York State Banker Association, and brings a financial industry perspective to his work.

8. The material in this concluding chapter section on "Communications Management" was initially developed by Thomas W. Thompson in a three-part series, "Managing Communications through Planning," that was published in the July, August, and September 1978 issues of the *United States Banker*. The charts in this section have been adapted from the *United States Banker* and used with permission.

12

Internal Marketing

The focus in previous chapters has been on external customers, that is, individuals or institutions purchasing financial services from financial institutions. In this chapter, we focus on a vital internal customer group, namely, the employees who buy job products from financial institutions.

That we are not accustomed to thinking of employees as customers is a function of tradition, not of reality. The "transaction" that occurs between employer and employee is as real as the one that occurs between company and consumer. Whereas consumers exchange financial resources for various goods and services, employees exchange their labors for various compensations, including the financial resources that they use to buy goods and services. The employee is no less a customer than the consumer purchasing Jif peanut butter or choosing to fly American Airlines. And just as a consumer can decide to switch from Jif to a new brand that costs less or is chunkier, so can an employee leave one financial institution for another, or leave the financial services industry altogether.

The philosophy, key ideas, and techniques of marketing can be of genuine value to financial institution executives as they address the challenge of human resources management. Thinking like a marketer need not be—and should not be—restricted to external marketing. In this chapter, we explore the dimensions of *internal marketing*.

PEOPLE MAKE THE DIFFERENCE

The pivotal difference between goods businesses and service businesses is that goods businesses sell things and service businesses sell performances. These performances are often labor-intensive, which means that human efforts constitute the actual "product" that customers buy. If the human efforts are responsive and competent, then the product is responsive and competent. If the human efforts are unresponsive and incompetent, then the product is unresponsive and incompetent. The building's architecture may be stunning, the ads may be slick, but the product is still unresponsive and incompetent. For financial institutions, people make the difference! This is true today. And it will be true tomorrow.

Many observers assume that the electronic banking movement will diminish the role and importance of people in financial service businesses. As machines do more, people will do less, or so the theory goes. The theory is wrong. In the best-managed institutions, machines will do more, but so will people. There may be fewer people in certain types of financial service jobs, and they may be different kinds of people than were used heretofore, but they will do more—and be more important to the success of the enterprise—than ever before.

In the best-managed institutions, electronic banking technologies will be used not only to lower service delivery costs but also to liberate employees from routine, mechanical tasks for creative, problem-solving, relationship-building tasks. Employees will be viewed in these institutions as *revenue-generating* resources rather than as *cost-generating* resources. Selling and serving—building and keeping the clientele—will be the dominant themes for contact personnel. Quality of service production and productivity will be the dominant themes for noncontact personnel.

Most financial institution jobs have a high "discretionary" content. The concept of discretionary effort can be understood as "the difference between the maximum amount of effort and care an individual could bring to his or her job, and the minimum amount of effort required to avoid being fired or penalized; in short, the portion of one's effort over which a jobholder has the greatest control."[1]

The jobs highest in discretionary content are customer-contact jobs, operations jobs involving nonroutinized judgments, and skill/knowledge jobs relying on new technologies.[2] By their very nature, high-discretion jobs place a premium on employee selection and motivation. Given a situation in which competing financial institutions offer essentially the same services, charge essentially the same fees, and pay essentially the same rates (not uncommon despite deregulation), having employees who make the discretionary effort—who are friendly and responsive, who ask that extra question or suggest that extra service, who take the time to listen—provides the competitive edge!

A *central* marketing opportunity in the financial services business concerns the performance of people. It is people who sell, who solve customer problems, who "build a clientele," who distinguish one financial institution from another. Machines will never be more important than people in the financial services business! It is a terrific advantage for a financial institution to have qualified people providing maximum rather than minimum efforts on an ongoing basis. Achieving this state, which is far from easy, is the objective of internal marketing.

INTERNAL MARKETING

The term *internal marketing* can be used in various ways. What all of these uses have in common is that the "customer" is inside the organization. In this chapter, the customer is the employee. We can think of internal marketing as *attracting, motivating, and retaining qualified internal customers (employees) through job-products designed to satisfy their wants and needs.*

The fundamental idea of internal marketing is that the best way to attract, motivate, and keep first-rate employees is to offer them job-products *worth buying.* Just as financial institutions compete for the best external customers, so do they compete for the best internal customers. How successful they are in competing for internal customers directly influences how successful they are in competing for external customers. Stated another way, a financial institution upgrades its capability for satisfying the wants and needs of its external customers by first satisfying the wants and needs of its internal customers. As Sasser and Arbeit wrote: "The successful service company must first sell the job to employees before it can sell its service to customers."[3]

What we think of when we think of marketing—marketing research, market segmentation, product development and positioning, pricing, advertising, and so forth—is actually external marketing. However, the same ideas and techniques that are applied in external marketing can be applied internally as well. Managers who are more customer-conscious and sales-minded toward employees are likely to have more customer-conscious and sales-minded employees.

THE INTERNAL CUSTOMER

Most Americans buying jobs today want to work. This is the conclusion of Daniel Yankelovich and John Immerwahr in their 1983 study *Putting the Work Ethic to Work.* Their research indicates that the work ethic has broader support in the United States than in many other industrialized countries, including Sweden, West Germany, and the United Kingdom. Yet American workers admit that they are not giving as much to their jobs as they could give. The problem, according to the researchers, is that U.S. management practices are not yet in sync with evolving worker values.[4]

The dominant work-related values of the 1950s and 1960s can be summed up as follows:[5]

- If women could afford to stay home and not work at a paid job, they did so.
- As long as a job provided a man with a decent living and some degree of economic security, he would put up with all its drawbacks, because it meant that he could fulfill his economic obligations to his family and confirm his own self-esteem as breadwinner and good provider.
- The incentive system—mainly money and status rewards—was successful in motivating most people.
- People were tied to their jobs not only by bonds of commitment to their families but also by loyalty to their organizations.
- Most people defined their identity through their work role, subordinating and suppressing most conflicting personal desires.
- For all practical purposes, a job was defined as a paid activity that provided steady full-time work to the male breadwinner with compensation adequate to provide at least the necessities and, with luck, some luxuries for an intact nuclear family.

The above listing no longer explains the values of most American workers.

- Today more than two fifths of the labor force are women. Although economic need is still a primary reason why many women work, the notion of "career" has replaced the notion of "job" for millions of them. That collegiate schools of business now attract as many female students as male students tells us plenty about changing values.
- Although job security remains an important value to many, especially in light of recent high unemployment rates due to recession and structural dislocation, there is much more interest today in the content of work. Millions of workers seek to develop themselves in their work, to learn new skills and new knowledge. It has also become important that the work be interesting, allow for autonomy and creativity, and be challenging.
- Good pay in and of itself is no longer a sufficient incentive. Also critical is pay tied to performance advancement opportunity, and nonfinancial recognition from superiors and "team" members.

- Loyalty to one's profession has tended to supplant loyalty to one's company.
- Fewer people define their identity through their work role ("I am a loan officer"). More common is the insistence that one's individuality be recognized ("I am more than a loan officer; I am myself").[6]
- Jobs are more than just a "paid activity." They are a way to contribute to organizations, to society; jobs are a way to make a difference.

Figure 12–1, based on the Yankelovich-Immerwanr research, isolates the 10 most important job values from a list of 46 items studied. Understanding internal customers is a critical first step in developing job-products to satisfy them. The consequences of not fitting job-products to wants and needs include turnover of those who can find more satisfying work elsewhere and low discretionary effort from those who are unable to leave.

THE INTERNAL PRODUCT

The idea takes getting used to, but the fact is that jobs are products. Jobs are bundles of benefits that people pay for through their labors. If the benefits bundle seems greater than its "costs"—and more attractive

---

FIGURE 12–1

The 10 Most Important Job Values

	percentage of sample who think item very important
Working with people who treat me with respect	88
Interesting work	87
Recognition for good work	84
Chance to develop skills, abilities, and creativity	83
Working for people who listen if you have ideas about how to do things better	83
Having a chance to think for myself rather than just carry out instructions	83
Seeing the end results of my efforts	82
Working for efficient managers	79
A job that is not too easy	78
Feeling well informed about what is going on	78

Source: Daniel Yankelovich and John Immerwahr, *Putting the Work Ethic to Work* (Public Agenda Foundation, 1983), p. 23.

than available alternatives—people buy it; that is, they accept the job. People shop for jobs, often become emotionally involved in the ones they buy, and may become sufficiently dissatisfied to quit—just as with an automobile, or a house and neighborhood, or even a hairdresser.

The job-product involves four key elements:

- Content.
- Valuation.
- Reporting relationship.
- Environment.

These are the elements of the internal marketing mix. They represent the "total" product that the internal customer buys. Weakness in any one element can diminish positive qualities associated with the other elements and lead to frustration, reduced commitment, low discretionary efforts, and quitting.

Content.   Job content concerns what *one does in the job.* Tasks. Roles. Responsibilities. Authority. Job content is more than procedures and techniques. It involves the creative possibilities of the job, the degree of autonomy, the extent of challenge, the variety of functions to be performed, and the opportunity for self-growth. The best job-products *stretch* people to their best efforts. They know that their job is important, that it matters to the company, and beyond the company, and that good performance is expected. Job satisfaction is more likely when the job requires excellence rather than tolerating mediocrity.

Valuation.   Valuation concerns what *the job is worth.* It is what management is willing to pay—directly and indirectly—for the work to be performed. Valuation is the barometer that organizational members use to assess the worthwhileness of given types of jobs in the eyes of management.

Valuation is a broader concept than pay, although pay is a key part of it. It involves management's *commitment* to a given type of job—for example, branch manager, or trust officer, or teller. Valuation is what management is willing to pay; it is the way management pays; it is management's willingness to make the effort to measure and recognize (financially and otherwise) superior performance; and it is the opportunity for advancement.

Valuation encompasses managerial response to performance. If everyone in a given job classification receives essentially the same raise—regardless of each individual's effort and effectiveness—the job can't really be very important to management. If the job were important, management would reward and recognize superior performers; management would act to encourage superior performance if superior performance mattered.

Reporting Relationship. The reporting relationship concerns *who one works for*. It is no fun working for a bad manager; placing the wrong person in charge of other people is a sure path toward lessening the appeal of a job-product. In research conducted with bank branch managers and branch employees, Schneider found that the attitudes and behaviors of managers were crucial in shaping the attitudes and behaviors of employees. In branches in which managers showed concern for customers, stressed interpersonal relationships with the staff, and flexibly applied work rules and procedures, branch employees were less dissatisfied and frustrated, experienced less role conflict, and were less likely to quit their positions. Significantly, the customers of these branches were more likely to report superior banking experiences.[7] Schneider writes:

> What management frequently perceives as employee disinterest or lack of motivation is really employees' lack of enthusiasm for carrying out management policies that are incongruent with their own desires. In fact, employees in this study seemed very interested in meeting customer needs, but less interested in satisfying management's bureaucratic needs.[8]

One of the gravest mistakes made by many financial institutions is that they put bureaucrats or technicians, rather than skilled managers, in charge of other people. And a key facet of the job—the superior/subordinate relationship—is shortchanged. It's more difficult to learn on the job if one's manager is uninterested in teaching or lacks knowledge to pass on. It's more difficult to be informed if one's manager fails to communicate. Managers who don't manage foul up job-products that might otherwise be appealing.

Environment. The environment concerns *what one is a part of*. It is the "package" that envelops the content/valuation/reporting relationship aspects of one's work. It is the physical work environment, to be sure, but it is much more than this. It is organizational culture and climate; it is what the company stands for; it is a company's central values.

One of the most compelling lessons of the best-seller *In Search of Excellence* is that excellent companies are governed, not by strict edict, but by one or more dominant values around which employees rally.[9] These values guide, unify, and inspire; they give employees something to grab hold of, something to believe in. A central value at IBM is to deliver outstanding customer service, to be easy to do business with. A central value at Neiman-Marcus is fashion education and leadership. At Perdue Farms, the central value is product quality. At the Friendly National Bank, a community bank is Oklahoma City, it is treating all customers with respect, dignity, and courtesy, regardless of the size of their balances or their mode of dress.

The concept ot "job environment" incorporates the notion of "team." Do people work together toward common goals? Are communications and feedback sessions intense and frequent? Is there peer pressure to perform well? Is there an air of informality, and even some horseplay from time to time?

People find the job-products they buy more satisfying to the extent that they *believe* in the organization employing them. Believing in the employing organization is what the concept of job environment is all about.

THINKING LIKE A MARKETER

Thinking like a marketer can pay off richly when managing people. What marketers know about research, human behavior, and communications directly relates to effective human resources management. In this section, we highlight some internal marketing applications.[10]

Marketing Research

Marketing research can be used to identify employee needs, wants, and attitudes just as it can be used to identify consumer needs, wants, and attitudes. Regularly surveying personnel concerning perceptions of supervision quality, working conditions, compensation and benefits, company policies, and other job-related matters provides direct feedback concerning the degree of internal customers' satisfaction with the job-products they are buying. This feedback helps isolate aspects of different jobs that need to be improved.

An active user of employee opinion research is Marriott Corporation, which systematically researches employees in each of its operating divisions. In the hotel division, employees from every hotel are surveyed annually. The results of each hotel's survey—trends and major concerns—are discussed with the general manager and personnel director and summarized for all employees. The changes to be made as a result of the survey are communicated to employees. Marriott's top management receives a summary of the research. Because the anonymity of the employee respondents is protected and the research is performed by corporate rather than hotel staff, Marriott's management believes that it receives candid feedback that is invaluable in improving the human resources management function.[11]

In addition to survey research, a research process known as "deep sensing" can be helpful. Deep sensing refers to efforts by management to learn what is on the minds of employees through small group dialogue sessions. These sessions enable senior managers to reach out to employees at various levels in the organization and learn firsthand their ideas, concerns, and sense of the company. Even the best of surveys do not convey the nuances, shadings, and insights that can be obtained when management meets face-to-face with the troops to *listen*. For this reason, employee opinion surveys and deep sensing methods are best viewed as complements rather than as alternatives.

Regardless of whether the focus of marketing is external or internal, its central purpose remains the same: the attraction, retention, and improvement of customer patronage through the satisfaction of customer needs and wants. Satisfying the needs and wants of internal customers requires that management first understand what those needs and wants entail. The tools of the marketing researcher—questionnaires, personal interviews, group discussions—provide a means for understanding employee needs and wants.

Market Segmentation

The underlying reason for segmenting markets is that customer prospects in the same market can be quite different in what and how they buy. Although members of a market share an overall need, they may prefer to satisfy that need in various ways; that is, their wants are different. So marketers segment markets, designing different marketing strategies for each segment of interest. Marketers know that to forgo this process of more precisely meeting wants is to risk losing customers to competitors that take full advantage of the potential of segmentation.

Having discussed the value of market segmentation in Chapter 5, we need not restate the argument for it here. The point that we wish to make at this juncture is that market hetereogeneity is just as real for internal markets as for external markets. People are just as different when they are at work as when they are shopping in Safeway or getting a haircut. It follows that internal market segmentation is a concept worthy of attention in all financial institutions.

Internal market segmentation revolves around two key issues. First, what types of internal customers to attract. Second, how to do it.

Few issues in a financial institution are as important as properly identifying internal market segments. It is quite amazing to us that so many financial institutions appear to take a casual approach to determining the optimum mix of backgrounds, skills, knowledge, and personal traits for specific types of positions. The people a financial institution hires *perform* the services it sells; the hiring decisions of a financial institution directly affect the quality of service that external customers receive and, ultimately, their willingness to do business with the institution. Thinking through who should be the internal customer is just as important as thinking through who should be the external customer.

Internal market segmentation decisions should be dictated, not by industry dogma, but by the institution's strategy and by the types of human resources that are needed to implement the strategy. For example, we like the spunk of the Oregon savings bank management that reduced the number of the bank's tellers by half; filled the remaining slots with college graduates, who were paid competitive salaries; and then allowed this group to design its own work flow and marketing plans.[12] "Those six women cost the bank no more than the 12 low-level people they replaced, but the production improved 500 percent and accounts at the branch grew 70 percent in the first year."[13]

Attracting the "business" of internal market segments, once they are identified, is easier when the offered job-products are tailored to them. In a period of demographic upheaval (more dual-career households, more singles, an older work force), it is more important than ever to recognize the heterogeneity of the labor force through segmentation. Flexible benefits programs and flexible work hour programs illustrate the potential of internal market segmentation.

Flexible Benefits. Flexible benefits programs (sometimes referred to as "cafeteria" benefits) allow employees to put together their own benefits package up to a specified dollar amount. In effect, employees select benefits that fit their specific situations and preferences, rather than employers force-fitting everyone into the same benefits.

The appeal of a flexible benefits approach stems from research indicating that what is a valued benefit to one employee is not necessarily a valued benefit to another. Factors such as age, marital status, and family size influence which benefits are preferred.[14] Married women in particular find uniform benefit plans biased against them because such plans duplicate certain benefits that the husband receives, for example, health insurance.[15]

A study conducted at Comerica Bank in Detroit showed that 94 percent of the over 4,000 participating employees in its flexible benefits program chose to rearrange the benefits that they had been receiving under the conventional benefits program.[16]

Flexible Work Hours. Flexible work hours (or flexitime for short) provide employees with greater freedom in selecting work hours than is customary in the 8-to-5 type of workday. Although still working the expected number of hours, employees on flexitime may vary starting and finishing times within certain prescribed boundaries. Typical flexitime systems involve "core time" (when all employees must be present) and "flexible time" (when work schedules are discretionary). Core time generally corresponds with peak workload patterns.

Among the benefits frequently reported for flexitime employees are increased job satisfaction; shorter commuting times; more time for leisure, personal business, and family activities; and added cross-training opportunity. Perhaps the outstanding characteristic of flexitime is that it shifts some control over working time to the employee, so that the job gains in dignity. In reporting on the flexitime experience at First National Bank of Maryland, Cottrell and Walker wrote:

> One other major benefit from the system was the creation of a more adult atmosphere. No longer did employees have to ask for time off for doctor or dentist appointments. Missed rides, traffic jams, or late babysitters no longer brought the pressure and frustration as they had with the traditional nine to five schedule. Without question, employees responded in a positive manner when given some control over their lives.[17]

Flexible benefits and work hour programs are market segmentation programs pure and simple. They may not be referred to in this fashion, but that is what they are. These concepts are working and growing in popularity because most employees like them. The job-product, at least in terms of fringe benefits and working hours, is what internal customers want it to be, or at least closer to the mark. And this helps the employer in marketing the job-product. There can also be direct economic gains for adopting companies. Half or more of the firms adopting flexitime programs experience economic gains; few experience net losses.[18] Many companies with cafeteria benefit plans have been able to reduce overall benefits costs.[19]

First Impressions Marketing

First impressions are important in marketing. The customer's earliest experiences with a product tend to carry disproportionate weight since the customer knows so little about the product. Clearly, the best time to develop a product's image is early, when the customer is more open-minded. The hotel that opens before its staff is fully trained makes a disastrous mistake. The new automobile model that is marketed before being debugged will probably suffer greatly from negative word-of-mouth communications.

Making the right first impressions is just as critical in internal marketing as in external marketing. Most financial institutions do not take full advantage of the opportunities available to make favorable first impressions on internal prospects and customers. Consider, for example, the typical financial institution's help-wanted advertising Such advertising is usually buried in the classified advertising sections of newspapers. Aside from being buried, it tends to be unimaginative and uninspiring. The ads generally say little or nothing about the institution's philosophy, its caliber, its specialness. They generally do little or nothing to make the case for the job-products being sold. They may be informative, but they are almost always short on persuasion.

Why not take a marketing point of view with regard to job-product advertising? The payoff may be more, and better, employment candidates. We advocate that job-product advertising be given the same care and talent that are normally given to external advertising campaigns. Indeed, job-product advertising should be viewed in the context of "campaigns" rather than "ads." It should be developed, or at least influenced, by the institution's advertising agency. At least some of the time, it should be placed in the main sections of the newspaper rather than the classified sections. Alternative media should be considered for selected campaigns. And more emphasis should be placed on selling the institution, on positioning it, on setting it apart, and on delineating the qualities of the people being sought.

Another opportunity to improve first impressions marketing lies in the interviewing process. Are the right people in the institution interviewing employment candidates? Are the interviewers sufficiently professional? Are they enthusiastic? Do they sell the institution? A terrific marketing opportunity is being wasted if the answers to the above questions are no.

Investing in the proper orientation of new employees is still another key element in first impressions marketing. Starting new employees off with a thorough grounding in the company's history, values, strategic objectives, and organizational structure provides a "context" into which they fit. The orientation period is a time to nurture company values, provide a "big picture" view of the institution, and make a favorable impression. It is an internal marketing opportunity that should not be missed. People who go to work for a Walt Disney theme park (regardless of whether they are entry-level employees or executives) must attend Disney University and pass "Traditions I" prior to receiving more specialized training. Traditions I is an all-day experience in which new employees learn the Disney philosophy of doing business, the company's history, and how the various park divisions—Operations, Food and Beverage, Entertainment, and so forth—relate to "the show."[20]

Remarketing

Attracting new customers is an *intermediate* step in the marketing cycle, a point stressed in the relationship banking chapter. Keeping customers—and making them better customers—is marketing too. This idea is no less relevant in internal marketing. Internal marketing should not stop once internal customers have been attracted to the institution.

Job-products should be continually "remarketed," which involves per-petuating company values, providing personal growth opportunities, sharing information, recognizing superior performance, and generating excitement. Well-conceived remarketing programs give internal cus-tomers multiple reasons for remaining with the institution; they reduce the probability that valued employees will be lured elsewhere by slightly higher salaries or wage rates. The tools of remarketing can be as varied as one's imagination and cleverness allow. Below we present three remarketing tools: advertising, employee reports, and excitement rallies.

Advertising. We discussed advertising as a means of attracting inter-nal customers in the last section; advertising can also be used to great advantage with existing employees. The fact is that a financial institu-tion's employees are a critical "second audience" for the advertising that the institution sponsors in external media. Such advertising can involve, educate, and motivate employees; it can shape their percep-tions about the institution, about the objectives it is trying to accom-plish, and about how they as employees relate to those objectives.

Indiana National Bank's "person-to-person" advertising campaign in the late 1970s illustrates how well-executeu advertising can perform the double duty of simultaneously reaching internal and external audi-ences. In this campaign, bank employees were featured in radio and television spots explaining in their own words what person-to-person banking meant. In follow-up research, over 90 percent of the bank's contact employees reported paying attention to the advertising. Nearly 75 percent indicated that because of the campaign they had become more concerned with pleasing the customer and were more likely to go out of their way for customers.[21]

Attempting to advertise to external customers and prospects in such a way that internal customers will want to perform the services being advertised is a worthwhile advertising objective. It is a form of remar-keting that should be considered.

Annual Employee Reports. Public companies publish annual stock-holder reports that review company financial results, programs, and developments during the preceding year. Some of these companies also publish annual employee reports that review the past year from an employee point of view. We believe that such a document represents a good opportunity to link employee involvement to a firm's financial performance, to recognize individual employee accomplishments, and to communicate the firm's philosophy, objectives, and plans for the future. One of the finest examples of an employee report that we have seen is First Interstate Bank of Arizona's 1983 *Report to Employees*. The 28-page document includes a statement of philosophy, goals, and corporate identity; a letter from the president; an overview of the bank's highlights and problems during the year; a user-friendly financial review (which is reproduced as Figure 12–2); written and pictorial recognition of outstanding employees under such headings as "teamwork," "customer service," and "productivity"; and, finally, a review of what to expect in 1984.

Excitement Rallies.   Peters and Waterman's research with excellent companies underscores a trait that many of these companies have: they seek out opportunities to gather the troops, celebrate accomplishments, reaffirm a sense of teamwork, spark excitement, and have some fun. Peters and Waterman describe the regular Saturday morning management meeting at Wal-Mart this way: "The buyer of the month receives a plaque. There are 'honor roll' stores, every *week*. And every week the 'SWAT' team that swoops down to remodel stores testifies to jobs well done. Mr. Sam [Walton, the company's founder] stands up and yells, 'who's number one?' And everyone, of course, yells back 'Wal-Mart.'"[22]

We are not suggesting that Wal-Mart's approach be mimicked by every financial institution. Rather, we are suggesting the benefits of bringing people together to rekindle their commitment to the organization and to one another. And we are suggesting periodically interrupting the work routine for some unabashed fun. Wal-Mart does this in its own special way.

Norwood W. "Red" Pope, marketing director of Sun Banks in Orlando, Florida, wrote a 1981 *American Banker* column in which he described the "Third Annual Walt Disney World Forklift Rally." All certified Disney World forklift drivers were invited to compete and demonstrate their skill in driving a forklift. Pope went on to state: "I've never been to a Proof Machine Olympics, or Teller Time Trials, or a Type-a-thon . . . because I've never heard of any being held. Maybe we should get on it?"[23]

Advertising, annual employee reports, and excitement rallies are just three of many remarketing possibilities. In effect, remarketing is the internal marketing equivalent of relationship banking. As George Rieder writes: "Management competes for the continued commitment of its people."[24]

CONCLUSION

Marketing's scope has traditionally been restricted to the exchange that occurs between organizations and customers. Yet marketing is just as

FIGURE 12-2

1983 Financiaı Review For First Interstate Bank of Arizona Employees

We Received ;;om Oι.; Customers $513,953,000 = 100%. Interest from loans, investments, and fees from services sold by First Interstate during 1983 amounted to $514 million.

Interest Cost o´ Funds ʼrom all Sources, $250,131,000 = 48.7%. In 1983, funds required to support growth and to generate loans cost First Interstate $250.1 million in interest. Included in the cost was $185 million for market rate deposits, $34.7 million for stable deposits, and $30.4 million for purchased funds.

The cost of funds purchased by First Interstate accounted for 48.7 cents of every income dollar received.

Cost of Employee Services, $84,713,000 = 16.5%. One of our largest expenditures was for wages, salaries, and benefits for more than 4,600 First Interstate employees amounting to $84.7 million. This included First Interstate's matching contribution to Social Security and the Employee Savings Plan, as well as to employee insurance plans and unemployment insurance.

Costs for employee services were up 11.6 percent over last year. They required 16.5 cents of every dollar we received from our customers.

Cost of Computer Services, $17,438,000 = 3.4%. The cost of our data processing service was $17.4 million, which included new programs, enhancements to existing systems, and daily production to service our customers. Costs were up 3.2 percent over last year and represent 3.4 cents of every dollar of income received.

Cost of Support Services, $88,673,000 = 17.2%. The cost of other items to support our income dollars was $88.7 million. Some of the major items in this category were supplies, $4 million; postage, $7.9 million; occupancy, $12.2 million; losses and shortages, $4.6 million; and loan loss provision, $21.8 million. Approximately 17.2 cents of each income dollar received was allocated for these items.

Cost of Payments to the Government, $20,998,000 = 4.1%. Taxes on income, $21 million, were paid to our state and federal government. The cost of these items accounted for 4.1 cents of each income dollar received.

Cost of Payments to Stockholder, $19,086,000 = 3.7%. In return for its investment, the stockholder of First Interstate Bank of Arizona received a portion of our bank's net income. In 1983, of the $52 million realized as net income, $19.1 million was paid in cash dividends to the stockholder, at $10.40 per share of stock.

These payments took 3.7 cents of every income dollar.

Money Available to Reinvest in the Bank, $32,914,000 = 6.4%. After payment of all the preceding costs, 6.4 cents of every income dollar we received was left over to reinvest in the bank. These funds were used for new branch construction and equipment, creation of new jobs, expansion and improvement in services, and a larger lending base. These investments were made so that we would remain competitʼ   and profitable.

Source: First Interstate Bank of Arizona's 1983 *Report to Employees*, p. 6. Reprinted with the permission of First Interstate Bank of Arizona, N.A.

relevant to the exchange that occurs between employers and employees. Employees are simply internal customers rather than external customers. They make a commitment to a job just as they make a commitment to an automobile or a neighborhood. And they can withdraw that commitment if not satisfied. The job is no less a product for which the consumer exchanges resources—in this case, labor—than the automobile or the neighborhood.

Although it is not customary to think of marketing in this way, it is useful because marketing's philosophy, central concepts, and tools have much to offer toward the attraction, retention, and motivation of internal customers. This is an especially important idea for a financial institution because its internal customers perform the services that its external customers are asked to buy. A financial institution competes on the basis of the quality of these performances.

We believe that *no* competitive weapon is more important to a financial institution in the no-holds-barred, deregulated financial wars of today and tomorrow than the quality of its people. The possibility that a competitor will offer to pay more for deposits or take less for loans is ever present. The way to compete in this kind of environment is to have the finest caliber of people—people who give maximum discretionary effort, who go the extra mile for customers when the extra mile is needed, who make the institution "easy to do business with." A financial institution cannot hope to practice relationship banking without first-rate people. Machines may provide informational and transactional convenience, but only people can provide the credibility, competence, and care that build client relationships.

Having great people allows a financial institution to compete on bases other than just rates and locational convenience. This is a reality not to be taken lightly in deregulatory times. It is in this spirit that we challenge you, our reader, to broaden your perspective of marketing's potential. Think internal marketing, not just external marketing.

NOTES

1. Daniel Yankelovich and John Immerwahr, *Putting the Work Ethic to Work* (New York: Public Agenda Foundation, 1983), p. 1.

2. Ibid., chap. 1, pp. 11–18.

3. W. Earl Sasser and Stephen P. Arbeit, "Selling Jobs in the Service Sector," *Business Horizons*, June 1976, p. 64.

4. Yankelovich and Immerwahr, *Putting the Work Ethic to Work*, chap. 2.

5. "Work: Changing Motivations and Values," a report of the Futures Research Unit, Security Pacific National Bank, October 1978, p. 12.

6. Ibid., p. 14.

7. Benjamin Schneider, "The Service Organization: Climate Is Crucial," *Organizational Dynamics*, Autumn 1980, pp. 52–65.

8. Ibid., p. 63.

9. Thomas J. Peters and Robert H. Waterman, Jr., *In Search of Excellence* (New York: Harper & Row, 1982), chap. 9.

10. Several paragraphs in this section are drawn from Leonard L. Berry, 'The Employee as Customer," *Journal of Retail Banking*, March 1981, pp. 33–40.

11 Telephone interview with René Mondonedo, Employee and Labor Relations Department, Marriott Corporation, October 27, 1982.

12. George A. Rieder, "Employee Strategies in the 80s," *Journal of Retail Banking*, June 1982, p. 60.

13. Robert O. Metzger, "Productivity and Profitability: A Trust Perspective," *American Banker*, October 13, 1981, p. 4.

14. Edward E. Lawler III, "New Approaches to Pay: Innovations That Work," *Personnel*, October–December 1976, p. 12.

15. Peter F. Drucker, *Managing in Turbulent Times* (New York: Harper & Row, 1980), p. 123.

16. "Flexible Employee Benefit Plans Can Be Boon to Banks," *American Banker*, August 2, 1983, p. 9.

17. Charles A. Cottrell and J. Mark Walker, "Flexible Work Days: Philosophy and Bank Implementation," *Journal of Retail Banking*, December 1979, p. 80.

18. Stanley D. Nollen, "What Is Happening to Flexitime, Flexitour, Gliding Time, the Variable Day? and Permanent Part-time Employment? and the Four-day Week?" *Across the Board*, April 1980, p. 10.

19. "Cafeteria Plans Mean More for Less," *Boardroom Reports*, January 1, 1984, p. 11.

20 Norwood W. Pope, "Mickey Mouse Marketing," *American Banker*, July 25, 1979, pp. 4, 14; and "More Mickey Mouse Marketing," *American Banker*, September 12, 1979, pp. 4, 5, 10, 14.

21. Franklin Acito and Jeffrey D. Ford, "How Advertising Affects Employees," *Business Horizons*, February 1980, pp. 58–59.

22. Peters and Waterman, *In Search of Excellence*, p. 247.

23. Norwood W. Pope, "At Walt Disney, Mickey Mouse Markets Inside, Too," *American Banker*, July 29, 1981, p. 6.

24. Rieder, "Employee Strategies in the 80s," p. 54.

PART FIVE

Lessons

"The excellent companies were, above all, brilliant on the basics. Tools didn't substitute for thinking. Intellect didn't overpower wisdom. Analysis didn't impede action. Rather, these companies worked hard to keep things simple in a complex world. They persisted. They insisted on top quality. They fawned on their customers. They listened to their employees and treated them like adults. They allowed their innovative product and service 'champions' long tethers. They allowed some chaos in return for quick action and regular experimentation."

Thomas J. Peters and Robert H. Waterman, Jr.,
from In Search of Excellence: Lessons from America's Best-Run Companies (New York. Harper and Row, 1982).

It's Still a People Business

Banking is, and for a long time to come will remain, a people business.

This conviction, as we have argued throughout *Marketing Financial Services: A Strategic Vision*, does not detract from the breathtaking possibilities propelled by technological innovation.

We are indeed awed by the promise of technology in expanding the horizons of the financial services business. We are acutely sensitive, for example, to the very real possibility that within a decade what most customers today mean by a "bank" could be stored in microchips on a plastic card and used worldwide to process routine consumer financial transactions. We are likewise impressed by mounting evidence that a business or retail customer will soon be no farther from a financial institution than the switch on an at-home or at-work terminal. The promise of technology is sweeping, profound.

Still, banking will remain a people business.

The leaps and bounds ahead fostered by technological innovation will be more than matched by product line extensions and customer-handling approaches demanding increasingly higher levels of customized, high-touch attention. High-touch will go hand in hand with high-tech. Dependence on *quality* people will intensify, not decline. It will become more important, not less so. This is the first and most important lesson of our book.

A NEW CULTURE

Quality people, to amplify this crucial distinction, will be aggressive and knowledgeable sellers of services, and no longer "9-to-2" order takers. They will be experienced in reaching out to a well-researched marketplace, rather than waiting expectantly for a customer's visit. They will be sensitive to the uniqueness of any customer's felt needs, rather than detached, aloof, conditioned to view customers as aggregates. They will understand the necessity of more fully serving existing customers, rather than focusing too narrowly on new customer development.

Accordingly, our second lesson is that the financial industry's culture will change profoundly in the years ahead. It will change profoundly because of technology, because of competition, because of new economic and social realities, and because customers have changed their thinking about the role and responsibilities of industry organizations. The culture will change because the industry's people will change. What will be different, clearly, is how and where people perform their tasks, how they are trained and educated, and how they are motivated and compensated.

It is difficult, for example, to believe that commercial banks and thrift institutions will not break with tradition and substantially upscale the wages paid to customer-contact personnel while also moving proven "salespeople" to an incentive system. How else will these organizations keep quality retail people from taking jobs with competitive financial service institutions that have developed a culture in which incentive pay is common for uncommon sales initiative? Intrinsic and extrinsic compensation programs must fit a changing culture—a *selling* culture, a *relationship* culture.

What will also be different is how quality bankers think about customers. Our contention is that quality people will come to define their fundamental job as *customer satisfaction engineering.* They will instinctively understand this necessity. They will be trained to think and act in these terms. They will be motivated by management to excel in satisfying customers, not just make loans, dispense credit cards, or acquire deposits. They will be conditioned to weigh decisions in human terms, not just in terms of portfolio aggregates.

Quality people will come to believe in and act on the principle that 'the customer is the business." *Believe in and act on.* Not pay it lip service, not apply it cosmetically, not merely mouth the proper wording in speeches, annual reports, and press releases, but make it actually happen on a continuing basis through real-time deeds.

TEACH MARKETING

Our third major lesson is that preparing quality people *explicitly* must emerge as a major marketing task in the world of Banking Tomorrow. Customer satisfaction engineering won't just happen. A selling culture won't just fall into place. Relationship banking won't just happen. Turning indifferent customers into loyal, multiservice clients won't just happen. These things, these necessary changes, have to be made to happen. In this critical sense, a primary task of marketing practitioners in the financial services industry will be to *teach marketing*.

Call it a heightened focus on *internal* marketing as distinct from external or customer marketing. Or simply link this task to the fundamental truth that people can't sell what they don't understand and won't sell what they don't believe in—be it products and services, what the institution is attempting to stand for, or the competitive enterprise system itself.

In the financial services business, in any modern business activity, marketing has only one purpose: *the creation of satisfied customers*. Here is what must be taught. This idea must come to permeate every aspect of institutional performance. Not just permeate, but define and characterize the role of employees. It must be taught to tellers and telephone operators at the front lines of customer contact and not only to personal bankers and loan officers. It must be taught to systems developers as they adapt the promise of technology to the everyday needs of countless customers who are confused by, if not actually overwhelmed by, electronic banking innovations.

"The creation of satisfied customers" as an underlying philosophy of doing business must be taught to managers creating new product lines. It must be taught to managers singling out customer niches for their institution to attack. It must be taught to managers determining credit allocation and credit scoring procedures. And it must be taught to managers deciding why and where to locate branch offices or why and where to close them down.

Even more than taught, *accepted*. In tomorrow's world, internal marketing—marketing to your own people—will be just as important as external customer marketing.

The notion that the purpose of marketing—indeed, the purpose of the institution itself—is the creation of satisfied customers must also dominate the thinking of senior management. The executive's concern, reasonably enough, is the bottom line of profit maximization. The truth is that profits depend on customer satisfaction; they are maximized by superior efforts at customer satisfaction.

MAKING A DIFFERENCE

There is one other reason for stressing the importance of quality people. They and they alone, we believe, will make the difference if their institution is to stand for something special in the marketplace. They will make the difference if their particular institution is to both survive and succeed.

Consider the principal characteristics of our current and projected operating environment:

- Commercial banks, thrifts, and the nonbank players in the retailing field such as Sears, Beneficial Finance, Prudential-Bache, or Merrill Lynch are pretty much alike in terms of services offered, rates charged or paid, and how and where they can perform.
- Each financial institution has the capacity to be an anywhere bank, an anytime bank, a relationship bank, and a selling bank. Each has the capacity, and each has the freedom to utilize that capacity.
- Each grouping of the financial services industry is starting to devise and implement a positioning strategy anchored in market segmentation and, in most cases, "narrow-band nichemanship." Each is moving away from an operating philosophy of being all things to all people and toward the necessity of becoming something special to some people and especially to preferred customer segments.
- Each grouping is becoming more technology dependent, either to enlarge markets and customer offerings or to reduce operational costs.
- Each grouping prices competitively based on market conditions.
- Each grouping basically promises a similar set of benefits in its ads, and the same holds true for primary product lines.
- And finally, the financial institutions in each grouping *look and act like* traditional banks from that critical perspective of the customer.

What's the *real* difference to a retail customer between a Sears Financial Center and a bank or savings and loan branch? What's the real difference to a customer? This is what bank marketing or thrift marketing now boils down to.

Not very long ago, commercial banks and their chief competitors were in fact substantially different. Law and custom mandated a difference. Law and custom assured commercial banks a transaction account monopoly. Law and custom dictated that savings and loans would acquire low-cost deposit funds and allocate low-cost home mortgage credits. Law and custom relegated the Bulls of Merrill Lynch to the narrow confines of brokering stocks and bonds largely to an upscale market. Law and custom specified the roles of finance companies and credit unions. Law and custom fragmented the financial services business into very distinct lines of commerce.

This was yesterday. Today fundamental distinctions in the retailing arena have all but disappeared. Probably, in fact, the majority view is that *basically* they have all vanished or blurred to the poir ' ˜ᶠ insignificance.

And tomorrow?

We find it hard to believe that such distinctions will reappear, the Continental Illinois scare notwithstanding. The clock won't be turned back, largely because the *customer* likes the way things are going. The customer is satisfied by more options. The customer is satisfied by a fuller range of services provided under a single roof. The customer is satisfied by the ability to conduct banking business when and where it is most convenient for him or her to do so—that is, his or her time, not traditional bank time. And in a "what's in it for me" pocketbook society, the customer is satisfied by market rates on savings and investment instruments.

This is the real-world environment that financial institution marketers and managers are being told to come to grips with. The clock won't be turned back. Nor will things simply stay as they are for some indefinite period of time. Technological innovation will assure the evolution of more and more profound change. So will the creativity on the part of bank managers that has been unleashed by existing levels of deregulation. So will the fact that interstate banking is not coming but has arrived. So will the fact that discount brokerage is conditioning commercial bank customers to accept banks as a point-of-purchase alternative for investment assets.

This is the real world. The challenge is coping. The challenge, we insist, is coping by standing apart as a distinctive performer in the business of customer satisfaction. The challenge is coping through meaningful differentiation.

QUALITY PEOPLE—THE QUALITY DIFFERENCE

For many, many financial institutions, the bottom-line challenge will be outright *survival.* The simple truth is that not all of today's 15,000 commercial banks will make it on their own to the year 2000 and beyond, or, at the very least, not in their present form. The same contention holds true for savings and loans, credit unions, and countless independent finance companies and brokerage firms. This is not a matter of conjecture on our part. Just listen to the quiet, behind-the-scene conversations at industry conferences or at trade association leadership meetings. Survival and not just success is the challenge hurled by the combining pressures of technology, deregulation, and intensifying competition.

The challenge, once again, is coping through successful differentiation in a world where financial institutions are pretty much alike. The response is people. *Quality people will make the difference.*

People will be the institutional differentiators. They will sell more effectively than the competition. A successful institution's people will reach out more diligently and more frequently to very carefully selected customer segments. They will perform in a most sensitive and caring manner as customer need evaluators, recognizing clearly that effective response is based on sound understanding.

Creative and motivated quality people will create product lines and servicing approaches that stimulate customer interest and motivate long-term customer allegiance. Managers will kindle a "spirit of innovation," and in their own right create a "climate of trying."

A successful institution's people will not only be more efficient in adapting new technology procedures to day-to-day operations but will also excel in preparing employees and customers to understand, believe in, buy, and utilize these innovations.

Quality people—not the clever name given an ATM program or a new investment account, not interstate economies of scale, not what's promised in a massive television ad campaign, and not press release sloganeering, but people, high-touch and caring quality people—will turn indifferent customers and customer prospects into concerned, satisfied, and loyal clients.

By quality people, we of course mean customer-contact staff at all levels. Very specifically, we mean a marketing officer who at long last discovers that this job involves teaching marketing as well as functionally creating ads, designing the annual report, or managing premium programs. We mean product development teams that are not graduates of the "copycat" and "follow-the-leader" schools of financial institution marketing. We mean market segmentation specialists who can look well beyond the shimmering brilliance of The Affluent Market to where the rest of the customers are.

And not just marketers. By quality people, we mean traditionally reclusive trust department officers sensible enough to realize that relationship banking is chiefly an extension of trust banking practices to the retail sector and that their well-honed trust skills are vital to its effective implementation. We mean credit officers who at long last come to grips with the customer-driven fact that perpetuating sex, race and ethnic distinctions is not only unconscionable but is also stupid banking. By quality people, we mean officers who are hungry to write sound loans and not just loan hungry. We mean "backroom" operations personnel who handle the customer's checks, who answer the customer's inquiries, who solve the customer's problem. And by quality people, we mean so much more at every level of the organizational structure.

IT STARTS AT THE TOP

We also are pragmatists. More so than most industries, the financial services industry is a top-down, management-down business. There may be any number of highly structured management layers. Still, the chief executive officer is commonly the organization's chief planner, its chief marketing officer, and its chief decision maker about how and where funds are raised and allocated. The CEO sets policy. The CEO ultimately determines that this product, this delivery system structure, this basic pricing schedule, and this major promotion scheme make sense. The CEO gives the final order, "Let's do it."

The man or woman at the top also sets the organization's style, the performance pattern that others emulate, the culture that subordinates give greater shape to and practice in the marketplace.

In this sense, marketing as a philosophy of doing business that permeates every nook and cranny of the organization is actualized because top management believes in it and insists on it. It is actualized because the chief executive officer commits to marketing, creates a systematic follow-through mechanism, and demands measurements of effectiveness and efficiency from quality people who *perform* marketing in the marketplace

Marketing Financial Services: A Strategic Vision addresses both the professional marketing practitioner and the financial institution executive officer. Each possesses and performs a critical role in the task of creating satisfied customers. The executive officer plots the course, gives orders to the ship's company, and assures that the orders are carried out. The marketer as helmsman steers through the sometimes turbulent and always uncertain waters of the marketplace.

THE PLANNING IMPERATIVE

Marketing and managing are two of the interdependent pillars on which successful banking operations are structured. The third is plan-

ning. Not giving lip service to the concept, not theorizing over "what if" scenarios, but systematically utilizing each of the various steps comprising the planning process in order to make informed managerial and marketing decisions that will optimize performance in an environment that will surely be characterized by change, by more rapid change than has occurred in the past.

Planning in our judgment can become all too easily a confused, stumbling, unproductive, wheel-spinning, hodgepodge activity unless there is a single, very basic reference point in the organization. There must be a framework that is understood and applicable equally in such *apparently* diverse areas as lending, trust, operations, marketing, personnel, and mortgage or securities portfolio management. There must be a unifying element that by its very nature demands that attention continually and systematically be directed toward change.

This reference point . . . framework . . . unifying element is the customer. It is the organization's *external* customer groups: consumers, corporations, the media and other customer influencers, the capital markets, and so many other customer groups that can be seen as a whole, as a major segment, or as a smaller but no less viable niche. This reference point is also an organization's *internal* customers—its own people, its *customer satisfaction engineers.*

The single, inexorable fact about the future is that it will be much different from today. More turbulent? Less? More competitive? Less? More impersonal? Less? We don't know for sure. Nor is this a major concern of our book. However, we do know that it will be different. What banking has been historically is not a given for tomorrow; it is not a monument graven in concrete. Knowing this is the why of strategic planning. It is the imperative to plan.

Marketing. Managing. Planning. These are the three building blocks of success in the marketplace.

Index

A

A priori segmentation, 80–82
Aaker, David A., 92
Account relationship manager; see Personal banker programs
Account representatives
  for new accounts, selling behaviors for, 187–88
  as relationship banking element, 119, 125–28, 131
Acito, Franklin, 245
Additions to existing service lines, 137
Advertising
  guidelines for, 195–99
  job product, 239–40, 241
  and personal selling, combination of, 185, 194–95
  and relationship banking, combination of, 115
Age of the People, 209–10
American Banker, 114, 209, 215, 242
American Telephone & Telegraph Company (AT&T), 72
Anderson, M. J., Jr., 40
Anderson, Rolph E., 201
Annual employee report, 241–42
Arbeit, Stephen P., 231, 244
Arms-race strategy, 38
Asset management department, creation of, 64
At-home banking, 159, 162–63, 174
Automated teller machines (ATMs)
  future of, 162, 174, 179, 180
  and revolution in delivery systems, 158–59
  and standardized service, 140
Avis, 109

B

Bank cards, 100–101, 158; *see also* Credit cards *and* Smart Card
Bankers Trust of New York, 35, 102
Bartling, Charles E., 181
Basic service providers, 103
Benefit segmentation, 82, 83–86
Benefits, flexible, 238
Berg, Stephen, 226
Bernstein, Peter, 91
Berry, Leonard L., 110, 132, 155, 200, 201, 245
Beynon, W. D., 74
Bird, Marv E., 74
Bonuses, in rewarding sales performance, 192
Borrowings, and external flexibility, 30, 31
Bowen, David E., 155
Bowers, Michael, 200
Brainstorming, 148
Branches, 101
Brokerage, 9, 99, 103
Brouillette, Geof, 226
Burnett, Leo, 195, 196
Buyer-seller relationship, focusing on, 54–55

C

Cafeteria benefits, 238
Calantone, Roger J., 85
Caldwell, L. A., 91
Calling officers, selling behaviors for, 187–88
Capital adequacy, and internal flexibility, 30, 31
Cecil, R., 87

Centralization/decentralization
   definition of, 61–62
   and function-oriented structure, 64,
      65, 69
   and innovation, 143, 144
   and market-oriented structure, 67,
      69
Chain of command
   in coordinating work, 59
   in function-oriented structure, 63–
      64, 69
   in market-oriented structure, 67, 69,
      73
Change Masters, The (Kanter), 141
Chase Manhattan Bank, 68
Chief executive officer; see Top man-
      agement
Citibank, 33, 129
Citicorp, 4, 9, 72
Citytrust Bancorp, 36
Client(s)
   education of, 131
   idea of, in relationship banking, 55,
      113
Climate of trying, 141–42, 153, 254
Cognitive and behavioral segmenta-
      tion, 83
Cole, Robert S., 226–27
Comerica Bank, 238
Commerce and Trade Division, in
      First Southeast model, 168–70
Commercial banking, dominance of, 6
Commissions, in rewarding sales per-
      formance, 192
Communications assignment, multi-
      plicity of, 210–13
Communications management
   concept of, 203–4
   guiding principles of, 205–15
   importance of, 204–5, 224
   as relationship banking element,
      119, 131
   steps in developing program of,
      215–25
Communicatons publics, identifying,
      215–19
Communications skills, in effective
      selling, 190

Community banking organization
   definition of, 98, 174–75
   market positioning example for,
      107–8
Compensation
   and evaluation, 234
   innovation in, 250
   and organizational structure change,
      73
   and work values, 232
Competitive equality, drive for,
      10–12
Competitive strength
   as dimension in portfolio planning
      matrix, 44–47
   as performance criterion, 29–31
Complementary services, 125–26
Comprehensive analysis of new ser-
      vices ideas, 146, 149–51
Concentration or specialist strategy, 35
Confrontation strategy, 37
Consumer banking department, in
      market-oriented structures, 66–67
Consumer orientations, 116–17
Consumerism, 210
Content, of jobs, 234
Contented follower strategy, 35–36
Continuity in advertising, 196
"Convenience store" banking, 102–3
Coordinating of work, 58–60, 61
Core services, as relationship banking
      element, 119, 121–25
Core time, 238
Corporate banking department, in
      market-oriented structures, 66–67
Corporate objectives; see Objectives
Corporate Relationship Offices, in
      First Southeast model, 168–69,
      174
Cotrell, Charles A., 239, 245
Cravens, David W., 56
Credit cards, 52–53; see also Bank
      cards
Crisis management, as communica-
      tions task, 211, 212, 217
Customer(s)
   as driving force of organization, 32–
      34 36, 86

Customer(s)—*Cont.*
feelings of concerning relationship banking, 116–18
as market positioning factor, 94, 96, 105–7
Customer-assisting machines, 158–59
Customer contact personnel, in new services development, 148, 154
Customer Financial Centers, in First Southeast model, 171–73, 174
Customer satisfaction engineering, 250–56

D

Dana Corporation, 72
DeButts, J. D., 72
Decision making, in market-oriented structures, 67, 69
Deep sensing, 236–37
Delivery systems; *see also* Technology
decisions on, as part of market positioning, 94, 100–101, 104, 107
and deregulation, 7–8
as driving force of organizations, 33
integrating elements in, 159–61
model for future, 162–79
problems concerning future, 179–81
revolution in, 157–59
DeMarco, William M., 200, 201
Demographic segmentation, 82, 83
Deposit mix, and external flexibility, 30, 31
Deregulation
consequences of, 6–10
reasons for, 4–6
strategic response to, 10–12
Development and testing of new services ideas, 146, 151–53
Direct financial rewards, for sales performance, 192
Discretionary content of jobs, 230–31
Disney, Walt, 240, 242
Distinctiveness in advertising, 196, 200
Distribution systems; *see* Delivery systems
Dividing of work, 58–59, 61

Dominant institutions, strategies for, 35, 36–37
Donnelly, James H., Jr., 56, 74, 91
Doyle, Stephen X., 200
Drexler, John A., 155
Drift strategy, 38
Driving force of organization, identifying, 28, 32–34
Drucker, Peter F., 245
Duncan, Robert, 74
Durland, L. V., Jr., 74

E

Education
as communications task, 131, 211, 217–19
marketing, importance of, 251–52
Edwards, Raoul D., 17, 110
Effectiveness
as dimension of organizational performance, 23–28
in market-oriented structures, 67–69
Efficiency
criterion of, in evaluating organizational performance, 29–31
as dimension of organizational performance, 23–28
in function-oriented structures, 64–66
in market-oriented structures, 69
Electronic funds transfer (EFT), 163, 179
Employee report, annual, 241–42
Employees; *see also* Internal customers; Internal marketing; Quality of financial institutions personnel; *and* Staffing
as communications public, 220–21
new services ideas from, 148
Entrepreneurship Management Centers, in First Southeast model, 168–69
Environment
characteristics of current and projected, 252–53
and function-oriented structure, 64, 65

Environment—*Cont.*
  of job product, 234, 235–36
  and managerial planning focus, re-
    lationship between, 21–23
  and market-oriented structure, 67
Everywhere bank, 95
Excitement rallies, 242
Expertise intensive banking, 102
Exploration stage, in new services
    development, 145–48
External customers
  as communications public, 217–19
  internal customers contrasted with,
    229
External flexibility, 29–31
External sources for new services
    ideas, 147–48
Extrapolative planning, 22

F

Fast-food chains, efficiency/effective-
    ness of, 26–27
Feigin, Barbara, 92
Financial analysts, as communica-
    tions public, 220–21
Financial forecasts, in new services
    development, 150–51
Financial Information Collection Cen-
    ter, in First Southeast model,
    164–66
Financial planning, as core service,
    123, 124–25
First-impressions marketing, 239–40
First Interstate Bancorp, 98
First Interstate Bank of Arizona, 241–
    43
First National Bank of Maryland, 239
First Nationwide Savings, 4
Flexibility, performance criterion of,
    29–31
Flexible benefit programs, 238
Flexible work hours (flexitime), 238–
    39
Focus groups, 147
Ford, Jeffrey D., 245
Ford, William, 74
Formalization, degree of
  concept of, 61–62

Formalization, degree of—*Cont.*
  and function-oriented structure, 64,
    65, 69
  and market-oriented structure, 67,
    69
Forum Corporation, 189
Franchising, 9, 98, 160
Friars, Eileen M., 110
Friendly National Bank, 235
Front, Sig, 110
Front runners, as market segment, 85,
    86
Full-service providers, 103
Function-oriented structures
  changing to market-oriented struc-
    tures, 70–73
  definition and characteristics of,
    63–66
  market-oriented structures con-
    trasted with, 67–70
Functional decisions and options, in
    institutional positioning, 96, 98–
    99, 100
Furash, Edward E., 181
Futrell, Charles, 200

G

Garn, Jake, 3, 17
Gay, John H., 117, 132
General Electric, 44
General Foods, 68
General media, 215
General Mills, 68
Geographic expansion, 11, 160
George, William R., 201
Gerstner, Louis V., Jr., 133
"Get-my-money's-worth" consumers,
    116–17, 124
Gibson, James L., 57, 74
Glass-Steagall Act, 8, 11
Goal setting, selling behavior con-
    trasted with, 187–88
Grant, W. T., 26, 29
Great Western Savings and Loan As-
    sociation, 197
Green, Paul E., 91
Greenberg, Herbert M., 200
Gregor, William T., 110

Growth
  as competitiveness measure, 29, 30
  as driving force of organization, 33–34
  new product, difficulty in forecasting, 42–43
  in portfolio planning matrix, 45, 50
Guiltinan, Joseph P., 56
Guppy strategy, 36

H

Haley, Russell I., 84, 91
Hamermesh, R. G., 40
Harris, J. E., 40
Help-wanted advertising, 239–40
Heublein Co., 27
Hit-another-home-run strategy, 38
Hixon, Carl, 201
Holiday Inns, 198
Homan, G., 87
Home mortgage package, 103, 123–26
Hope-for-a-better-day strategy, 38
Housing Department, in First Southeast model, 172
Human resources; see Staffing

I

"I am an individual" consumers, 117, 127–28
IBM Corp., 72, 185, 235
Idea seeding, 142
Image creation, as communications task, 211, 212, 217
Immerwahr, John, 231–33, 244
Impalpability, 51–53; see also Intangibility
In Search of Excellence (Peters and Waterman), 72, 235, 247
Incentive programs, 192, 250
Income, as basis for segmentation, 81, 83, 120–24
Independent financial industry media, 215–17
Indiana National Bank, 241
Indirect financial rewards, for sales performance, 192–93
Industry Relationship Offices, in First Southeast model, 168–69

Informing, as communications task, 210–11, 212, 217
Innovation(s); see also New services
  funds for, 142
  major, 136
  ways of encouraging, 141–45
Institutional positioning, 94, 96, 97–100, 104, 107
Institutional Services Division, in First Southeast model, 166–68
Insurance
  as financial institutions service, 9, 125
  marketing of, by insurance companies, 50, 53–54, 197
Intangiblity, 50–55, 138–39, 197
Interest rate(s)
  advertising of, 200
  custom, 129–30
  and deregulation, 4, 5
Internal customers; see also Employees
  as communications public, 217–19
  employees as, 229
  work values of, 231–33
Internal flexibility, 29–31
Internal marketing
  applications of, 236–42
  concept of, 229, 231
  future importance of, 251
  and job product, 233–36
Internal sources for new services ideas, 148
International banking, 98, 105
Interstate banking, 9, 160, 163
Interviewing of job applicants, 240
Introduction stage for new services, 146, 153
Investment department, creation of, 64–65
Investment portfolio, and external flexibility, 30, 31
Investors' bank, 95
Ivancevich, John M., 74

J

Jacobs, Donald, 74
Job enrichment, 63

Job promotions, 73, 192–93
Job security, 232
Jobs
    discretionary content of, 230–31
    new, in market-oriented structures, 68
    as products, key elements of, 233–36
Jolson, Marvin A., 145, 155

K

Kahn, Herman, 209
Kami, M., 40
Kanter, Rosabeth Moss, 141, 155
Keep-the-offensive strategy, 37
Kemmer, Rick, 74
Kendall, Richard, 184, 200
Key services, repromoting, 196–97
Kimball, Ralph C., 117, 132
Klaisle, William J., 75
Kotler, Philip, 40
Krane, Robert A., 110

L

Lawler, Edward E., III, 155, 245
Lehr, Lewis, 155
Levi Strauss, 142
Levitt, Theodore, 141
Life cycle stage, as basis for segmentation, 120–22, 123–24
Line-of-business considerations, in customer markets positioning, 105
Line-stretching, 137
Lipp, Robert I., 1, 110
Liquidity, and internal flexibility, 30, 31
Loan department, in function-oriented structures, 64–65
Loan mix, and external flexibility, 30, 31
Loan seekers, as market segment, 85, 86
Local office network, in First Southeast model, 173–78
Locational considerations, in customer markets postioning, 105

Looper, Eugene, 62–63, 74
Losing-hand strategy, 39
Losing strategies, 35, 37–39

M

McDonald's, 140–41
McFadden and Douglas Act, 8, 11
McGuire, Al, 114
McKinsey & Co., 110
McPherson, René, 72
Maginn, Michael D., 200, 201
Mainline banking, selling contrasted with, 184
Maintenance strategy, 37
Major innovations, 136
Management, see Communications management; Managers; and Top management
Management by objectives, 63
Managerial positioning, 96, 99–100
Managers
    for "big bank" delivery systems, 180
    and customer satisfaction engineering, 251
    market, 143–44
    and organizational performance, 57–58
    product, 68, 143–44
    reporting relationship to, 235
Market
    attractiveness of, as dimension in portfolio planning matrix, 44–47
    as driving force of organization, 32–34, 36, 86
    managerial positioning as response to, 99–100
    media as, 222–24
    stable/changing, and managerial planning focus, 22–23
Market analysis, of new services ideas, 150–51
Market feedback, 151–52
Market managers, and innovation, 143–44

Market-oriented structures
  changing function-oriented structures to, 70–73
  definition and characteristics of, 63, 66–70
Market positioning
  choices in, 93–96
  elements of, 94, 96–108
  implementing steps for, 108–9
  importance of, 8
  as stage in segmentation process, 87–89
Market segmentation
  a priori versus post hoc, 80–82
  and advertising, 195
  bases for, 82–87
  importance of, 8, 77–78
  internal, 237–38
  and new services development, 145
  process of, 78–90
  as relationship banking element, 119–21
  strategy of, 89–90
Market share
  and competitive strength, 29, 30
  product objective for, 47
  ways of increasing, 115
Marketing department
  creation of, 65–66
  and new services, 144
  and selling effectiveness, 191
Marketing expenditure level, decision on, 48
Marketing mix
  developing, 48, 78, 90
  internal, 234
Marketing plan, as stage in comprehensive analysis, 150–51, 154
Marketing planning, and strategic planning, relationship between, 41–42
Marketing research
  internal, 236–37
  for segmentation, 80–82
  as source of new services ideas, 147
Marketing strategies
  developing, 47–48
  and intangibility, 51–55

Marriott Corporation, 236
Mass market, 81, 100
Mayer, David, 200
Me-too advertising, 196
Me-too strategy, 37
Measurable market segment, 89–90
Media
  as communications public, 215–17, 220–21
  as concern of public relations, 204
  as market, 222–24
  print versus audiovisual, 213–15
Mergers, 9, 160
Merit raises, for sales performance, 192
Method of sale, as driving force of organization, 32
Metzger, Robert O., 40, 245
Middle market, 81
Middlemen, in intangibles marketing, 51, 52
Mix-and-match banking, 102
Moag, Joseph, 74
Modifications of existing services, 137–38
Mondonedo, René, 245
Montgomery, Jim, 226
Moriarty, Rowland T., 117, 132
Mortgage loan package, 103, 123–26
Motivation, and selling, 188–89
Myers, D. F., 143
Myers, Patricia W., 155

N

Naisbitt, John, 17, 181, 209
National organizations, 97–98, 105
Nationwide Savings, 98
Natural resources, as driving force of organization, 33
Needs and wants
  customer, 80, 106
  employee, 237
Negri, Robert, 201
Networking, 9, 98, 160
New services
  encouraging ideas for, 141–45
  importance of, 135–36
  problem of planning, 42–43

New services—Cont.
  repromotion of, 196
  systematic development of, 145–53
  types of, 136–38
Newspaper Advertising Bureau, 86
Nollen, Stanley D., 245
Nonfinancial rewards, for sales performance, 193

O

Objectives
  corporate translated into communications, 217, 219–22
  product, 47
  strengths/weaknesses assessment in establishing, 29
O'Connor, David A., 181
Office, and new technology, 101
Olson, Dennis, 74
One-stop bankers, as market segment, 85, 86
Operations department, in function-oriented structures, 64–65
Order-taking banking, relationship banking contrasted with, 112–13
Organizational performance
  criteria for, 29–31
  dimensions of, 21, 23–28
  management's role in achieving, 57–58
  and organizational structure, 61–63
Organizational structure; see also Function-oriented structures and Market-oriented structures
  characteristics of, 60–61
  and innovation, 143–45
  and performance, 61–63
  purposes of, 58–60
Ott, Leland, 92
"Ours-is-better-than-theirs" strategy, 35
Oversegmentation, 137

P

Parasuraman, A., 201
Paul, Gordon W., 56
Pay; see Compensation
Penn Central, 26, 29
Penn Square, 212

People positioning, 94; see also Staffing
Performance; see also Organizational performance and Sales performance
  and discretionary effort, 230–31
  reviews of, 142
  and valuation, 234
Personal banker programs
  in First Southeast model, 173, 178
  in mix-and-match banking, 102
  and relationship banking, 124, 127–28
  and revolution in delivery systems, 158
Personal selling
  difficulty of, for financial institutions, 184–85
  importance of, 185
  steps to improve, 186–94
Personality of manager, and organizational change, 72
Peter, J. Paul, 91
Peters, Thomas J., 39, 72, 155, 242, 245, 247
Physical and intangible products contrasted, 50–51
Planning; see also Strategic planning
  effect of environment on, 21–24
  extrapolative, 22
  importance of, 8, 255–56
  need to shift focus of, 24–25
Point-of-sale (POS) terminals, 159, 174
Polaris E-Z Go Division of Textron, 143
Pope, Norwood W. "Red," 114, 132 209, 226, 242, 245
Popgun strategy, 39
Poppen, Jon C., 110
Portfolio planning matrix, 44–47; see also Product portfolio analysis
Position-to-be-a-financial-conglomerate strategy, 37
Positioning; see Market positioning
Positioning-to-be-acquired strategy, 36
Post hoc segmentation, 80–82, 86

Pricing
  decisions and options on, in market
      positioning, 94, 96, 104–5, 107
  and deregulation, 7
  relationship, 119, 128–30
Priorities, establishing, in portfolio
    planning matrix, 46–47
Privacy, 180
Prizes, in rewarding sales perform-
    ance, 192
Product(s)
  classification of, in portfolio plan-
      ning matrix, 44–46
  decisions and options concerning,
      in market positioning, 94, 96,
      103–4, 107
  as driving force of organizations,
      32–34
  knowledge of, 189–90
  offered by financial institutions, 7,
      11, 160
Product managers
  and innovation, 143–44
  role of, 68
Product objectives, establishing, 47
Product portfolio analysis
  definition and functions of, 42, 43
  guidelines for using, 48–50
  phases of, 43–49
Product positioning; see Market posi-
    tioning
Product proliferation, 137
Productivity; see Efficiency and Per-
    formance
Profitability
  as driving force of organization, 33,
      34
  as market positioning factor, 94, 96,
      106
  of new products, difficulty in fore-
      casting, 42–43
  performance criterion of, 29–31
  product objective for, 47
Promises, making keepable, in adver-
    tising, 198
Promotion, 8, 183; see also Advertis-
    ing; Job promotion; and Personal
    elling

Psychographic segmentation, 82, 83,
    86–88
Public relations, communications
    management contrasted with,
    204, 212–13
Putting the Work Ethic to Work
    (Yankelovich and Immerwahr),
    231–33

Q–R
Quality of financial institutions per-
    sonnel, 102, 230–31, 244, 249–56
Quality circles, 63
Railroad industry, planning in, 24–
    25, 33
Reachable market segment, 89–90
"Reaching out," meaning of, 157–59
Real estate banking department, in
    market-oriented structures, 66–67
Regional Administrative Centers, in
    First Southeast model, 164–65,
    170–72
Regional organizations, 97–98, 105
Regulation Q, 5, 8
Related services, 125–26
Relationship banking
  benefits to customers of, 116–18
  benefits to institutions of, 113–16
  definition of, 95, 112–13
  elements of, 119–31
  personal selling in, 185
  pricing in, 104, 119, 128–30
  relationship skills development for,
      189
Remarketing of job products, 240–41
Report to Employees (First Interstate
    Bank of Arizona), 241–43
Reporting relationship, 234, 235
Representation, as communications
    task, 211, 212–13, 217
Responsiveness to marketing, of mar-
    ket segment, 89–90
Return/profit; see Profitability
Reward system
  and effective selling, 192–93
  and organizational structure change
      72–73
Rieder, George, 191, 201, 242 245

Rosenberg, Richard, 181
Rosenbloom, Bert, 201
Ross, J., 40
Rules of risk, 142–43

S

Sales behaviors,, defining, 187–88
Sales champions, 186
Sales culture, 186, 192
Sales knowledge and skill develop-
 ment (SK/SD), 188–91
Sales managers, turning supervisors
 into, 193
Sales performance
 facilitating, 191
 measuring, 187–88, 191–92
 rewarding, 192–93
Sales representatives, role of, 68
Sasser, W. Earl, 231
Sawyer, Alan G., 85
Schneider, Benjamin, 155, 235, 244
Schroeder, Michael, 132
Screening of new services ideas, 147,
 148–50, 154
Secondary City Administrative Of-
 fices, in First Southeast model,
 164–65, 170–71
Selected service specialists/brokers,
 103
Self-service machines, 158–59; see
 also Automated teller machines
 (ATMs)
Selling, as communications task, 211–
 12, 217; see also Personal selling
Selling bank, 95–96
Service augmentation, 130
Services; see also New services
 inseparability of production and
  consumption in, 139–40
 intangibility of, 50–55, 138–39, 197
 packages of, 53, 122–25
 variability potential in, 140–41
Shain, John H., 74
Shapiro, Benson P., 200
Shapiro, R. D., 74
Shared facilities, in First Southeast
 model, 176–78

Shareholders, as communications
 public, 220–21
Shea, Francis X., 74
Shostack, G. Lynn, 132, 139, 153, 155
Silberman, Lee, 206–7, 226
Simplicity in advertisng, 197–98
Situation analysis, 79–80
Size, as driving force of organization,
 33
Smart Card, 160–61, 163
Snell, Susan, 132
Specialist or concentration strategy, 35
Specialization/despecialization
 definition of, 61–62
 and function-oriented structure, 64,
  65, 69
 and market-oriented structure, 67,
  69
Specialized media, 217
Spokesmanship, as communications
 task, 211, 212–13, 217
Spreads on loans, and need for relationship banking, 114
Stability
 as competitiveness measure, 29, 30
 as market attractiveness component, 45, 50
 of organizational structure, 70
 of performance measures, 31
 of technology/market, and managerial planning focus, 22–23
Staffing; see also Employees
 decision on, in market positioning,
  96, 102–3
 for sales effectiveness, 186–87
Stansby, J. G., 92
State Farm Insurance, 197
Stickler, Kent, 193
Strategic marketing, aspects of, 77
Strategic planning
 focus on effectiveness in, 27–28
 importance of, 21
 key concepts of, 28–39
 as prior to marketing planning,
  41–42
Strategy; see also Marketing strategies
 and Strategic planning

Strategy—*Cont.*
communications management, 217, 222
marketing mix, 90
as prior to structure, 71, 73
role of new services in, 145–47, 149
segmentation, 89–90
selection of, during planning, 28, 34–39
Strengths/weaknesses, institutional assessment of, 28–32
Strickland, A. J., III, 40
Structural decisions and options, in institutional positioning, 96, 97–98, 100
Structure of organization; *see* Organizational structure
Sullivan, Michael P., 181
"Supercustomers," financial needs of, 120–21
Supervisors, turning into managers, 193
Survival, objective of, 6–7, 29, 253–54
Swiss watch industry, efficiency/effectiveness in, 27, 33

T

Tactics, in communications management, 217, 222–24
Take-away strategy, 38
Target market, decision on, as part of marketing strategy, 48; *see also* Market segmentation
Teaching; *see* Education
Technology; *see also* Delivery systems
and competitive equality, 11–12
as driving force of organizations, 32, 33
identification of needs and wants for new, 80
in marketing mix positioning, 100–102
people versus, 102–3, 230–31, 249–50
and revolution in delivery systems, 158–59, 179–80

Technology—*Cont.*
stable/changing, and managerial planning focus, 22–23, 24
Telecommunications Center, in First Southeast model, 164–66
Tellers, selling behaviors for, 187–88
Test marketing, 151–53, 154
Test-the-water strategy, 38
Thompson, A. A., Jr., 40
Thompson, Thomas W., 17, 110, 132, 181, 227
3M Co., 142, 145
"Time-buying" customers, 116–17
Toffler, Alvin, 209, 210
Top management
and customer satisfaction engineering, 251–52, 255
and organizational change, 70–71
and portfolio planning, 50
Training, as communications task, 217–19; *see also* Education
Trans-America Corporation, 197
Tregoe, B. B., 39
Trust department
creation of, 59, 64–65
in First Southeast model, 171
and retail banking organization, merger of, 124

U

"Umbrella" campaigns, 197
Underdog institutions
product positioning for, 87
strategies for, 35–36, 39
Upscale market segments, 81, 120–21
Use testing, 152

V

Vacant niche strategy, 35
Valuation, 234
Value seekers, as market segment, 85, 86
Values
governing companies, 235–36
work, 231–33
Variability of services, 140–41

Venture capital funds, 142
Venture groups, 143, 144–45
Vittas, Dimitri, 130
Volume, product objecive for, 47

W

Wachovia Bank, 102, 115
Waite, Donald C., III, 110
Wal-Mart, 242
Walker, J. Mark, 239, 245
Wall Street Journal, The, 206, 215
Wants; see Needs and Wants
Waterman, Robert H., 39, 72, 155, 242, 245, 247
Watson, T. J., 72
Weems, M. Marshall, 201
Wells, W., 87, 88
Wels, Alena, 74

Wendy's, 198
White goods industry, planning in, 22–23
Wholesale customers, 117–18, 130
Wind, Yoram, 91
Women, in work force, 232
Work, dividing and coordinating, 58–60, 61
Work hours, flexible, 238–39
Work values, 231–33
Wriston, Walter, 72

Y–Z

Yankelovich, Daniel, 231–33, 244
Young, Shirley, 92
Zeithaml, Valarie, 201
Zimmerman, J. W., 39

Impossible is not a fact. It's an opinion.
Impossible is not a declaration. It's a dare.
Impossible is temporary. Impossible is nothing.
-MUHAMMAD ALI-

AMERICA NOW...
FERGUSON 2014

TRAYVON
JORDAN DAVIS
ERIC GARNER
MICHAEL BROWN

Now your place is with those seated next to God.
To anyone who wants to understand, you explain...

"Boxing was nothing. It wasn't important at all.
Boxing was just meant as a way to introduce me to the world."

WHAT DO YOU THINK OF MUHAMMAD ALI?

THEN IT'S NELSON MANDELA'S TURN TO FINALLY SEE HIS DREAM COME TRUE: MEETING YOU. MOVED, YOU EMBRACE LIKE TWO YOUNG BOYS.

YOU WILL MEET AGAIN MANY TIMES, IN THE U.S. AS WELL AS IN SOUTH AFRICA, TO ARRANGE FOR THE FUNDING OF A SCHOOL FOR IMPOVERISHED CHILDREN.

THEN COMES THE MOMENT WHEN YOU RETURN YET AGAIN TO THE WHITE HOUSE--ONLY THIS TIME YOU ARE MEETING THE FIRST AFRICAN AMERICAN PRESIDENT.

YOU ARE BEAMING WITH JOY. OBAMA IS PLEASED TO TELL YOU THAT HE USED TO WORK WITH YOUR PORTRAIT HANGING ABOVE HIS HEAD.

IN 1972, AFTER J. EDGAR HOOVER'S DEATH, CHARLIE CHAPLIN WAS FINALLY GIVEN A STAR ON HOLLYWOOD BOULEVARD...

...BUT IT'S ONLY IN 2002 THAT YOURS IS INSTALLED, NOT ON THE GROUND BUT ON THE WALL OF THE KODAK THEATER, BECAUSE YOU REFUSE TO LET ANYONE WALK ON THE PROPHET'S NAME.

MUHAMMAD ALI

IN 2001, IN A NEW YORK TIMES INTERVIEW, YOU APOLOGIZE TO JOE FRAZIER AND HIS FAMILY FOR EVERYTHING YOU SAID ABOUT HIM.

FRAZIER ACCEPTS.

HOWEVER, IN HIS HEART...

...THE WOUND WILL NEVER HEAL.

1986

YOU DIVORCE VERONICA.

LONNIE, THE DAUGHTER OF A FRIEND OF BIRD'S YOU'VE KNOWN SINCE THE AGE OF FIVE, DECIDES TO COME TO YOUR RESCUE. YOU ARE SINKING INTO SADNESS.

SINCE THEN SHE HAS DEVOTED HER LIFE TO YOU AND CONVERTED TO ISLAM SO THAT YOU COULD CELEBRATE YOUR MARRIAGE.

SHE HAS ALWAYS LOVED YOU, AND SHE TAKES MATTERS INTO HER OWN HANDS.

JIMMY CARTER IS THE FIRST TO INVITE YOU TO THE WHITE HOUSE. EVERY PRESIDENT WHO FOLLOWS WANTS TO INVITE YOU AT LEAST ONCE. BUSH SR. WILL BE THE ONLY ONE YOU DON'T VISIT.

THE ILLNESS TAKES OVER YOUR FACE, THEN THE REST OF YOUR BODY, SO RAPIDLY THAT YOU FEEL HOPELESS.

THREE YEARS EARLIER YOU WERE STILL BOXING. YOU EVEN CLIMBED EIGHT FLOORS OF A BUILDING AT TOP SPEED TO CONVINCE A MAN SITTING ON A LEDGE NOT TO COMMIT SUICIDE.

YOU ALSO REMEMBER THE EVENINGS WHEN YOU WOULD STOP YOUR CAR IN FRONT OF A FACTORY TO GREET THE EXHAUSTED WORKING WOMEN, GIVE THEM ALL HUGS, SO THEIR DAY MIGHT SUDDENLY BECOME A KIND OF DREAM.

YOU ARE NOT THAT GUY ANYMORE. YOU ARE NOT YOU. SILENCE OVERWHELMS YOU.

THEN YOU BECOME SOMEONE ELSE.

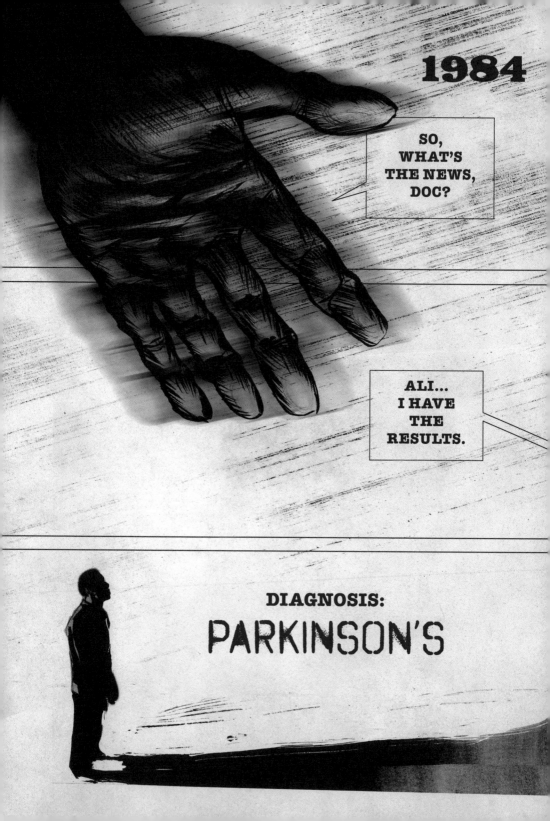

"I WAS ALI'S SPARRING PARTNER FOR YEARS, IN ZAIRE, AT DEER LAKE, EVERYWHERE. HE WAS MY IDOL, BUT I COULDN'T PASS THE OPPORTUNITY TO FIGHT HIM. IT MADE MY CAREER. A LONG CAREER.

"THAT NIGHT AFTER THE FIGHT, I FELT REALLY BAD. I WAS GOING FOR THE CLEAN CUT, FAST VICTORY. BUT I COULDN'T KNOCK HIM OUT. HE WAS A TOUGH GUY, THAT ALI.

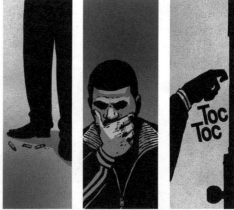

"SO I WENT TO SEE HIM AT HIS HOTEL. THE ATMOSPHERE WAS DEATH. I KNEW ALL THE GUYS WHO WERE WAITING OUTSIDE THE DOOR. BUT NO ONE WANTED TO LOOK AT ME.

"AS IF THEY HAD FORGOTTEN THAT ALI'S CAREER WAS ABOUT TAKING HITS AND BEING REALLY, REALLY WELL PAID TO DO IT. AND I'M SURE THAT FOR THIS FIGHT, NOT HALF OF THEM HAD BET ON HIM.

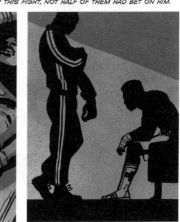

"ALI WAS SURPRISED TO SEE ME. HE GOT UP WITH DIFFICULTY, BUT IT WAS REAL OBVIOUS THAT I WAS THE ONE WHO WAS SUFFERING THE MOST IN THAT ROOM.

"AND HE TOLD ME THAT WE SHOULD DO IT AGAIN AND THAT NEXT TIME, HE WOULD BEAT ME LIKE HE HAD BEATEN THE OTHER TOUGH GUYS.

"YOU KNOW HOW YOU RECOGNIZE A GREAT MAN? EVEN WHEN DEFEATED, HE INSPIRES YOU."
                                        --LARRY HOLMES

JOHN SCHULIAN
-AUTHOR, BOXING EXPERT-

IF HERBERT HAD ANY AFFECTION FOR ALI, HE WOULD HAVE DISCOURAGED HIM FROM GETTING INTO THE RING. INSTEAD OF THAT, HE SENT HIM IN TO GET HIS BRAIN BEAT TO A PULP.

AS FOR THAT MOTHERFUCKER DON KING, HE'S JUST A PIECE OF TRASH WITH A ROCK FOR A HEART. ALL THEY DID WAS SACRIFICE ALI. THIS FIGHT WAS SIMPLY A HUMAN SACRIFICE FOR MONEY AND POWER.

LARRY HOLMES
-HEAVYWEIGHT WORLD CHAMPION, 1980-1985-

WHAT CHOICE DID I HAVE? IF I WON, IT WAS AGAINST AN OLD GUY. IF I LOST, I WAS A REAL LOSER.

AFTER ALI, I REMAINED INVINCIBLE FOR FIVE YEARS. I DESERVED MY TITLE.

CUS D'AMATO
-FLOYD PATTERSON'S TRAINER-

I WENT TO SEE *ALI VS. HOLMES* WITH MY PROTÉGÉ. AND *ALI* WAS SLAUGHTERED. THE KID WAS CRYING. HE DIDN'T SAY A WORD ON THE WAY HOME.

SO I CALLED UP ALI:

"ALI, I HAVE A KID HERE. HE'S GONNA BE THE NEXT HEAVYWEIGHT WORLD CHAMPION. PLEASE, SAY A FEW WORDS TO HIM..."

CUS D'AMATO
-FLOYD PATTERSON'S TRAINER-

AND HIS EYES FULL OF TEARS, HE SAID:

"WHY DID YOU LET THAT IDIOT BEAT YOU LIKE THAT?

"YOU SHOULD HAVE PICKED UP YOUR FISTS. WHEN I'M STRONG ENOUGH, *I'LL TEAR HOLMES APART FOR YOU.*"

AND THAT KID WAS...

MIKE TYSON
-HEAVYWEIGHT WORLD CHAMPION, 1984-1989-

IN 1988 I WAS HEAVYWEIGHT WORLD CHAMPION, AND I FOUGHT LARRY HOLMES.

BEFORE THE FIGHT, ALI CLIMBED INTO THE RING TO GREET THE FIGHTERS, AND HE WHISPERED IN MY EAR, "GET HIM FOR ME."

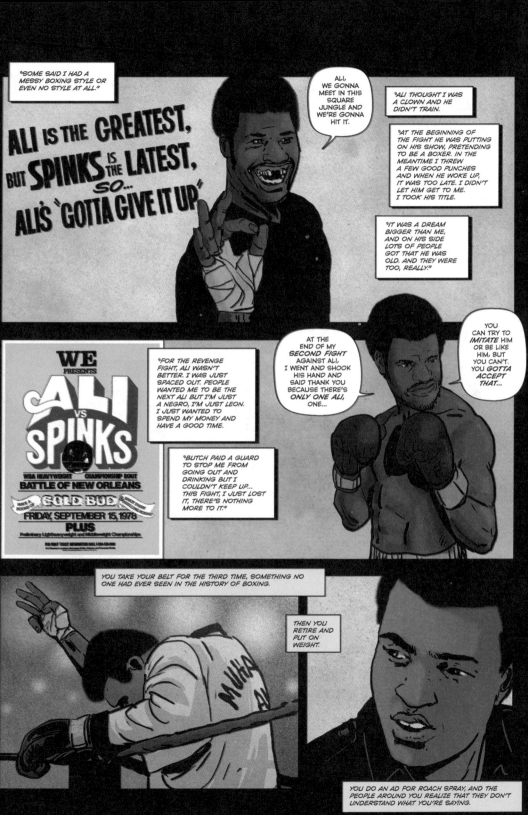

THE YEAR 1976 STRETCHES OUT STRANGELY AS YOUR FIGHTS SHOW OBVIOUS SIGNS OF DECLINE. YOU SEEM SLOW AND APATHETIC.

1977

YOU TRY TO HIDE YOUR DESIRE TO QUIT BY USING YOUR AURA AND YOUR COLOSSAL FAME TO PUT ON A SHOW. BUT BOXING ISN'T IN YOU ANYMORE.

AND YET YOU CAN'T STOP, BECAUSE YOUR WORK FEEDS NEARLY 150 MOUTHS.

YOU DIVORCE BELINDA AND CAN FINALLY MARRY VERONICA.

SHE WILL GIVE BIRTH TO TWO GIRLS, HANA AND LAILA. BUT IN THE RING NOTHING CHANGES. YOU'RE DEPLETED. YOU BECOME AN ACTOR PLAYING A CARICATURE OF YOURSELF.

ALI, PLEASE LISTEN TO ME, FOR GOD'S SAKE. YOU CAN'T GO ON LIKE THIS. YOU'RE GETTING BEATEN UP BY MEN HALF YOUR AGE. IT'S GOING TO CAUSE SERIOUS HARM, IF IT HASN'T ALREADY.

I'M INJECTING YOUR HANDS WITH NOVOCAIN SO YOU CAN STAND THE PAIN WHEN YOU'RE BOXING. I'M A DOCTOR, GODDAMMIT... NOT A SORCERER.

I KNOW YOU WON'T LISTEN TO ME, BUT YOU'RE GOING TOO FAR. EITHER YOU STOP...OR I LEAVE.

...

OKAY, FINE, YOU ASKED FOR IT. I CAN'T STAND HERE AND WATCH THIS. I CAN'T.

"ONCE I GOT IN THE CAR, IT TOOK ME FIVE MINUTES TO START THE ENGINE. AS IF I COULDN'T CLOSE THE DOOR ON THE MOST EXCITING PERIOD OF MY LIFE."

--DR. FERDIE PACHECO

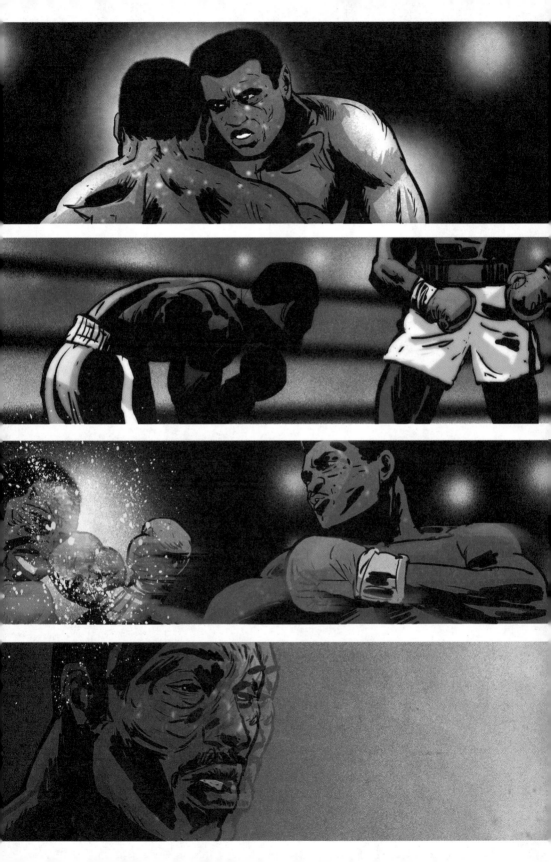

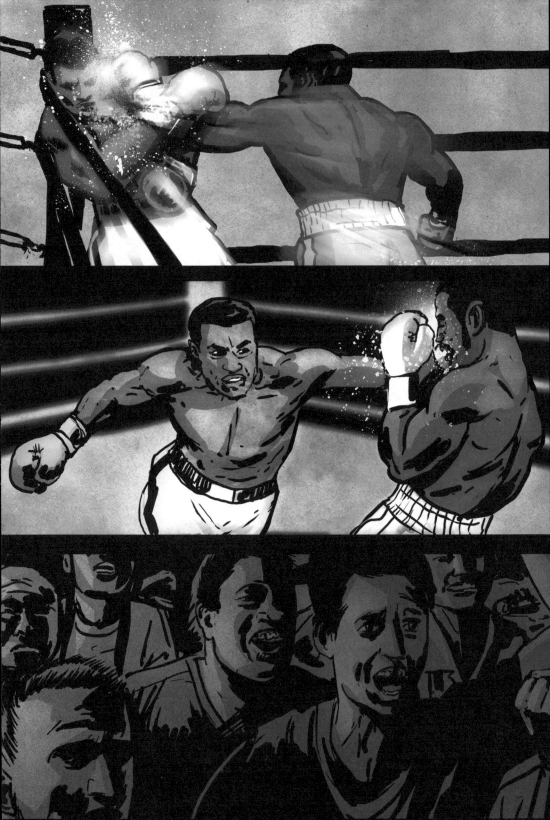

ROUND 11

THE CROWD IS FEELING HOPELESS, THINKING THE FIGHT WON'T END UNTIL ONE OF YOU IS DEAD.

IT IS BECOMING OBVIOUS THAT JOE ISN'T HUMAN, AND YOU LET OUT A SIGH.

FRAZIER, HIS FACE COVERED IN BLOOD, CONTINUES TO RAM INTO YOU LIKE A SUICIDAL MANIAC.

ROUND 13

YOU STRUGGLE LIKE A MADMAN, FILLED WITH THE COURAGE OF THE SOLDIER WHO ISN'T READY TO DIE, AND YOU THROW A JAB THAT SENDS FRAZIER'S MOUTH GUARD FLYING INTO THE CROWD, FEVER-ISH AND SCREAMING YOUR NAME. JOE STAGGERS, YOU STUMBLE, YOU BOTH THROW A SERIES OF PUNCHES SO VICIOUS THAT WHEN THE BELL RINGS, THE REFEREE SEPARATES YOU WITH A HORRIFIED LOOK ON HIS FACE.

ROUND 14

YOU LOOK LIKE TWO OLD, DRUNKEN SAILORS HANGING ONTO EACH OTHER, THEN YOU GIVE ALL YOU'VE GOT AND PRAY FOR IT TO BE OVER.

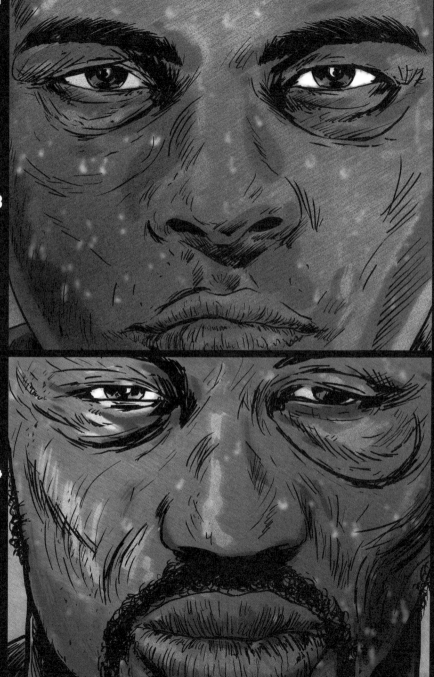

ROUND 5

HE'S PINNED YOU TO THE ROPES AGAIN, AND YOU ALREADY LOOK TIRED, WHEREAS FRAZIER SEEMS INEXHAUSTIBLE.

ROUND 7

YOUR CHEEK IS SWOLLEN. YOU START DANCING.

YOU BRING OUT YOUR BEAUTIFUL COMBINATIONS, BUT NOTHING WORKS, AND YOUR FACE REVEALS DISMAY AND DISAPPOINTMENT.

ROUND 8

THIS IS A REAL PUNCHING COMPETITION. FRAZIER IS WORKING YOUR BODY, THE LIVER, THE HEART, TO HURT YOU AS MUCH AS POSSIBLE.

ROUND 9

YOU'RE GLUED TO THE ROPES, UTTERLY EXHAUSTED.

YOUR SKIN IS GRAY, YOUR ATTACKS ARE DESPERATE, YOU MISS YOUR PUNCHES--JOE TOO, BUT EVERYONE SEES HE'LL NEVER GIVE UP.

AT THE END OF THE ROUND, YOU ARE ON THE VERGE OF COLLAPSING, AND YOU THROW YOURSELF ON THE STOOL.

ROUND 1

ON SEPTEMBER 30, 1975, THE HUMID TROPICAL WEATHER REACHES 104°F. YOU CLIMB INTO THE RING IN THE NOISE OF THE FRENZIED CROWD YOU YOURSELF PROVOKED.

JOE STARTS THE LOCOMOTIVE.

JOE CHARGES AND YOU HAVE TO BRING OUT YOUR BEST GAME RIGHT AWAY.

SOON HE HAS YOU PINNED AGAINST THE ROPES, AND YOU TAKE A COUNTLESS NUMBER OF HITS. BUT YOU STRIKE BACK, AND IT BECOMES CLEAR THAT THIS IS ABOUT SETTLING A SCORE.

ROUND 4

JOE THRUSTS HIS HEAD AGAINST YOUR CHEST LIKE A BATTERING RAM.

YOU SAY:

WHAT'S IN THAT LITTLE BLACK HEAD OF YOURS?

HE ANSWERS:

FUCKING STONES.

"A THRILLA IN MANILA"

THE PRESS IS FOCUSED ON THE FIGHT BETWEEN BELINDA AND VERONICA, AND ON THE 50 ROOMS YOU BOOKED AT THE HILTON FOR YOUR UNRULY ENTOURAGE. FRAZIER ONLY ASKED FOR 17.

PRESIDENT MARCOS POKES FUN AT YOU, SAYING HIS WIFE IS IN LOVE WITH YOU BECAUSE SHE HAS A WEAKNESS FOR EFFEMINATE MEN, AND THAT IF YOU HAD BEEN FILIPINO, HE WOULD HAVE HAD TO KILL YOU BECAUSE YOU ARE TOO POPULAR.

BUT AS USUAL, YOU ARE IN THE MIDST OF A PSYCHOLOGICAL WAR, BONA FIDE VERBAL WARFARE THAT IS EATING AWAY AT JOE'S CORE.

YOU KEEP ADDING FUEL TO THE FIRE: JOE IS A SMELLY GORILLA, A SHAME TO ALL THE BLACK BROTHERS, AN ILLITERATE, AN UNCLE TOM... DON KING IS RELISHING THIS FROM ATOP HIS THRONE.

YOU ARE SO CRUEL THAT A FEW REPORTERS ARE NOW FORCING THEMSELVES TO LAUGH. THEY'RE EMBARRASSED...TO TOP IT OFF, YOU EVEN FIRE A FEW SHOTS UNDER YOUR OPPONENT'S ROOM. YOU'VE CROSSED THE LINE. JOE HATES YOU SO MUCH HE CAN ONLY THINK OF ONE THING: CRUSHING YOU (BUT SLOWLY, SO YOU SUFFER AS MUCH AS POSSIBLE...).

DING

Muhammad Ali joins Sunni Islam

Muhammad Ali makes his pilgrimage to Mecca

I AM THE GREATEST. ALLAH IS BY MY SIDE IN THE RING. I'M NOT SCARED OF ANYTHING OR ANYONE.
I TELL MY FANS, VISIT THE CLOSEST MOSQUE, READ ELIJAH MUHAMMAD'S TEXTS.
HOW DID I BEAT HIM? HA...HEY, I WAS BLOCKING HIS PUNCHES. I HAVE A BUILT-IN RADAR-- I KNOW HOW TO JUDGE PUNCHES.
DIDN'T I TELL YOU I'M GOING TO FLOAT LIKE A BUTTERFLY AND STING LIKE A BEE?
HIS HANDS CAN'T HIT WHAT HIS EYES CAN'T SEE.
YES, I'M GOING TO RETIRE. I'M JUST GOING TO HOLD MY TITLE A FEW MORE MONTHS...
...THEY TOOK MY TITLE AWAY UNJUSTLY, BUT I'M THE REAL CHAMPION OF THE WORLD, I TOLD YOU.
I WANT YOU TO ALL RECOGNIZE THAT I AM AN EXCEPTIONAL BOXER.
I AM THE GREATEST.
AND HELLO TO ALL MY FRIENDS IN LOUISVILLE, KENTUCKY, WHERE IT ALL STARTED...

THERE, NOW.

THE FIRST RIGHT HOOK MAKES HIM STAGGER...

HE LOWERS HIS GUARD...

SUDDENLY 80,000 PEOPLE ARE SCREAMING TOGETHER.

YOU GIVE HIM A BEAUTIFUL COMBINATION...

HE LOSES HIS BALANCE. IT'S THE LAST BLOW...

FOREMAN FALLS...

YOU WATCH HIM FALL AT YOUR FEET...

YOU HOLD BACK YOUR FINAL PUNCH. YOU ARE IN COMPLETE CONTROL.

EVEN FOREMAN WILL LATER ADMIT THAT YOU DIDN'T HIT HIM AS HE FELL.

THAT'S THE MARK OF A CHAMPION, WHICH YOU ARE, ONCE AGAIN, TONIGHT, IN FRONT OF THE WHOLE WORLD.

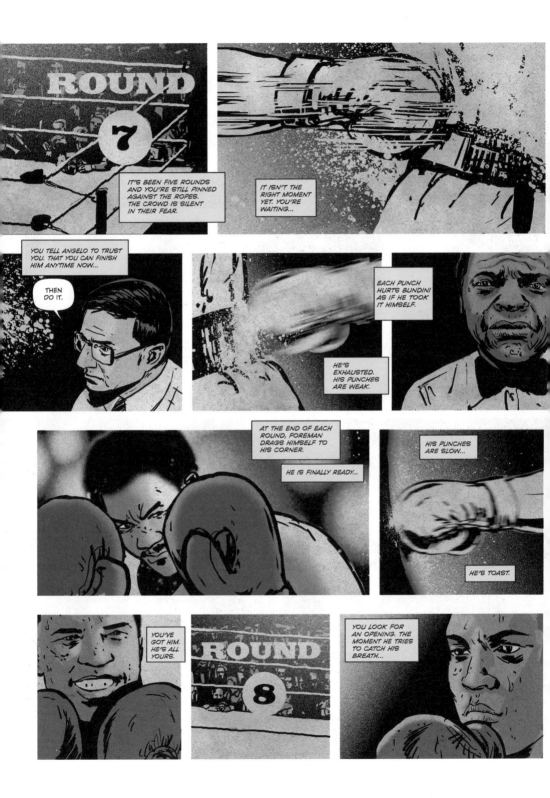

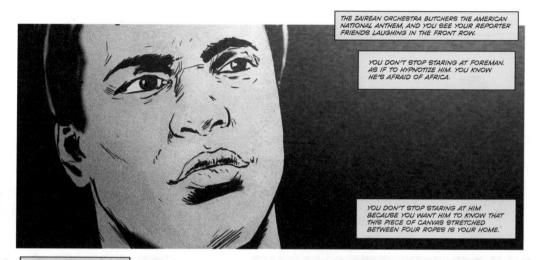

THE ZAIREAN ORCHESTRA BUTCHERS THE AMERICAN NATIONAL ANTHEM, AND YOU SEE YOUR REPORTER FRIENDS LAUGHING IN THE FRONT ROW.

YOU DON'T STOP STARING AT FOREMAN. AS IF TO HYPNOTIZE HIM. YOU KNOW HE'S AFRAID OF AFRICA.

YOU DON'T STOP STARING AT HIM BECAUSE YOU WANT HIM TO KNOW THAT THIS PIECE OF CANVAS STRETCHED BETWEEN FOUR ROPES IS YOUR HOME.

GEORGE SEEMS ALOOF. BUT WITH HIM IT'S HARD TO KNOW IF HE'S THINKING OF ANYTHING OTHER THAN MAKING YOU SUFFER LIKE HE DID FRAZIER AND NORTON...

TRUE ENOUGH, YOU BEAT THEM TOO, BUT HE SHATTERED THEM, NEVER LOSING A SINGLE MATCH.

ROUND 1

YOU JUMP ON FOREMAN LIKE A MADMAN...

...AND YOU LEAD WITH A RIGHT-HAND PUNCH. THE SUPREME INSULT FOR A BOXER.

IT MEANS: "YOU'RE TOO SLOW, GEORGE."

THE CAMERAS ARE FLASHING. EVERYONE IS AWARE OF THE INSULT YOU THREW AT THE MUMMY...

...WHO HAS BETTER FOOTWORK THAN YOU EXPECTED.

YOU PUNCH, AND THE CRIES OF THE CROWD CAN BE HEARD ALL THE WAY TO CHINA.

AND YOU AREN'T DANCING.

OCTOBER 30

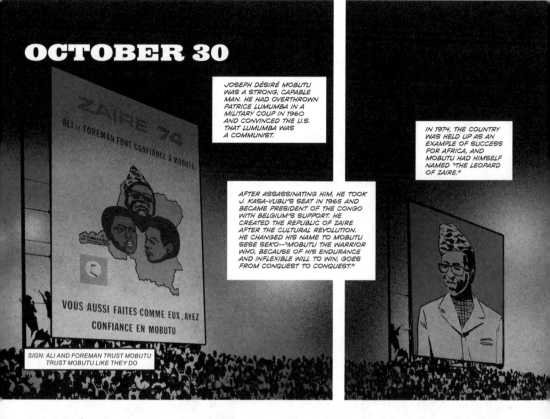

JOSEPH DÉSIRÉ MOBUTU WAS A STRONG, CAPABLE MAN. HE HAD OVERTHROWN PATRICE LUMUMBA IN A MILITARY COUP IN 1960 AND CONVINCED THE U.S. THAT LUMUMBA WAS A COMMUNIST.

IN 1974, THE COUNTRY WAS HELD UP AS AN EXAMPLE OF SUCCESS FOR AFRICA, AND MOBUTU HAD HIMSELF NAMED "THE LEOPARD OF ZAIRE."

AFTER ASSASSINATING HIM, HE TOOK J. KASA-VUBU'S SEAT IN 1965 AND BECAME PRESIDENT OF THE CONGO WITH BELGIUM'S SUPPORT. HE CREATED THE REPUBLIC OF ZAIRE AFTER THE CULTURAL REVOLUTION. HE CHANGED HIS NAME TO MOBUTU SESE SEKO--"MOBUTU THE WARRIOR WHO, BECAUSE OF HIS ENDURANCE AND INFLEXIBLE WILL TO WIN, GOES FROM CONQUEST TO CONQUEST."

SIGN: ALI AND FOREMAN TRUST MOBUTU TRUST MOBUTU LIKE THEY DO

TO WELCOME THE BOXING CHAMPIONS, HE HAD A HUGE STADIUM BUILT, USEFUL BOTH FOR BIG SPORTING EVENTS THAT KEPT PEOPLE BUSY AND FOR LOCKING UP DISSIDENTS AND EXECUTING THEM.

A RISE IN CRIME WAS PLAGUING THE COUNTRY. THERE WAS NO WAY HE COULD LET THESE CRIMINALS ATTACK THE TOURISTS AND TARNISH THE LEOPARD'S ACHIEVEMENTS.

SO HE HAD 300 CRIMINALS ARRESTED AND LOCKED UP IN THE WINGS BELOW THE STADIUM, THEN HAD 50 OF THEM EXECUTED BEFORE HE LET THE OTHERS GO. THEY WERE SO TERRIFIED THAT EVERYONE TOED THE LINE.

BUT WHEN THE FIGHT TOOK PLACE, THE SMELL OF BLOOD AND DEATH PREVAILED IN THE CHANGING ROOMS THAT LOOKED LIKE PRISON CELLS.

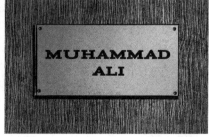

MUHAMMAD ALI

THEN THERE IS A TURN OF EVENTS: GEORGE INJURES HIS EYE. THE FIGHT IS POSTPONED FIVE WEEKS. HE WANTS TO GO HOME AND ASKS DON KING IF THEY CAN FIGHT ON THE GOOD OLD SOIL WHERE HE WAS BORN. IN ANY CASE, HE'S CONVINCED THAT SOMEONE IS POISONING HIS FOOD AND WATER.

I WON THE OLYMPIC GOLD MEDAL, ALI WON ONE, FRAZIER TOO. I SAW FRAZIER IN THE RING AND *HE WAS A MACHINE.*

HE MADE ME WANT TO BECOME A CHAMPION. BUT I DIDN'T THINK I WOULD GET THERE UNLESS FRAZIER HAD AN ACCIDENT.

AND HE DID. I *WAS THE ACCIDENT.*

THE TENSION IS SO PALPABLE THAT MOBUTU SOLVES THE PROBLEM BY SEIZING EVERYONE'S PASSPORTS. EVERYONE IS WORRIED ABOUT THE COMING RAINY SEASON, BUT YOU'RE CALM. EVEN BETTER, YOU SEEM TO EXULT IN THE LOVE OF THE PEOPLE. YOU RUN IN THE STREETS AND THE CHILDREN FOLLOW YOU FOR HOURS, LAUGHING. THEY CAN'T BELIEVE THEY'RE SEEING YOU AND TOUCHING THE CHAMPION OF THE WORLD--AND HE'S JUST LIKE THEM. YOU DON'T WANT TO BE ALONE, BECAUSE YOU DON'T WANT TO THINK ABOUT THE WORST...

PACHECO'S FIRST-AID KIT HAS BEEN STOLEN, AND HE IS SO TERRIFIED OF THE FIGHT THAT HE SECRETLY CHARTERS A PLANE TO FLY YOU TO A NEUROLOGY CLINIC IN MADRID, IN CASE OF EMERGENCY. NOT ONE JOURNALIST IS BETTING ON YOU. EVEN NORMAN MAILER (WHO ADORES YOU) DOESN'T BELIEVE IN YOU, WHICH REALLY GETS ON BUNDINI'S NERVES.

BUT YOU ARE THE GREATEST. YOU'RE ENJOYING EVERY SECOND--PROBABLY ALSO BECAUSE YOU JUST MET VERONICA.

FIRST SHE THOUGHT YOU WERE ONLY THE BIG-MOUTH YOU PLAY ON T.V. DON KING HIRED HER TO PROMOTE THE FIGHT, BUT SHE SOON FALLS FOR YOU. WHO WOULDN'T WANT TO BE WRAPPED UP IN YOUR GENTLENESS, YOUR KINDNESS, AND ALL THE REST THAT SETS YOU APART?

ZAIRE 1974

DON KING IS CHOSEN TO ORGANIZE THE FIGHT. HE PROMISES YOU AND GEORGE FOREMAN FIVE MILLION DOLLARS EACH.

I HAVE WRESTLED WITH AN ALLIGATOR.

I DONE TUSSLED WITH A WHALE.

I DONE HANDCUFFED LIGHTNING, THROWN THUNDER IN JAIL. THAT'S BAD.

ONLY LAST WEEK I MURDERED A ROCK, INJURED A STONE, HOSPITALIZED A BRICK!

I'M SO MEAN I MAKE MEDICINE SICK!

LAST NIGHT I CUT THE LIGHT OFF IN MY BEDROOM, HIT THE SWITCH, AND WAS IN THE BED BEFORE THE ROOM WAS DARK.

THE PROBLEM IS THAT HE'S BROKE. SO HE ASKS MOBUTU TO SPONSOR HIM. THE ZAIREAN DICTATOR, WHO SEES A PERSONAL INTEREST IN THIS, ACCEPTS. SO BEGINS THE LEGEND OF DON KING, A DOUBLE-EDGED REPUTATION--EVERYONE KNOWS THAT HE HAD BEEN IMPRISONED FOR MURDER. HE DOESN'T HIDE THE FACT THAT HE IS BETTING ON FOREMAN. HE IS REALLY THE ONLY ONE WHO IRRITATES YOU.

IF GEORGE *"THE MUMMY"* DREAMS OF BEATING ME, HE BETTER *WAKE UP AND APOLOGIZE.*

WRITE THAT DOWN IN YOUR NOTE-PADS...

IF YOU THINK YOU WERE SURPRISED WHEN NIXON RESIGNED...

WAIT TILL YOU SEE THE MUMMY'S ASS AFTER I WHUP IT.

AS FOR GEORGE, HE'S GRUFF. HE STANDS APART FROM THESE PEOPLE, WHO DON'T LOVE HIM, AND FEELS LIKE A STRANGER IN THIS COUNTRY. YOU CONTRIBUTE TO THIS, OF COURSE, BY SHOWING THEM THAT HE IS ONE OF THE INVADERS. HE HAS HIS FAVORITE DOG BY HIS SIDE--DAGO, A GERMAN SHEPHERD--JUST LIKE THE BELGIAN POLICE OFFICERS...YOU UNDERSTAND EARLY ON THAT GEORGE IS A BRUTE WITH A FRAGILE MENTALITY. THAT WILL BE HIS ACHILLES' HEEL.

HAVE YOU EVER *SPOKEN* TO AN OPPONENT IN THE RING LIKE ALI?

NO, I'VE *NEVER BEEN THE CHATTY TYPE.* AND I DON'T SEE HOW YOU CAN ANYWAY.

YOU'VE JUST MET THE GUY... *AND THE FIGHT IS ALREADY OVER.*

DURING TRAINING, YOU ACT AS IF YOU'LL DANCE AND GEORGE WILL NEVER BE ABLE TO CATCH YOU. BUT WHEN THEY SEE FOREMAN HIT THE PUNCHING BAG, PEOPLE JUST THINK THAT YOU'RE GOING TO DIE.

ALI HAS NEVER BEEN IN BETTER SHAPE THAN IN *ZAIRE.* THERE'S NOTHING LEFT TO DO.

WE'RE RELAXING IN THE GYM.

AND FOREMAN HASN'T BOXED A TOTAL OF 15 ROUNDS SINCE 1972.

WELCOME TO
MUHAMMAD
★ ALI ★
▶TRAINING CAMP

AT DEER LAKE, YOU'RE RUNNING AT 8 A.M., DOING YOUR EXERCISES, STAYING IN THE ROPES TO GET USED TO TAKING THE PUNCHES, ALL IN FRONT OF THE MIRRORS YOU HUNG ON THE WALLS.

OUTSIDE, YOU HAD THE NAMES OF FAMOUS BOXERS PAINTED ON BIG ROCKS...

...NOW IT IS AS IF YOU, LIKE PERSEUS, TURNED YOUR ENEMIES INTO STONE.

EVERY DAY, HIGH-CLASS PEOPLE COME TO VISIT. SOME EVEN STEAL BATH TOWELS, VASES, OR ASHTRAYS AS SOUVENIRS.

YOU GIVE MONEY TO ANYONE WHO ASKS, ANYWAY. YOU PAY FOR FOOD AND DRINKS, AND WOMEN NEED GIFTS...HOWARD CHEWS YOU OUT, BUT YOU DON'T CARE. YOU DON'T LISTEN TO HIM. AREN'T YOU A LORD?

SONNY LISTON

YOU, AT LEAST, ARE MUSLIM. YOU INTEND TO MAKE YOUR BROTHERS AND SISTERS HAPPY, AND YOU COULD CARE LESS ABOUT THIS STUFF. THEY CAN TAKE YOUR BATHROBES AND SELL THEM ON THE BLACK MARKET, YOUR SHEETS, YOUR UNDERWEAR. YOU HAVE TO TRAIN, BEAT THEM ALL, BECAUSE AFTER PERSEUS, YOU WILL BE ACHILLES, THE GREATEST FIGHTER OF ALL TIME.

1973

"ALI TOOK ME FOR GRANTED, AND THE PEOPLE ONLY KNEW ME AS FRAZIER'S SPARRING PARTNER.

"EVERYONE TOLD HIM HE WOULD WIN HANDS DOWN, SO HE DIDN'T TRAIN MUCH.

"AND HE HAD HURT HIMSELF PLAYING GOLF. SINCE HE COULD HIT THE BALL WHILE WALKING HE THOUGHT HE WOULD UPDATE THE GAME AND HIT IT WHILE RUNNING. THAT'S HOW HE TWISTED HIS ANKLE, ACTING FOOLISH AND ALL.

"WHEN HE CLIMBED INTO THE RING HE WASN'T IN GOOD SHAPE AND HIS LEGWORK WAS REALLY WEAK...

"HIS JAW WAS BROKEN DURING ROUND 4, EVEN IF ANGIE DUNDEE SAYS IT WAS IN ROUND 2. I KNOW WHERE I'M HITTING.

"BUT BECAUSE TO HIM I WAS ABOVE ALL A U.S. MARINE, HE WOULDN'T GIVE UP. HE WASN'T GOING TO LET A GUY WHO HAD BEEN IN THE MILITARY GET TO HIM, MOSTLY 'CAUSE OF THE VIETNAM WAR GOING ON.

"SO HE PREFERRED TO CONTINUE TO SUFFER... I COULD SEE HE WAS IN PAIN AND HE WASN'T PUNCHING. AT THE END HE WAS ALMOST WHITE...

"BECAUSE OF THIS FIGHT I WON $50,000. I WAS ABLE TO GET BACK ON MY FEET.

"EVERYONE UNDER-STOOD THAT HE WASN'T INVINCIBLE ANYMORE."

IT'S TIME FOR EVERYONE TO GO HOME, CRYING, AND NURSE THEIR HANGOVERS.

YOU ARE TAKEN TO THE HOSPITAL FOR AN X-RAY OF YOUR JAW, BUT YOU REFUSE TO STAY A MINUTE MORE. IT WOULD GIVE FRAZIER TOO MUCH PLEASURE TO KNOW HE SENT YOU THERE. AND WHILE SOMEONE STEALS THE X-RAYS FERDIE JUST LOOKED AT...

...RICHARD NIXON DOES A HAPPY DANCE ON THE THICK CARPET OF THE OVAL OFFICE.

SINCE JOE IS THERE TO PROVE THAT HE DIDN'T STEAL THE CHAMP'S BELT...

HE WORKS YOUR BODY INTO THE ROPES.

YOU AREN'T DANCING ANYMORE. YOU'RE JUST HOLDING ON.

YOU LAND SOME MAGNIFICENT JABS BUT, IN THE FIFTEENTH ROUND, FRAZIER THROWS AN EXTRAORDINARY LEFT HOOK THAT DROPS YOU TO THE MAT.

SO, WHEN YOUR POMPOMS SWEEP THE CANVAS LIKE DECORATIONS AFTER A PARTY, THE AUDIENCE GASPS IN HORROR, A GASP COMMENSURATE WITH THE HOPES THEY HAD IN YOU.

THE REFEREE COUNTS TO FOUR.

BUT YOU ARE ALREADY ON YOUR FEET, THOUGH YOUR EYES ARE GLAZED, THOUGH YOUR CHEEK IS SWOLLEN.

AND FOR THE FIRST TIME IN YOUR CAREER...

...YOU HAVE LOST.

WINNER BY UNANIMOUS DECISION

JOE FRAZIER

DING

AND SO IT BEGINS.

YOU PUT IN YOUR MOUTH GUARD, AND YOUR FACE METAMORPHOSES INTO THAT OF A WILD BEAST, A MONSTROUS, BEAUTIFUL BEAST...

...THEN THE CEREMONIAL RED POMPOMS YOU TIED TO YOUR SHOES FOR THE OCCASION START MOVING TO THE RHYTHM OF YOUR DANCING.

FROM THE START, FRAZIER MOVES TOWARD YOU LIKE A BULLDOZER.

HE HITS, YOU RETALIATE, HE TAKES IT, NEVER TAKING A STEP BACK.

IT FEELS LIKE HIS FISTS ARE AS HARD AS ROCKS.

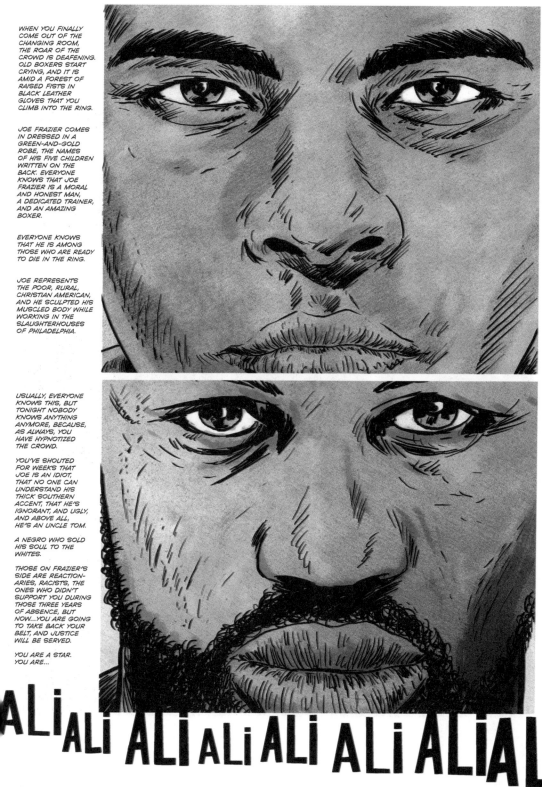

WHEN YOU FINALLY COME OUT OF THE CHANGING ROOM, THE ROAR OF THE CROWD IS DEAFENING. OLD BOXERS START CRYING, AND IT IS AMID A FOREST OF RAISED FISTS IN BLACK LEATHER GLOVES THAT YOU CLIMB INTO THE RING.

JOE FRAZIER COMES IN DRESSED IN A GREEN-AND-GOLD ROBE, THE NAMES OF HIS FIVE CHILDREN WRITTEN ON THE BACK. EVERYONE KNOWS THAT JOE FRAZIER IS A MORAL AND HONEST MAN, A DEDICATED TRAINER, AND AN AMAZING BOXER.

EVERYONE KNOWS THAT HE IS AMONG THOSE WHO ARE READY TO DIE IN THE RING.

JOE REPRESENTS THE POOR, RURAL, CHRISTIAN AMERICAN, AND HE SCULPTED HIS MUSCLED BODY WHILE WORKING IN THE SLAUGHTERHOUSES OF PHILADELPHIA.

USUALLY, EVERYONE KNOWS THIS, BUT TONIGHT NOBODY KNOWS ANYTHING ANYMORE, BECAUSE, AS ALWAYS, YOU HAVE HYPNOTIZED THE CROWD.

YOU'VE SHOUTED FOR WEEKS THAT JOE IS AN IDIOT, THAT NO ONE CAN UNDERSTAND HIS THICK SOUTHERN ACCENT, THAT HE'S IGNORANT, AND UGLY, AND ABOVE ALL, HE'S AN UNCLE TOM.

A NEGRO WHO SOLD HIS SOUL TO THE WHITES.

THOSE ON FRAZIER'S SIDE ARE REACTION-ARIES, RACISTS, THE ONES WHO DIDN'T SUPPORT YOU DURING THOSE THREE YEARS OF ABSENCE, BUT NOW...YOU ARE GOING TO TAKE BACK YOUR BELT, AND JUSTICE WILL BE SERVED.

YOU ARE A STAR. YOU ARE...

ALI ALI ALI ALI ALI ALI ALIAL

NORMAN MAILER
-NOVELIST-

THE WAR IN VIETNAM HAD DIVIDED THE COUNTRY IN TWO AND NIXON WAS LOOKING FOR A WAY TO CALM PUBLIC OPINION.

IN THE END, HE THOUGHT IT WAS PREFERABLE TO MAKE ALI A BOXER AGAIN INSTEAD OF A MARTYR.

CUS D'AMATO
-FLOYD PATTERSON'S COACH-

I HAVE A LOT OF RESPECT FOR ALI, BUT I NEVER SAW A TOP ATHLETE, THREE YEARS INACTIVE, MAKE A GOOD COMEBACK.

AFTER THE ALI-FRAZIER MATCH, WE'LL FINALLY FIND OUT HOW MUCH HE'S WORTH.

ANGELO DUNDEE
-MUHAMMAD ALI'S COACH-

WITH THIS KID, YOU NEVER KNOW. HE NEVER DOES THE SAME THING IN TRAINING AND IN THE RING.

I DIDN'T TEACH ALI ANYTHING. I ONLY HELPED HIM CORRECT HIS MISTAKES.

TRYING TO IMAGINE THE IMPACT THIS FIGHT HAD ON THE PEOPLE IN THOSE DAYS IS A DIFFICULT TASK. IT SEEMS LIKE SUCH A LONG TIME AGO THAT EVERYONE WAS FOCUSED ON BOXING--AND THE CIVIL RIGHTS MOVEMENT.

BECAUSE ON MARCH 8, 1970, THE WHOLE WORLD IS THERE TO SEE YOU. ITS HEART HAS BEEN POUNDING FOR DAYS. IT'S RESTLESS AS AN ANIMAL BEHIND BARS, FEVERISH WITH THE ANTICIPATION OF SEEING YOU CLIMB INTO THE RING.

THE CROWD POURING OUT ONTO MADISON SQUARE GARDEN IS LIKE A PSYCHEDELIC HALLUCINATION. THE RICH BLACKS ARE DRIVING THEIR COLORFUL LIMOUSINES, WEARING THEIR SUNDAY HATS. EVERY INCH OF SKIN IS FLASHING WITH JEWELS, AND MINK COATS SWEEP THE FLOORS LIKE THE CLOAKS OF ROYALTY.

IT'S A SHOW, A DISPLAY MEANT TO IMPRESS THOSE WHO STILL BELIEVE THAT THE BLACK SOCIAL CLASS CONSISTS ONLY OF TRASH...LIKE JOE FRAZIER?

BUT WHITES ARE RUSHING IN AS WELL: SINATRA, WOODY ALLEN, ELVIS PRESLEY, SALVADOR DALI, THE BEATLES...IN THE MEANTIME, THE LOWER CLASSES THAT CAN'T AFFORD A SEAT AROUND THE RING ARE CROWDING INTO MOVIE THEATERS BECAUSE, OF COURSE, THE FIGHT WILL BE BROADCAST IN CLOSED CIRCUIT--A HISTORIC, MULTIMILLION-DOLLAR MATCH CALLED...

"THE FIGHT OF THE CENTURY."

AFTER **3** YEARS **7** MONTHS **3** DAYS THE SUPREME COURT AUTHORIZES MUHAMMAD ALI TO BOX AGAIN. HIS LICENSE IS RETURNED.

YOU LEARN THE NEWS EARLY IN THE MORNING AS YOU ARE FILLING A BAG WITH ORANGES AT THE CORNER STORE. THE SHOPKEEPER SUDDENLY JUMPS INTO YOUR ARMS WITH CRIES OF JOY, THE ORANGES FALL ON THE SIDEWALK, WOMEN DELICATELY AVOID THEM, CHILDREN USE THEM AS BALLS, THEY ROLL ONTO THE ROAD AND EXPLODE UNDER THE CARS' WHEELS LIKE BURSTING SUNS.

THE ASSASSINATION OF MARTIN LUTHER KING HAD IGNITED THE STREETS. ROBERT KENNEDY DECIDED TO RUN FOR PRESIDENT. HE HAD THE BLACK VOTE, MORE THAN 12 MILLION AMERICANS.

JOHN CARLOS AND TOMMIE SMITH MEDALED IN THE 200-METER RACE. BOTH MILITANTS OF THE OLYMPIC PROJECT FOR HUMAN RIGHTS (O.P.H.R.) WHO HAD WANTED TO ORGANIZE A BOYCOTT OF THE OLYMPIC GAMES BECAUSE OF THE POLITICAL SITUATION IN MEXICO, THEY DECIDED TO MAKE A DRAMATIC STATEMENT.

KNOWING THEY WOULDN'T BE HANDED A MICROPHONE AND THAT A PICTURE IS WORTH A THOUSAND WORDS...

THEY TOOK OFF THEIR SHOES IN PROTEST AGAINST POVERTY IN THE UNITED STATES.

TOMMIE WORE A SILK SCARF AND JOHN WORE A PEARL NECKLACE TO REPRESENT THE BLACKS WHO HAD BEEN LYNCHED.

THEY RAISED THEIR BLACK-GLOVED FISTS DURING THE NATIONAL ANTHEM TO SYMBOLIZE THEIR TIES TO THE CIVIL RIGHTS MOVEMENT.

ON THE PODIUM WITH THEM, PETER NORMAN, A WHITE AUSTRALIAN ATHLETE, WORE A SIMPLE O.P.H.R. BADGE.

TOMMIE AND JOHN WERE SUSPENDED FROM THE AMERICAN OLYMPIC TEAM. THEIR EVERYDAY LIVES--AS WELL AS THOSE OF THEIR FAMILIES--WERE RADICALLY CHANGED AND SHADOWED BY DEATH THREATS.

BLAM

ONCE AGAIN, A BULLET STOPPED ANOTHER SURGE OF HOPE. NIXON WAS ELECTED IN 1969... IN 1974, HE RESIGNED AMID THE WATERGATE SCANDAL.

mexico 68

ON OCTOBER 2 IN MEXICO CITY, THOUSANDS OF PEOPLE, AMONG THEM STUDENTS AND TRADE UNIONISTS, PROTESTED IN THE PLAZA DE LAS TRES CULTURAS IN TLATELOLCO, CRYING, "¡NO QUEREMOS OLIMPIADAS, QUEREMOS REVOLUCIÓN!" (WE DON'T WANT THE OLYMPIC GAMES, WE WANT A REVOLUTION!). 5,000 SOLDIERS AND 200 TANKS CRACKED DOWN ON THE PROTEST, KILLING DOZENS AND ARRESTING OVER A THOUSAND.

SOME SAY IT'S ALL OVER FOR YOU. THEY SAY YOU'RE BOUND HAND AND FOOT, HAVEN'T GOT A DOLLAR IN YOUR POCKET, THAT YOU ALLOWED A BURGER CHAIN TO USE YOUR NAME JUST SO YOU COULD GET FREE MEALS THERE...

BUT OTHERS SAY YOU ARE SITTING ON MILLIONS OF DOLLARS THAT ALLOW YOU TO SATISFY YOUR ECCENTRICITIES.

AFTER ALL, WHO ELSE COULD HAVE GIVEN ELIJAH MUHAMMAD ENOUGH MONEY TO BUILD A MOSQUE IN MIAMI?

SOME SAY IT ISN'T TRUE...

IT CAN'T BE YOU, SINCE YOUR ENTOURAGE HAS BEEN SWINDLING YOU, FLEECING YOU...THEY SAY THE DEVIL'S FOOD CAKE IS BIG ENOUGH FOR EVERYONE, THAT YOU STUFF DOLLAR BILLS IN THE POCKETS OF ALL THE BLACKS YOU PITY.

BECAUSE YOU ALSO WANT TO HELP--TO FEED, TO MEND, TO ERADICATE POVERTY IN THE GHETTOS.

PEOPLE EVEN SAY YOU GO OUT AT NIGHT TO PUT ON YOUR "SHOWS"...IN THE STREETS CROWDED WITH BLACK PEOPLE, IN THE MIDST OF THEIR HOT, CLAMMY MISERY, YOU DO EVERYTHING, ABSOLUTELY EVERYTHING YOU CAN TO MAKE THEM SMILE...

AND IT'S MUTUAL. THEY STILL LOVE YOU, AND THAT MEANS A LOT TO YOU.

SOME IN THE PRESS STAND UP FOR YOU. AND MANY ICONS CHALLENGE THE AUTHORITIES, ASKING THEM TO RETURN YOUR LICENSE. WHEN THE PHOTOGRAPHER GEORGE LOIS HAS YOU POSE LIKE THE MARTYR SAINT SEBASTIAN FOR THE COVER OF ESQUIRE, IT STIRS UP CONTROVERSY--BUT NOT AS MUCH AS IN 1963 WHEN SONNY LISTON WAS SANTA CLAUS...

APRIL 1968
PRICE $1

Esquire
THE MAGAZINE FOR MEN

The Passion of Muhammad Ali

WHEN YOU MEET *BELINDA BOYD* IN A BAKERY--SHE IS ONLY 17--AND, JUST A FEW DAYS LATER, ASK HER TO MARRY YOU, *SHE ACCEPTS*. BECAUSE YOU ARE SO EASY TO LOVE.

SHE LIKES WEARING A VEIL. IT MAKES HER FACE LOOK AS WISE AS HER HEART ALREADY IS. THEN SHE BEARS YOUR CHILDREN.

WITH THEM, YOU ARE LIKE THEM, BECAUSE YOU WERE ALREADY LIKE THEM ANYWAY, BUT NOW YOU DON'T HAVE TO PRETEND ANYMORE.

SOMETIMES, HOWEVER, YOU *PLAY THE ADULT*. YOU TRY TO LOOK AT THEM STERNLY WITHOUT LAUGHING. YOU ALSO TRY TO SAY "*NO*," WHICH IS ALMOST IMPOSSIBLE BECAUSE WITH THEM, "*YES*" IS THE ONLY WORD YOU KNOW.

YES, YOU CAN HAVE A THIRD ICE CREAM. YES, YOU CAN POUR WATER ALL OVER THE HOUSE, THEN SLIDE ON THE COOL, TILED FLOOR TO FORGET THE HEAT.

YES, OF COURSE YOU CAN SLEEP IN MY ARMS AND EVEN IN THE HAMMOCK WITH ME, *FOREVER*, AND WHEN WINTER COMES WE'LL COUNT THE STARS, BAREFOOT ON THE ROAD.

YES, YOU CAN SCREAM, THEN CRY, THEN LAUGH, AND EVEN DO ALL THREE AT ONCE *IF YOU WANT*.

WHEN YOU ARE SEPARATED FROM THEM, WHEN YOU NEED TO *GO BACK TO YOUR LIFE AS A MAN*, THE OTHER LIFE YOU CAN'T PART WITH, YOU TALK TO THEM OVER THE PHONE.

WITH THAT OTHER VOICE, YOUR REAL VOICE. IT IS *SO TIMID AND SO GENTLE* IT SOUNDS LIKE IT'S FROM A FARAWAY PLACE, UNHURRIED, LANGUID AS AN AWAKENED SLEEPER.

"I FOUGHT AGAINST ALI IN 1966 BECAUSE I WAS ACTUALLY FILLING IN FOR ERNIE TERRELL, WHO PULLED OUT.

"AT THE TIME HE WORKED FOR TONY ACCARDO, THE BOSS OF THE CHICAGO MAFIA.

AIR CONDIT...
BEAUMONT
CITY AUDITORIUM

BOXING

THE SECOND RECKONING

MONDAY
MAY 1 9:00 P.M.

MUHAMMAD

ALI

—VS—

GEORGE

CHUVALO

NO HOME TV OR RADIO

TICKETS ON SALE AT CENTRAL TICKET OFFICE
GOLDEN TRIANGLE ARENA, 1005 ORLEANS, BEAUMONT

1966

"THE FIGHT WAS TOUGH BUT I HELD ON FOR 15 ROUNDS.

"NO ONE HAS EVER KNOCKED ME OUT IN ALL MY CAREER, NOT EVEN ALI.

"BERNIE GLICKMAN, WHO TOOK CARE OF TERRELL—WELL, WHO PLAYED THE ROLE OF A FAKE MANAGER—WENT TO HERBERT MUHAMMAD AND THREATENED HIM:

"IF ALI WINS AGAINST TERRELL, YOU'LL END UP AT THE BOTTOM OF LAKE MICHIGAN,' HE SAYS TO HIM.

"SO THEN, HERBERT SENDS HIS GUYS TO BEAT UP THAT IDIOT BERNIE...HE WENT FROM THE HOSPITAL TO THE ASYLUM, WHERE HE DIED.

"IN ANY CASE, I WON A LOT OF MONEY BECAUSE OF THAT FIGHT. BUT ON THAT DAY, HE WAS JUST BETTER THAN ME.

"LIKE SCHULBERG SAID, HE WAS NUREYEV IN SHORTS."

"THAT'S WHY I ENDED UP FILLING IN.

3

- JUSTICE -

EQUAL·JUSTICE·UNDER·LAW·

ROUND 1

SONNY IS UNABLE TO TOUCH YOU BECAUSE, DESPITE THE BOOING AUDIENCE, YOU DANCE, YOU PLAY, YOU DODGE, AS IF MOUNTED ON SPRINGS.

AT 1 MINUTE AND 42 SECONDS, LISTON DROPS LIKE A ROCK, K.O.

YOU SCREAM AT HIM TO GET BACK UP, AND IN A SINGLE FLASH, THE MOST FAMOUS PICTURE IN THE HISTORY OF SPORTS IS CREATED. THE MYSTERY OF "THE PHANTOM PUNCH" IS LAUNCHED.

DOES HE WANT TO STOP NOW SO HE DOESN'T END UP IN THE HOSPITAL LIKE LAST TIME, WHEN HE FINALLY REALIZED THAT YOU WERE BIGGER AND FASTER THAN HIM?

WAS HE THREATENED BY THE NATION OF ISLAM?

SONNY LISTON WILL ALWAYS REMAIN A MYSTERY...

NO ONE KNOWS WHEN HE WAS BORN. ONE OF A FAMILY OF 23 CHILDREN, HE ENDED UP IN PRISON, WHERE HE QUICKLY LEARNED THAT HE WAS THE BIGGEST BRUTE AROUND AND THAT HE COULD MAKE MONEY WITH THAT.

HE WAS A HENCHMAN IN THE MAFIA FOR A WHILE. IT DIDN'T TAKE THEM LONG TO START INVESTING IN HIM.

BUT YOU ARE OPPOSITES...

WITH A FACE ONLY HIS WIFE COULD LOVE, THE MEDIA NEVER STOPS MOCKING HIM...EVEN WHEN HE BECOMES CHAMPION OF THE WORLD.

LOSING TO YOU PUTS THE BRAKES ON HIS CAREER.

HE WILL START BOXING AGAIN IN A FEW YEARS, BUT HE ISN'T WHAT HE USED TO BE.

ON MARCH 5, 1970, WHILE HIS WIFE IS ON A TRIP, HE IS FOUND IN HIS HOME, DEAD FROM A HEROIN OVERDOSE.

AFTER GETTING A CALL FROM THE NEIGHBORS BECAUSE OF THE SMELL, THE LAS VEGAS POLICE LET HIM ROT THREE MORE DAYS, WHICH SHOWS HOW MUCH HE WAS LOVED BY THE LOCAL OFFICERS OF THE LAW.

HIS TIES TO ORGANIZED CRIME AND HIS PHOBIA OF NEEDLES LEAD TO RUMORS ABOUT THE CIRCUMSTANCES OF HIS DEATH.

HIS EPITAPH READS:

CHARLES "SONNY" LISTON
-A MAN-

THE REMATCH BETWEEN MUHAMMAD ALI AND SONNY LISTON IS STILL TALKED ABOUT TO THIS DAY.

NOBODY KNOWS WHAT REALLY HAPPENED... BUT YOU KNOW.

THIS TIME, YOU DECIDE TO TRAIN WITH *STEPIN FETCHIT.*

AN ACTOR AND FRIEND OF JACK JOHNSON, THE FIRST, AND MOST HATED, BLACK HEAVYWEIGHT CHAMPION.

AS FOR STEPIN, HE WAS THE FIRST BLACK ACTOR TO BECOME A MILLIONAIRE, AND WHO CARES THAT HE REPRESENTS THE WHITES' FAVORITE STEREOTYPE OF THE STUPID, LAZY BLACK MAN. EVEN HIS NAME IS A JOKE.

FOR MANY, IT'S ALREADY A STEP UP TO HAVE A REAL BLACK MAN IN COSTUME, NOT ONE OF THOSE DAMN WHITES WEARING SHOE POLISH ON THEIR FACES.

WHEN HE DECLARES BANKRUPTCY, HE TURNS TO THE NATION OF ISLAM, AND YOU ADOPT HIM.

HE TELLS YOU STORIES ABOUT HOLLYWOOD AND EVERYTHING HE KNOWS ABOUT JACK JOHNSON.

HE TEACHES YOU HIS SECRET WEAPON: *THE ANCHOR PUNCH.*

A FAST, SWIVELING HOOK THAT DESTROYS THE ENEMY.

YOU ARE ECSTATIC. YOU TRAIN LIKE MAD TO PULL IT OFF. LISTON HASN'T GOT A CHANCE.

YOU TELL EVERYONE NOT TO BE LATE ON THE BIG NIGHT, BECAUSE IT WILL BE OVER IN A FLASH.

MIAMI

YOU PACE IN CIRCLES IN YOUR HOTEL ROOM, PROTECTED LIKE YOU'RE THE PRESIDENT, LEAVING ONLY TO TRAIN.

WAKE UP, CHAMP. THOSE BLACK MUSLIMS ARE A *DANGER TO THE PUBLIC* AND THEY'RE ON YOUR HEELS MORE OFTEN THAN YOUR SOCKS.

CAN'T YOU SEE YOU'RE IN A TIGHT SPOT? *TWO BLACK MUSLIMS WERE ARRESTED FOR MURDERING MALCOLM,* AND YOU STILL WANT TO FOLLOW THEM?

YOUR ROOM BURNS UP, SONJI IS TERRIFIED, AND YOU GO ON LIKE *NOTHING IS HAPPENING.* I'M TELLING YOU, THEY JUST WANT *YOUR DOUGH.* THAT'S ALL THEY CARE ABOUT, *YOUR GLORY AND YOUR MONEY,* AND WE'RE RISKING OUR LIVES.

HE'S RIGHT, CHAMP. I HATE TO SAY THIS, AND YOU KNOW I'M NOT CRITICIZING YOUR RELIGION, BUT *THEY WANT YOU TO GET A DIVORCE.*

AND ME? SAME THING. THEY WANT TO SEPARATE US BECAUSE I DON'T WANT TO *CONVERT* AND I'M MARRIED TO A WHITE WOMAN.

I CAN'T BELIEVE YOU WANT TO *DISTANCE YOURSELF* FROM EVERYONE WHO LOVES YOU FOR *ALL THESE EX-CONS.*

...THEY EVEN SUSPECT *ANGELO* OF WANTING TO HARM YOU.

SHUT UP--YOU DON'T KNOW ANYTHING. ANYWAY, I DON'T LISTEN TO PEOPLE WHO AGREE TO USE THEIR SLAVE NAME THEIR WHOLE LIFE.

MALCOLM WAS DEAD, AND A FEW MONTHS EARLIER SAM COOKE, YOUR FRIEND, WAS KILLED ALSO, SHOT UNDER STRANGE CIRCUMSTANCES AT A SORDID MOTEL IN L.A.

BUNDINI DROPPED OUT OF CIRCULATION FOR A WHILE...FORTUNATELY HE WAS JUST DROWNING HIMSELF IN ALCOHOL. HE SOLD YOUR CHAMPIONSHIP BELT FOR 500 DOLLARS, BUT WHEN HE CAME BACK, YOU FORGAVE HIM.

HOWARD STAYED AND CONTINUED TO PHOTOGRAPH YOU, THOUGH THE INNOCENCE SEEN ON YOUR FACE IN HIS FIRST IMAGES WAS GONE.

YOU START TRAINING FOR A REMATCH WITH LISTON AFTER A SIX-MONTH BREAK DURING WHICH YOU HAD AN OPERATION FOR A HERNIA (THAT'S WHEN YOUR OPPONENT STARTS DRINKING AGAIN).

THE ATMOSPHERE IS OPPRESSIVE. WHITE AMERICA HATES YOU. MUCH OF BLACK AMERICA WANTS YOU DEAD BECAUSE YOU HAVE SIDED WITH MALCOLM X'S MURDERERS.

ONE NIGHT, WHEN YOU ARE AT A RESTAURANT WITH SONJI, YOUR HOTEL ROOM IS SET ON FIRE. ELIJAH MUHAMMAD SENDS YOU EVEN MORE BODYGUARDS.

YOU AND SONJI ARE HARDLY EVER ALONE ANYMORE...THE BLACK MUSLIMS FIND HER SKIRTS TOO SHORT, HER MAKEUP TOO HEAVY, AND HER MANNERS IMPROPER.

THEY KEEP TELLING YOU SHE ISN'T THE ONE FOR YOU, AND YOU START WONDERING WHY SHE BOUGHT THAT INAPPROPRIATE SKIRT, WHY SHE WEARS THAT GAUDY RED LIPSTICK, AND WHERE WAS SHE THE OTHER NIGHT WHEN YOU CAME HOME LATE FROM THE GYM?

WHAT DOES SHE DO WHEN SHE ISN'T BY YOUR SIDE? WHO DOES SHE THINK SHE IS TO DEFY YOU? YOU STILL LOVE HER, BUT YOU HAVE EVERY REASON TO BELIEVE YOU MADE A MISTAKE.

BLAM

HE COLLAPSED ON THE FLOOR WHILE TWO ACCOMPLICES OF THE MURDERER CONTINUED TO SHOOT HIM. ACCORDING TO THE POLICE, 21 BULLETS ENTERED THE VICTIM'S BODY.

MALCOLM X, BORN MALCOLM LITTLE, BREATHED HIS LAST BREATH ON THE WAY TO THE HOSPITAL. POLICE SOURCES SAY THE AUDIENCE THREW THEMSELVES ON THE KILLER--A MAN CALLED THOMAS 15X JOHNSON-- AND CAME VERY CLOSE TO LYNCHING HIM.

HE WAS QUICKLY ARRESTED. THE OTHER TWO CRIMINALS GOT AWAY...BUT WE ALREADY KNEW THEY WERE BLACK MUSLIMS.

ON FEBRUARY 14, THE SHABAZZ RESIDENCE HAD BEEN FIREBOMBED, WHICH LEADS ONE TO QUESTION THE AUTHORITIES' ABILITY TO PROTECT THE MEMBERS OF THIS FAMILY.

MALCOLM X MURDERED

EVERYONE NOW HOPES THAT THE COUNTRY WON'T BE SET ABLAZE BY RIOTS. SOME COUNTRIES HAVE OFFERED THEIR CONDOLENCES UPON HEARING THE NEWS.

THE BLOW TO THE BLACK CAUSE IS CLEAR. IT SHOVES THE HOPES OF THESE MEN AND WOMEN INTO DARK CORNERS WHERE THEY HAVE NOTHING TO HOLD ONTO BUT THE MEMORY OF THEIR BLACK PRINCE.

THIS WAS THE DAY THE ASSASSINATION OF A LEADER SHOOK THE WORLD, THE ASSASSINATION OF THE CONTROVERSIAL BLACK LEADER MALIK EL-SHABAZZ, BETTER KNOWN AS...MALCOLM X.

KA-KLAK

HE WAS IN MANHATTAN AT THE AUDUBON BALLROOM TO DELIVER A SPEECH TO THE ORGANIZATION OF AFRO-AMERICAN UNITY...

A QUARREL SEEMED TO HAVE BROKEN OUT IN THE AUDIENCE. A MAN YELLED, "TAKE YOUR HAND OUT OF MY POCKET."

A FEW SECONDS LATER, AS MALCOLM X'S VOICE CALLED FOR SILENCE...

...A MAN STEPPED FORWARD WITH A SAWED-OFF SHOTGUN, OPENING FIRE AND HITTING THE FAMOUS ORATOR IN THE STOMACH.

BOOM

HOOVER EVEN HAS A BEEF WITH DR. KING BECAUSE HE'S CONVINCED THAT MOSCOW IS BEHIND HIS ACTIONS...

COINTELPRO IS THE BUREAU'S BEST-KEPT SECRET. ITS MAIN GOAL IS TO STOP THE ACTIVITIES OF POLITICAL GROUPS DEEMED SUBVERSIVE, AND BY ANY MEANS NECESSARY: INFILTRATION, WIRETAPPING, FALSE INFORMATION AND SCANDALOUS RUMORS, RANDOM ARRESTS, AND EVEN ROBBERIES.

COINTELPRO IS A PROGRAM THAT MAKES IT POSSIBLE TO SOLVE "PROBLEMS" WITHOUT HAVING TO GO TO COURT.

COINTELPRO, LIKE FIGURE SKATING, IS A PROGRAM WITH TOTAL FREEDOM...

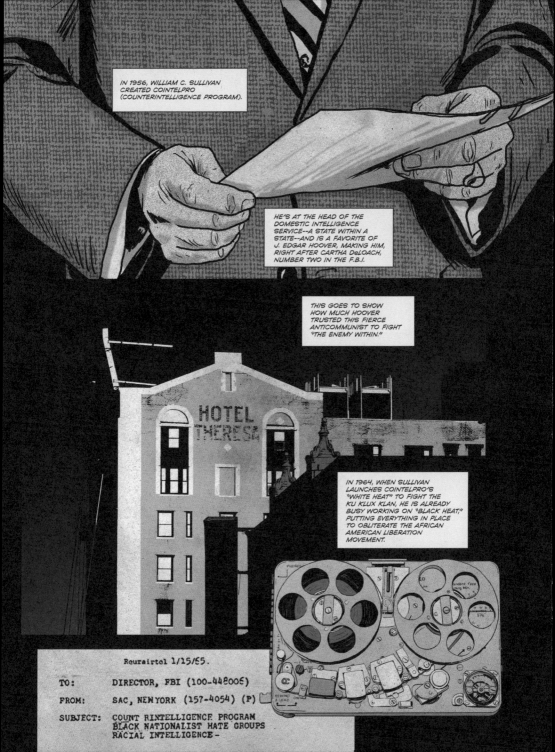

IN 1956, WILLIAM C. SULLIVAN CREATED COINTELPRO (COUNTERINTELLIGENCE PROGRAM).

HE'S AT THE HEAD OF THE DOMESTIC INTELLIGENCE SERVICE--A STATE WITHIN A STATE--AND IS A FAVORITE OF J. EDGAR HOOVER, MAKING HIM, RIGHT AFTER CARTHA DeLOACH, NUMBER TWO IN THE F.B.I.

THIS GOES TO SHOW HOW MUCH HOOVER TRUSTED THIS FIERCE ANTICOMMUNIST TO FIGHT "THE ENEMY WITHIN."

HOTEL THERESA

IN 1964, WHEN SULLIVAN LAUNCHES COINTELPRO'S "WHITE HEAT" TO FIGHT THE KU KLUX KLAN, HE IS ALREADY BUSY WORKING ON "BLACK HEAT," PUTTING EVERYTHING IN PLACE TO OBLITERATE THE AFRICAN AMERICAN LIBERATION MOVEMENT.

Reurairtel 1/15/65.

TO: DIRECTOR, FBI (100-448006)

FROM: SAC, NEW YORK (157-4054) (P)

SUBJECT: COUNT RINTELLIGENCE PROGRAM
         BLACK NATIONALIST HATE GROUPS
         RACIAL INTELLIGENCE-

"YOU DON'T SCARE NEGROES TODAY WITH NO BADGE, OR NO WHITE SKIN, OR NO WHITE SHEET, OR NO WHITE ANYTHING ELSE.

"THE POLICE THE SAME WAY. THEY PUT THEIR CLUB UPSIDE YOUR HEAD AND THEN TURN AROUND AND ACCUSE YOU OF ATTACKING THEM.

"EVERY CASE OF POLICE BRUTALITY AGAINST A NEGRO FOLLOWS THE SAME PATTERN.

"THEY ATTACK YOU, BUST YOU ALL UPSIDE YOUR MOUTH, AND THEN TAKE YOU TO COURT AND CHARGE YOU WITH ASSAULT...

"WHAT KIND OF DEMOCRACY IS THAT? WHAT KIND OF FREEDOM IS THAT? WHAT KIND OF SOCIAL OR POLITICAL SYSTEM IS IT...

"...WHEN A BLACK MAN HAS NO VOICE IN COURT.

"HAS NOTHING ON HIS SIDE OTHER THAN WHAT THE WHITE MAN CHOOSES TO GIVE HIM.

"MY BROTHERS AND SISTERS, WE HAVE TO PUT A STOP TO THIS. AND IT WILL NEVER BE STOPPED UNTIL WE STOP IT OURSELVES.

"THEY ATTACKED THE VICTIM, AND THEN THE CRIMINAL WHO ATTACKED THE VICTIM ACCUSES THE VICTIM OF ATTACKING HIM.

"THIS IS AMERICAN JUSTICE, THIS IS AMERICAN DEMOCRACY AND THOSE OF YOU WHO ARE FAMILIAR WITH IT KNOW THAT IN AMERICA, DEMOCRACY IS HYPOCRISY.

"NOW IF I'M WRONG, PUT ME IN JAIL."

--MALCOLM X

CAIRO, EGYPT

PRESIDENT NASSER INVITES MALCOLM X TO CAIRO BECAUSE HE WOULD LIKE HIM TO BE A MINISTER IN HIS GOVERNMENT.

AS MALCOLM IS SIPPING A *CHAI TEA*, HE THINKS HE RECOGNIZES THE WAITER (HOW IS THAT POSSIBLE?), BUT HE IS SUDDENLY PLAGUED BY *AGONIZING STOMACH PAINS*...

HE WILL ONLY REMEMBER THE WAITER WHEN HE IS LYING ON A HOSPITAL BED AFTER HAVING HIS STOMACH PUMPED.

KNOWING THE N.O.I. DOESN'T HAVE THE FUNDS TO TAKE ACTION ABROAD, MALCOLM X SUSPECTS THAT HE IS FACING A *BIGGER THREAT.*

IT'S TRUE THAT MALCOLM HAS BEEN WORKING ON A *LARGER SCALE* SINCE HE LEFT THE N.O.I.

NOW FREE TO ACT AND SPEAK ON HIS OWN TERMS, HE IS VISITING NUMEROUS COUNTRIES HE WOULD LIKE TO SEE UNITE AGAINST THE OPPRESSORS. AND HE ALSO HAS A NEW AND CONVINCING THEORY: JUST LIKE ANY OTHER COUNTRY, THE UNITED STATES HAS ONLY *ONE VOICE* IN THE U.N. IF SEVERAL AFRICAN COUNTRIES UNITE, TOGETHER THEY CAN *ACCUSE THE U.S. OF GENOCIDE* AGAINST THE BLACK PEOPLE.

MALCOLM IS VERY ACTIVE. HE THINKS HE SAW THE WAITER IN NEW YORK, BUT IT MAY HAVE BEEN ELSEWHERE--HE ISN'T QUITE SURE... WHAT IS CERTAIN IS THAT HIS DAYS ARE NUMBERED.

MAROC | ALGERIE

EGYPTE

SENEGAL

SOUDAN

NIGERIA

LIBERIA

ETHIOPIE

NIGERIA

YOU KNOW HE LEFT FOR MECCA BECAUSE HE NOW FOLLOWS TRADITIONAL ISLAM. YOU MUST MAKE A DECISION. YOU ALSO KNOW THAT HE WILL BE CREATING HIS OWN POLITICAL MOVEMENT, SO YOU'LL TELL HIM...YOUR PATHS WILL SURELY CROSS AGAIN...

...BECAUSE YOU ARE THE CHAMPION OF THE WORLD. THE WHOLE WORLD WANTS TO SEE YOU AND TOUCH YOU.

YOU DECIDE TO TRAVEL TO AFRICA, THEN EGYPT.

WHEN YOU MEET THE PRESIDENTS, WHEN YOU LOOK AROUND YOU, IN EVERY CITY YOU SEE BLACK MEN, PROUD AND FREE. YOU SPEND HOURS WITH THEM, DECLARING HOW INVINCIBLE YOU ALL ARE.

YOU HOLD THE CHILDREN TIGHTLY IN YOUR ARMS, AND EVERY TIME YOUR HEART BECOMES PURE AGAIN.

AND THEN, ONE DAY, IN THE PARKING LOT OF A HOTEL, WHAT WAS BOUND TO HAPPEN HAPPENS...

WHAT HAD BEEN DISCUSSED MANY TIMES, REFLECTED UPON, BROODED OVER TO EXHAUSTION, HAPPENS...

YOU KNOW THAT YOU HAVE NO CHOICE. YOU ARE BOUND HAND AND FOOT.

HE IS HERE.

HE'S CALLING YOUR NAME. HE APPROACHES. HE SPEAKS TO YOU.

WE DON'T JUDGE A MAN BECAUSE OF THE COLOR OF HIS SKIN. WE DON'T JUDGE YOU *BECAUSE YOU'RE WHITE.* WE DON'T JUDGE YOU *BECAUSE YOU'RE BLACK.* WE DON'T JUDGE YOU BECAUSE YOU'RE BROWN. WE JUDGE YOU BECAUSE OF *WHAT YOU DO AND WHAT YOU PRACTICE.*

AND *AS LONG AS YOU PRACTICE EVIL,* WE'RE AGAINST YOU. AND FOR US, THE WORST FORM OF EVIL IS THE EVIL THAT'S BASED UPON *JUDGING A MAN BECAUSE OF THE COLOR OF HIS SKIN.*

WE ARE LIVING IN A SOCIETY THAT IS BY AND LARGE CONTROLLED BY *PEOPLE WHO BELIEVE IN SEGREGATION.* WE ARE LIVING IN A SOCIETY THAT IS BY AND LARGE CONTROLLED BY A *PEOPLE WHO BELIEVE IN RACISM, AND PRACTICE SEGREGATION AND DISCRIMINATION AND RACISM.*

IF YOU STICK A KNIFE NINE INCHES INTO MY BACK AND PULL IT OUT SIX INCHES, *THAT IS NOT PROGRESS.*

EVEN IF YOU PULL IT ALL THE WAY OUT, THAT IS NOT PROGRESS.

WE'RE FOR PEACE. BUT THE PEOPLE THAT WE'RE UP AGAINST ARE FOR VIOLENCE. *YOU CAN'T BE PEACEFUL WHEN YOU'RE DEALING WITH THEM.*

PROGRESS IS HEALING THE WOUND, AND AMERICA HASN'T EVEN BEGUN TO PULL OUT THE KNIFE.

THEY WON'T EVEN ADMIT THAT THE KNIFE IS THERE.

AS USUAL, MALCOLM'S MEETINGS ARE SWARMING WITH REPORTERS LOOKING TO FIND THE NEXT CONTROVERSY THAT WILL SELL MORE PAPERS. MALCOLM LEAVES THE NATION OF ISLAM...

THE END OF THE RELATIONSHIP BETWEEN MALCOLM X AND ELIJAH MUHAMMAD IS OFFICIAL...

NOW THAT HE HAS BROUGHT TO LIGHT THE CORRUPTION INSIDE THE N.O.I.--THE PROPHET'S LIFE OF LUXURY AND, ABOVE ALL, HIS MANY MISTRESSES AND HIDDEN CHILDREN (AT LEAST 13)--MALCOLM HAS DAMNED HIMSELF IN THE EYES OF THE NATION OF ISLAM, AND ELIJAH CAN'T STAND THAT YOU ARE STILL SPEAKING TO HIM...

THE NEXT DAY, YOU HOLD A PRESS CONFERENCE TO ANNOUNCE THAT YOU ARE CONVERTING TO ISLAM AND CHANGING YOUR NAME--YOU ARE NOW MUHAMMAD ALI, "PRAISED ONE." YOU EXPLAIN THAT YOU HAVE THE RIGHT TO BE WHOEVER YOU WANT.

IT IS A MATTER OF MINUTES BEFORE YOU BECOME A *DESPISED CHAMPION*. THE PEOPLE FEEL BETRAYED. *THE SEEDS OF DISCORD* ARE SOWN.

ROUND 6

YOU'RE FEELING BETTER AND YOU WANT REVENGE. YOU BRING OUT YOUR MAGIC BOXING. PERFECT COMBINATIONS.

RIGHT, RIGHT, LEFT, RIGHT. STRAIGHT RIGHT, HOOK, JAB.

SONNY IS DONE FOR. HE'S A WRECK. IT LOOKS LIKE HE'S STANDING BECAUSE HE DOESN'T KNOW WHAT ELSE TO DO, AND HIS EYES ARE AS SWOLLEN AS A FAT FROG'S.

LISTON'S CORNERMEN ARE PUTTING ICE ON HIS HEAD. THEN YOU SEE HIM WHEN IT'S TIME TO GO BACK OUT. YOU QUICKLY GET UP...BUT HE DOESN'T.

HE STAYS GLUED TO THE STOOL, SOMETHING NO ONE HAS SEEN SINCE JESS WILLARD, AND HE SPITS OUT HIS MOUTH GUARD.

HOWARD COSELL SHOUTS IN HIS MICROPHONE: "LISTON ISN'T COMING OUT."

WHILE YOU HOLLER DOWN AT THE REPORTERS: "EAT YOUR WORDS, EAT, EAT."

AND YOUR FAMOUS: "I'M GONNA UPSET THE WOOOORLD."

YOU KEEP IT UP FOR HOURS, BECAUSE YOU ARE THE WORLD HEAVYWEIGHT CHAMPION, AND ALSO BECAUSE THAT'S HOW YOU MANIPULATE THE BEASTS YOU FACE.

BUT SUDDENLY, DURING THE BREAK, YOU RUSH TO YOUR STOOL. YOU'RE CRYING LIKE A BABY, YOU'RE BLINKING YOUR EYES, YOU'RE SCREAMING THAT YOU CAN'T SEE ANYTHING, THAT YOU WANT TO STOP. IT STINGS--IT'S THE STING OF A SETUP.

ANGELO SPONGES YOUR EYES AND YELLS AT YOU:

"ARE YOU KIDDING? ARE YOU CRAZY? THIS IS YOUR BIG DAY. GET UP AND GO FIGHT. AND DON'T GET CLOSE TO HIM. RUN."

ROUND 5

YOU GO BACK IN BLIND, YOU TAKE HIS PUNCHES, YOU EVADE HIM BY PUSHING BACK AS BEST YOU CAN.

YOU AREN'T BOXING BUT YOU AREN'T ON THE MAT EITHER, AND THAT REALLY GETS TO SONNY. HE LOOKS LIKE HE'S AGED TEN YEARS. HE LOOKS EXHAUSTED.

SAVED BY THE BELL. ANGELO CHANGES HIS SPONGE TO RINSE OUT YOUR EYES BECAUSE THE BLACK MUSLIMS IN THE FRONT ROW WILL THINK THE DIRTY TRICK IS HIS DOING.

HE'S WHITE, AND ITALIAN TO BOOT.

BUT WE SAW LISTON WHISPERING INTO HIS COACH'S EAR. THEY COATED HIS GLOVES WITH A BLINDING SUBSTANCE-- IT ISN'T THE FIRST TIME.

YOU LOOK TO YOUR RIGHT AND YOU SEE THE WHITE PEOPLE WHO WANT YOU TO FALL. YOU LOOK TO YOUR LEFT AND YOU SEE MALCOLM, CASH, BIRD, AND SONJI.

ROUND 2

HE HITS YOUR SHOULDER. YOU MOVE BACK, RATTLED, NOT KNOWING THAT HIS SHOULDER HURTS TOO. THEN HE MISSES ALL OF HIS NEXT PUNCHES, SO HE THROWS HIMSELF ON YOU TO KNOCK YOU INTO THE ROPES AND HITS YOUR KIDNEYS AND YOUR EAR. HE OVERFLOWS WITH CHARACTERISTIC RAGE.

YOU ESCAPE HIM AND JUMP FROM ONE CORNER OF THE RING TO ANOTHER, LIKE A CAT IN A BATH.

THE RICH WHITES IN THE FRONT ROW, WHO PAID $250 TO SEE YOU BITE THE DUST, ARE SCREAMING THEIR HATRED. THIS SOOTHES THEM.

ROUND 3

YOU GIVE HIM A GOOD BEATING, AND SONNY SEES RED. HIS LEFT EYE IS MESSED UP. HE GETS EVEN WITH A STRAIGHT RIGHT THAT CLEARS YOUR HEAD.

YOU TELL YOURSELF IT DOESN'T HURT THAT MUCH. YOU CAN BEAT HIM...

ROUND 4

AS LISTON TRIES TO JAB HIS THUMB IN YOUR EYE, YOU TAKE HAND-TO-HAND FIGHTING TO NEW HEIGHTS. YOU TOUCH HIM LIKE A SNAKE, YOU STING HIM BETWEEN THE EYES, YOU THROW A FEW DECISIVE PUNCHES, AND THEY CRACK LIKE WHIPS. THAT'S HOW YOU PLAY WITH THE BEAST IN FRONT OF YOU.

ROUND 1

THIS MOMENT IS THE OUTCOME OF ALL THE YEARS OF TRAINING.

EVERY DROP OF SWEAT, EVERY MILE, AND EVERY VICTORY HAS ONLY BROUGHT YOU HERE.

SUGAR RAY ROBINSON IS HERE TO SEE YOU, ROCKY MARCIANO TOO--EVEN JOE LOUIS IS WATCHING, ALTHOUGH HE'S ON LISTON'S SIDE.

THE CROWD MAY BE BOOING YOU, BUT YOU'LL SHOW THEM HOW WRONG THEY ARE. YOU WON'T DROP LIKE A FLY IN FRONT OF THE GIANT WITH A STONE FACE.

YOU DANCE. YOU BOUNCE AROUND LIKE A PING-PONG BALL. LISTON HAS TO RUN AFTER YOU.

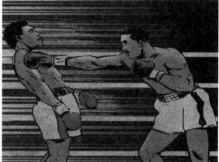

WHEN HE THROWS A PUNCH, YOU DODGE IT BY LEANING WAY BACK, BECAUSE THAT'S HOW YOU ENCOURAGE BRASH BEHAVIOR WITHOUT SAYING A WORD. HE THROWS A POWERFUL JAB AND MISSES BY 20 INCHES, WHICH THROWS HIM OFF COMPLETELY.

YOU TAKE THIS OPPORTUNITY TO HAMMER HIM.

WHEN THE BELL RINGS, YOU'RE STILL FIGHTING. HE'S FURIOUS NOW, JUST LIKE YOU WANTED.

FROM YOUR STOOL, YOU MAKE FACES AT THE RAVING CROWD, AT THE REPORTERS WHO ALREADY SENSE THAT THIS WON'T BE LIKE THE PATTERSON FIGHT.

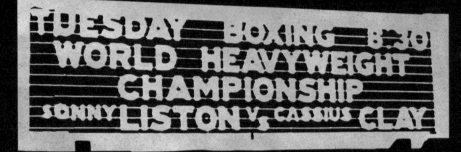

"HE'LL BE MINE
IN ROUND NINE.

IF HE MAKES ME SORE,
I'LL GET HIM IN ROUND FOUR.

IF THAT DON'T DO,
I'LL GET HIM IN TWO.

IF HE RUN,
I'LL GET HIM IN ONE.

IF MY HEART CAN BELIEVE IT--
THEN I CAN ACHIEVE IT."

--CASSIUS CLAY

"CASSIUS, YOU'RE MY MILLION
DOLLAR BABY, SO PLEASE DON'T
LET ANYTHING HAPPEN TO YOU
BEFORE TOMORROW NIGHT."

--SONNY LISTON

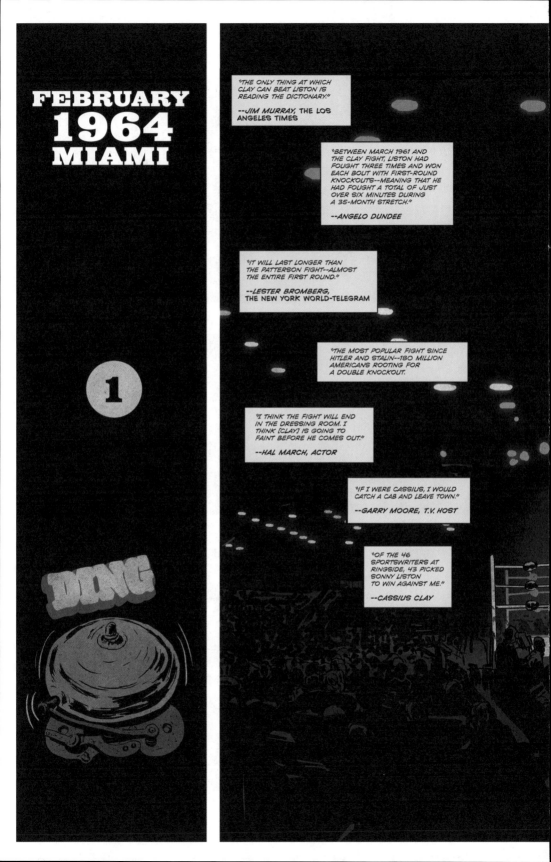

FEBRUARY 1964 MIAMI

1

DING

"THE ONLY THING AT WHICH CLAY CAN BEAT LISTON IS READING THE DICTIONARY."

--JIM MURRAY, THE LOS ANGELES TIMES

"BETWEEN MARCH 1961 AND THE CLAY FIGHT, LISTON HAD FOUGHT THREE TIMES AND WON EACH BOUT WITH FIRST-ROUND KNOCKOUTS--MEANING THAT HE HAD FOUGHT A TOTAL OF JUST OVER SIX MINUTES DURING A 35-MONTH STRETCH."

--ANGELO DUNDEE

"IT WILL LAST LONGER THAN THE PATTERSON FIGHT--ALMOST THE ENTIRE FIRST ROUND."

--LESTER BROMBERG, THE NEW YORK WORLD-TELEGRAM

"THE MOST POPULAR FIGHT SINCE HITLER AND STALIN--180 MILLION AMERICANS ROOTING FOR A DOUBLE KNOCKOUT.

"I THINK THE FIGHT WILL END IN THE DRESSING ROOM. I THINK [CLAY] IS GOING TO FAINT BEFORE HE COMES OUT."

--HAL MARCH, ACTOR

"IF I WERE CASSIUS, I WOULD CATCH A CAB AND LEAVE TOWN."

--GARRY MOORE, T.V. HOST

"OF THE 46 SPORTSWRITERS AT RINGSIDE, 43 PICKED SONNY LISTON TO WIN AGAINST ME."

--CASSIUS CLAY

THE HEAVYWEIGHT WEIGH-IN IS A SACRED RITUAL, AN OPPORTUNITY FOR REPORTERS
TO WRITE THEIR BEST STORIES AND TAKE THEIR BEST PICTURES.

AT 218 LBS.
AND 6 FT. 1 IN.
31 WINS, 24 BY K.O.
1 LOSS...

THE HEAVYWEIGHT
CHAMPION OF THE WORLD...

**SONNY
LISTON**

ABOVE ALL, THIS IS A MEDIA EVENT. IF ONE OF THE BOXERS TAKES OFF HIS ROBE
TO STAND ON THE SCALES AND OBVIOUSLY HAS PUT ON WEIGHT, IT WON'T CHANGE A THING.

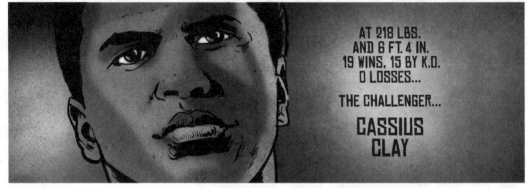

AT 218 LBS.
AND 6 FT. 4 IN.
19 WINS, 15 BY K.O.
0 LOSSES...

THE CHALLENGER...

**CASSIUS
CLAY**

THEY CAN TAUNT YOU, SAY YOU'LL BE CRAWLING IN THE RING, ADJUST THEIR BETS...
IN THE MIDST OF THIS MAYHEM, THE QUIBBLING, THE THIRST FOR VENGEANCE, THEY'LL AVOID
CONJURING UP MEMORIES OF THE SLAVE MARKETS OF THE PAST.

I
GOT YOU,
FUCKER.

BUT YOU DON'T CARE ABOUT THIS CIRCUS--
YOU'RE FINALLY GOING TO FACE LISTON IN THE RING. YOU'VE SUCCEEDED...

ALI's technique

When they are in a ready position, most heavyweight boxers take the same stance:

Head back toward the shoulders.

ALI's back is straight.

ALI's arms hang at his sides.

ALI stands on his toes.

Left fist forward as protection against the devastating right hook.*

Right foot forward to throw the left.

*Starting a match with a right hook is the supreme insult. It says, "You are an amateur. I'm going to knock you out."

ALI IS QUICK

ALI is so fast that he dodges blows to his face by moving his head less than four inches.

ALI is so nimble that he evades right hooks just by pulling back.

His opponents wear themselves out punching air.

ALI IS ALWAYS MOVING

Heavyweights rely on their power to finish the match.

They keep their two feet pinned to the ground.

ALI is constantly shifting his weight. It is impossible to guess where his next punch will come from.

ALI moves around so quickly that it is very difficult to land a damaging hook on his chin.

But ALI doesn't lack power...

Once his foot is anchored on the ground, he can throw a right that takes more than one opponent by surprise.

ALI IS A PUNCHER

Everyone sees ALI as a dancer who wears out his opponents, but he is a powerful puncher who, out of 56 fights as a professional, won 37 by KO.

ALI uses his exceptional footwork to surprise his opponents with a blow that, combined with a hip twist, allows him to use the muscles of his leg along with the muscles in his arm.

ALI IS BIG

6ft. 9in.

ALI has an advantage in his reach. He can hit his opponent and then quickly move back out of harm's way.

6ft. 4in.

ALI is a heavyweight who moves like a middleweight but hits like a heavyweight.

I'M THE GREATEST!

I AM A POET!

I AM A PROPHET!

I AM THE SAVIOR OF THE BOXING WORLD!

WITHOUT ME THIS SPORT WOULD BE DEAD!

AFTER A SURPRISE VISIT FROM LISTON AT THE FIFTH STREET GYM, YOU TAKE ADVANTAGE OF HIS VISIT TO PROVOKE HIM. YOUR LIPS ARE TREMBLING WITH FEAR, BUT YOU'RE STUCK--YOU CAN'T BACK OUT. "I'M THE FASTEST THING ON TWO FEET, MAN," YOU TELL HIM...

ONE THING IS CERTAIN--YOU'RE NOT GOING TO BOX IN OBSCURITY. EVEN IF RIGHT NOW YOU'VE ONLY HAD A FEW PROFESSIONAL FIGHTS, YOU WANT TO CLIMB TO THE TOP AS FAST AS YOU CAN. SO YOU START THE BEAR HUNT.

IN JULY 1963, WHEN LISTON RAISES A VICTORIOUS ARM AFTER BEATING PATTERSON IN ONE ROUND, YOU JUMP INTO THE RING TO TELL HIM THAT, AS LONG AS HE HASN'T BEATEN YOU, HE ISN'T REALLY THE CHAMPION OF THE WORLD. WHILE THE COPS HOLD YOU BACK, YOU SHAKE EIGHT FINGERS AT HIM IN PREDICTION.

AFTER MONTHS OF PRESSURE, SONNY CRACKS AND ACCEPTS THE CHALLENGE FROM YOU, THE BRAT, THE KID WHO SNORTS MILK FROM HIS NOSE, WHO'LL GET A GOOD SPANKING. FOR MONTHS YOU HARASS HIM ON T.V., IN THE NEWSPAPERS, ON THE BEACH OR AT THE GAMBLING HALL, EVEN ALL THE WAY TO HIS TRAINING CAMP. AND EVERY TIME AMERICA LAUGHS... OR GRINDS ITS TEETH.

SO YOU EACH HAVE AN AFRICAN WIZARD STAFF, BLACK SUNGLASSES, AND BECAUSE HE'S ALWAYS SUCKING ON MINTS, YOU TAKE UP THE HABIT. JUST LIKE HIM, YOU START TILTING YOUR HEAD TO THE SIDE TO THINK BEFORE TALKING.

JUST LIKE HIM, YOU NOW TAKE PICTURES, CLICK, CLICK, AT EVERY MOMENT, CLICK. MALCOLM SMILES OFTEN, BUT WITHOUT EVER LOSING HIS NATURAL CLASS, CLICK.

HE IS RADIANT, IMPRESSIVE, AND FORMIDABLE, AND YOU GET ALONG BECAUSE YOU ARE TOO... EXACTLY LIKE HIM.

"MALCOLM X AND ALI WERE LIKE VERY CLOSE BROTHERS. IT WAS ALMOST AS IF THEY WERE IN LOVE WITH EACH OTHER."--FERDIE PACHECO

THAT'S WHEN PEOPLE START UNDERSTANDING THAT A CHANGE IS COMING. MALCOLM AND YOU...

...YOU AND SONJI.

THIS GIRL IS AS DELICIOUS AS THOSE CREAM CAKES YOU LOVE SO MUCH.

YOU MET HER AT A PARTY...

...AND AT NIGHT SHE LETS YOU TOUCH HER BODY, SO YOU ASK HER TO MARRY YOU, OF COURSE...

TWO MONTHS LATER, AGAINST THE ADVICE OF YOUR ENTOURAGE...

...SONJI IS YOUR WIFE, AND YOU ARE NO LONGER A CHILD.

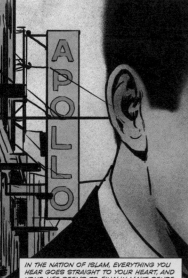

IN THE NATION OF ISLAM, EVERYTHING YOU HEAR GOES STRAIGHT TO YOUR HEART, AND YOUR LIFE SEEMS TO FINALLY MAKE SENSE. FOR YOU AND YOUR BROTHER, IT IS ALL REVELATIONS AND INFINITE HOPE.

AND THEN YOU MEET MALCOLM X...

ALL OF HARLEM IS READY TO FOLLOW HIM, BUT YOU ARE THE ONE HE CHOOSES.

YOU LIKE HIM AS MUCH AS HE LIKES YOU, AND HE KNOWS HOW TO PUT YOUR THOUGHTS INTO WORDS. YOU NEVER LEAVE HIS SIDE, YOU ARE LIKE SOULMATES FINDING EACH OTHER IN A SENTIMENTAL MOVIE.

EVER SINCE YOU MET MALCOLM, YOU NEVER FEEL LONELY. BECAUSE OF HIM, YOU BECOME A MAN. A BLACK MAN THAT THE WHITE PEOPLE WON'T FOOL.

PEOPLE SEE YOU TOGETHER EVERYWHERE, NIGHT AND DAY. AT BREAKFAST AT YOUR HOTEL, IN THE EVENING AFTER DINING WITH HIS FAMILY, HIS GIRLS ARE ON YOUR KNEES, IN YOUR ARMS, HANGING FROM YOUR NECK.

MALCOLM OFTEN TELLS YOU THAT YOU ARE MORE THAN A BOXER, YES, MORE THAN THAT--A BLACK LEADER WHO, LIKE HIM, WILL MAKE HISTORY...

THAT'S WHAT YOU WOULD LIKE-- TO BE LIKE HIM AT ALL TIMES.

Elijah Muhammad, self-proclaimed prophet of the NOI.

THE NATION OF ISLAM:
RELIGION OR CULT?

IS THE NOI EXPANDING?
Founded in 1930 by Wallace Fard Muhammad, the Nation of Islam is a sect that is based equally on African American nationalism and on the precepts of Islam. In 1934, Mr. Elijah Muhammad took the lead, succeeding Fard, who disappeared without a trace and has since been considered the Messiah to the members of this organization—an organization which continues to grow and gain strength thanks to leaders like Malcolm X, although its tenets are often questionable . . . In fact, the NOI advocates black separatism; its ultimate goal is to create an independent black state. This is why the followers of Martin Luther King, supporters of integration, do not wish to associate with their "brothers" of the NOI.

AIRCRAFT RHETORIC
If you are able to attend a meeting of the NOI (you must be black, as white people are not allowed), know, dear readers, that you'll be confronted with a very precise, immutable ideology repeated day after day by the venerable Elijah . . .

"Islam is the religion of the black man and is reserved exclusively for colored people. Christianity is the religion of slavery.

When there were only black people on this earth, Yacub, a black scientist, artificially created the white race of demons, in rebellion against the dark gods. The prophecies announce the end of their reign . . .

The white devils' world will be destroyed by the Mother Plane. It contains more than 1,500

flying saucers flown by black people who have known since the age of six what their mission will be. America will burn for 390 years. Clean air will be sucked in through huge tubes so that our brothers survive, and the great Babylon will perish in the flames thanks to Allah. It will take 610 years for the earth to completely cool down."

THE NATION OF ISLAM, A THREAT?
The NOI is everywhere, and its men in three-piece suits (an imposed uniform representing the desire for upward mobility) are now part of our everyday life. And then there's the world champion boxer Cassius Clay, who hit the headlines by announcing his conversion to Mr. Elijah Muhammad's Islam, explaining that he now wanted to be called Muhammad Ali. This sudden turn of events does not scare the top man in the NOI. A trusted source says that not long ago he refused to associate with "this clown" because:

"Boxers behave like slaves. They are under the yoke of big white men who smoke and drink and steal their money."

It was certainly the brilliant Malcolm X who managed to persuade his superior to take on a new recruit such as young Cassius; he is, after all, his best friend. The boxer is now well guarded—the "Fruit of Islam" never leave his side and stare coldly at anyone who approaches. Indeed, the NOI has a "military wing" mainly composed of convicts that takes care of the security of its members. In the end, if you don't threaten the NOI, it won't threaten you.

MALCOLM X

by HENRY
WALLACE

Malcolm X is the spokesman of the NOI. Charismatic and intelligent, he appeals to the black youth.

In 1925, Malcolm Little was born to a Baptist preacher father advocating the return of African Americans to Africa, and a West Indian mother with Scottish origins. They would have seven children. Among them, Malcolm inherited the finest complexion, and he would think all his life that was the reason his mother was tougher with him than with her other children, for she hated every drop of the white people's blood. In 1931, Malcolm's father was found dead on the tram tracks, but the wounds on his head were proof that he was hit from behind. When his widow tried to collect his life insurance, the criminal investigation ruled it a death by suicide, and she wasn't able to collect a single dollar. As for Malcolm, he believed his father was murdered by white supremacists.

After the tragedy, his mother was depressed. She was institutionalized in 1938 and her children placed in foster homes scattered throughout the country. Although he was an excellent student in a "very white" grade school in Mason, Malcolm dropped out of school after coming to the realization that he wouldn't ever have access to a career he was interested in because he was black. He did his best to straighten his reddish hair, but nothing changed for him. In 1943, he lived in New York but was part of the underworld and involved in drug trafficking, extortion, and robberies. He went out with white women, called himself "Detroit Red," and was also addicted to cocaine.

Arrested and sentenced to eight years in prison, he began a new life when he started reading everything he could find. He would later explain that he did not feel locked up, but rather completely free, because of his reading.

He was nicknamed "Satan" by other inmates because of his dislike of religion. Then his brother introduced him to the Nation of Islam. He decided to correspond with its leader, Elijah Muhammad, and then converted. Upon his release five years later, he joined the movement and was chosen to lead Temple Number 7 in Harlem.

Charismatic and brilliantly intelligent, Malcolm defends black people with unusual intensity. He has risen to number two of the NOI, and his fame has increased across the United States. Malcolm, who advocates radical values, fascinates black people . . . and terrifies white people.

AN
EXCEPTIONAL
MAN.
A LEADER.

November 22

PRESIDENT JOHN FITZGERALD KENNEDY IS ASSASSINATED.

WHITE AMERICA NEVER REALLY RECOVERED, AND MANY PEOPLE WROTE THAT THERE WAS A BEFORE DALLAS AND AN AFTER DALLAS...

THE AMERICANS WERE FORCED TO LIVE WITH THIS NIGHTMARISH VISION, PERMANENTLY TRAUMATIZED BY A SPLATTER OF BRAINS ON A CHANEL SUIT. AS THE YEARS WENT BY, NO ONE EVER KNEW WHO KILLED THE PRESIDENT BECAUSE OF THE OBSCURE TRAJECTORY OF A "MAGIC" BULLET.

IN ANY CASE, IN 1963, WHITES WERE UTTERLY DEVASTATED. J.F.K. WAS, IN THEIR EYES, A KNIGHT IN SHINING ARMOR. SOME BLACKS THOUGHT HIS DEATH WOULD HURT THEIR CAUSE, WHILE OTHERS ALREADY UNDERSTOOD THAT IT WOULDN'T CHANGE A THING. AS FOR MALCOLM X, HE RESPONDED IN AN INTERVIEW WITH A TYPICAL AMERICAN SAYING...

CHICKENS COMING HOME TO ROOST NEVER DID MAKE ME SAD. THEY ALWAYS MADE ME GLAD.

WHICH SIMPLY MEANT THAT THE COUNTRY HAD REAPED WHAT IT HAD SOWN. FOR J.F.K., THE RESULT WAS AN UNDERHANDED, VIOLENT DEATH.

HOWEVER, MALCOLM X WAS PUNISHED BY ELIJAH MUHAMMAD, WHO FORBADE HIM TO SPEAK PUBLICLY FOR 90 DAYS. J.F.K. WAS HONORED AS A HERO, AND TO THIS DAY THAT IS THE IMAGE WE HAVE OF HIM...

"IN ONE INTERVIEW, ALI SAID, 'ENGLAND HAS A QUEEN, BUT NOT YET A KING.' SO HE CLIMBED INTO THE RING WITH A MINK COAT AND A GOLDEN CROWN.

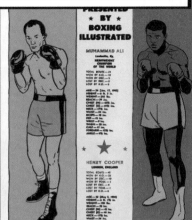

"HE COULDN'T HELP DOING IT THE AMERICAN WAY.

1963

"AFTER THAT, HE JUMPED AROUND LIKE A YOUNG GOAT TO AVOID MY PUNCHES WHEN THE BLOOD WAS RUNNING DOWN MY FACE, BUT I WAS ABLE TO GIVE HIM A HARD LEFT HOOK AND THE KID BIT THE DUST LIKE HE SHOULD. THE REFEREE COUNTED UP TO FOUR BUT THE BELL RANG FOR THE BREAK.

"RIGHT FROM THE START, I VICIOUSLY ATTACKED HIM AND I MADE HIS NOSE BLEED...

"...BUT HE QUICKLY RECOVERED AND CUT MY EYEBROW.

"THAT WAS ONE OF HIS THINGS, CUTTING HIS OPPONENTS...

"BECAUSE HE WAS GROGGY, DUNDEE USED THE SMELLING SALTS EVEN THOUGH IT WAS AGAINST THE RULES. THEN HE STARTED WHINING ABOUT CLAY'S GLOVE BEING RIPPED...THEY HELD BACK UNTIL THEY FINALLY REALIZED THAT THEY DIDN'T HAVE A SPARE GLOVE, AND SO THE KID HAD PLENTY OF TIME TO RECOVER.

"SO THEN, BECAUSE HE HAD PREDICTED THAT HE WOULD BEAT ME IN ROUND 5, HE WENT ALL IN TO LIVE UP TO HIS PROMISE. I COULD HAVE HAD THE UPPER HAND BUT THE REFEREE DECIDED TO STOP ME BECAUSE I WAS BLEEDING TOO MUCH. THEY WERE VERY SMART ACTUALLY.

"I WAS STILL THE FIRST ONE THAT SENT HIM TO THE CANVAS, AND NOBODY CAN EVER TAKE THAT AWAY FROM ME.

"HE WAS GOODHEARTED, HAD A SOLID CHIN, AND HE WAS FAST. WHAT MORE COULD YOU ASK FOR? THERE'S NOTHING BETTER."

"...A SYSTEMATIC TRICK THAT OFTEN HELPED HIM WIN AT THE LAST MOMENT.

FLOAT LIKE
A BUTTERFLY!

STING LIKE
A BEE!

RUMBLE,
YOUNG MAN!
RUMBLE!

ALTHOUGH BUNDINI IS A HOPELESS DRINKER, HE HAS HIS GOOD QUALITIES. YOU LIKE HIS *JOIE DE VIVRE*, AND SINCE YOU ARE OFTEN QUIET AND INTROVERTED, HE TEACHES YOU HOW TO BREAK OUT OF YOURSELF WHEN NEEDED, TO TALK AND SHOUT AS LOUD AS HE DOES. EVERYONE KNOWS YOU TRAIN HARD, AND NOW YOU WORK EVEN HARDER...YOU NEVER GET BORED WITH HIM, AND WHEN PEOPLE WATCH YOUR FIGHTS, THEY HEAR HIS DEEP VOICE ENCOURAGING YOU, CALLING YOU "SHORTY," WHICH IS HIS NAME FOR GOD.

SUGAR RAY ROBINSON
- HEAVYWEIGHT CHAMPION OF THE WORLD, 1940-1944 -

WHAT HE NEEDED WAS SOMEONE WHO WOULD WATCH OVER HIM. I SENT HIM *DREW BUNDINI BROWN*, WHO TOOK CARE OF ME.

CLAY IMMEDIATELY HIT IT OFF WITH HIM. HE LOVED TO LAUGH AND BUNDINI KNEW HOW TO MAKE HIM LAUGH.

ANGELO DUNDEE
-ALI'S COACH-

BUNDINI IS THE ONLY GUY I KNOW WHO CAN TALK FASTER THAN CLAY.

IF YOU TRY TO UNDERSTAND WHAT HE'S SAYING, YOU GO BONKERS... I'VE NEVER TRIED.

YOU MEET ONE OF THE BIG STARS OF YOUR TIME: GORGEOUS GEORGE.

A WRESTLER WITH BLOND CURLS WHO ENTERS THE RING DRESSED IN SILKS AND FURS, HIS VALET PERFUMING THE MAT WITH CHANEL N°5. HE IS ABOVE ALL A GENIUS OF SELF-PROMOTION.

PEOPLE EITHER ADORE HIM OR HATE HIM, AND YOU UNDERSTAND THAT IT HAS TO BE THE SAME FOR YOU.

YOU TOO WANT TO BRING IN A FULL HOUSE. YOU WANT PEOPLE TO FIGHT OVER THE TICKETS BECAUSE THEY WANT TO SEE IF SOMEONE WILL FINALLY SUCCEED IN SHUTTING YOU UP.

2

-ISLAM-

IN MIAMI, EVERYTHING IS DIFFERENT.

NOT YOUR LIFE, BECAUSE IT IS DEDICATED TO TRAINING WITH ANGELO, WHO IS A PERFECT FIT FOR YOU, AS YOU ARE FOR HIM...

BUT THE ESSENCE OF YOUR LIFE, BECAUSE EVERYONE IS STARTING TO BELIEVE THAT WHATEVER YOU SAY IS TRUE.

THE WOMEN FIND YOU BEAUTIFUL AND CHARMING, AND THE MEN THINK YOU BOX LIKE A GENIUS.

NO, NOT THE ONES WHO SAY YOU JUMP LIKE A DAMN SQUIRREL AND DODGE PUNCHES LIKE A FAG, THAT YOU DON'T HIT BACK...

THE ONES WHO UNDERSTAND THAT YOU ARE DANCING.

FERDIE PACHECO, THE DOCTOR WHO TENDS THE BOXERS AT THE FIFTH STREET GYM, WHERE YOU SWEAT BLOOD (VERY LITTLE) AND WATER (A HUGE AMOUNT), RECKONS THAT IF THE ALIENS WANTED TO TAKE WITH THEM THE MOST BEAUTIFUL SPECIMEN OF THE HUMAN RACE, IT SHOULD BE YOU.

ANYWAY, YOU WIN EVERY SINGLE FIGHT...

AND HE'S RIGHT. THAT'S EXACTLY WHAT YOU THINK YOURSELF.

FROM SADEBONG, A SIX-FOOT-TALL HAWAIIAN WHO CAN'T EVEN TOUCH YOU AND TRIES TO BITE YOUR EAR TO MAKE YOU CRY...

...TO SONNY BANK'S, WHO SENDS YOU TO THE CANVAS IN THE SECOND ROUND--AT THAT MOMENT, ANGELO TURNS WHITE AS A SHEET--BUT YOU JUMP BACK UP AND WIN IN THE FOURTH.

AS A MATTER OF FACT, IN MIAMI EVERYTHING IS DIFFERENT BECAUSE YOU AND YOUR BROTHER COME INTO CONTACT WITH THE NATION OF ISLAM.

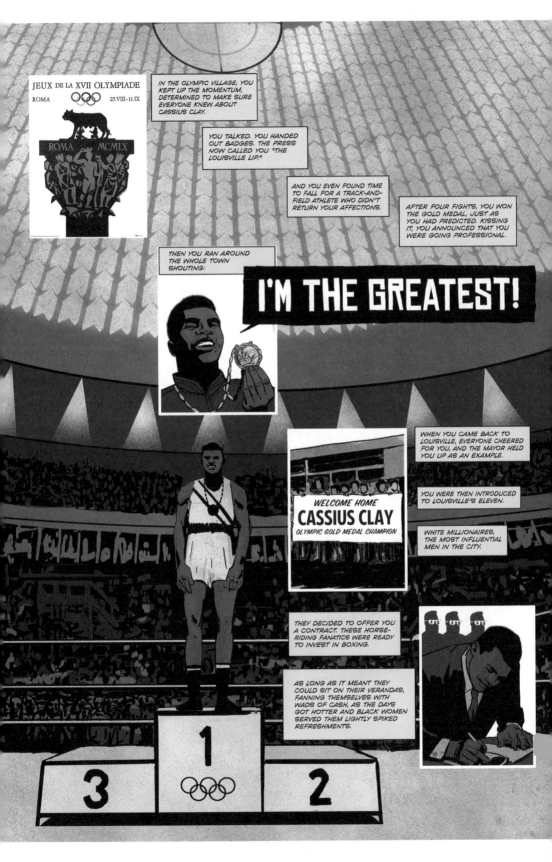

PEOPLE WOULD TALK ABOUT YOU, YOU KNOW, THE GUY WHO DRANK WATER WITH GARLIC, THE GUY WHO WENT RUNNING IN BIG WORK BOOTS...*CASSIUS CLAY?*

THE GUY WHO *BOXED ALL THE TIME,* SHADOWBOXING AND GRUNTING. THE GUY WHO HAD SOMETHING, SOMETHING SPECIAL... THAT GUY *WAS YOU.*

EVEN THOUGH YOU *TRAINED* EVERY DAY, NEVER WENT OUT WITH A GIRL, NEVER EVEN TOOK A SIP OF SODA, YOU HAD TO ADMIT THAT THERE WAS A *CLOUD ON THE HORIZON...*

CORKY BAKER.

CORKY TERRIFIED THE NEIGHBORHOOD AND REIGNED SUPREME WITH HIS *MASSIVE MUSCLES.* HE SCARED YOU TO DEATH.

YOU KNEW THAT YOU WOULD HAVE TO *CONFRONT HIM...*

...IN THE *RING.*

EVEN THOUGH BOXING WAS DEAD, CORRUPTED, RIGGED...

EVEN THOUGH IT WAS A CIRCUS GAME FOR THE MAFIA, A GAME WHERE, WHEN YOU'D HAD ENOUGH TO DRINK, YOU COULD EVEN THROW TOMATOES AT THE LOSERS, AT THE TWO GOATS WALLOPING EACH OTHER IN THE FILTHY RING.

YOU DECIDED THAT BOXING WOULD BE YOURS, AND YOU WOULD "BECOME" BOXING.

WHEN DAWN CAST A YELLOW HUE ON THE WITHERING NIGHT, YOU WOULD GO OUT JOGGING IN YOUR STEEL-TOED WORK BOOTS.

AT EIGHT O'CLOCK, YOU'D ENTER THE SCHOOL, WHERE YOU COULD DOZE AND REST YOUR GROWING LEGS, THEN YOU WOULD GO TO NAZARETH COLLEGE TO HELP THE NUNS AT THE LIBRARY.

AT SIX P.M., FINALLY, YOU WOULD GO TO JOE MARTIN'S GYM AND CONTINUE TRAINING UNTIL MIDNIGHT, WHEN YOU WENT HOME TO BED, EXHAUSTED, AND FELL ASLEEP IMMEDIATELY, ONLY TO START ALL OVER AGAIN THE NEXT DAY.

ON SUNDAYS, PEOPLE COULD SEE YOU ON A LOCAL T.V. SHOW CALLED TOMORROW'S CHAMPIONS.

YOU EARNED FOUR DOLLARS FOR YOUR FIRST FIGHTS, WHICH YOU THOUGHT WAS A GOOD DEAL FOR A 13-YEAR-OLD.

YOUR BIKE WAS STOLEN WHILE YOU WERE STUFFING YOUR MOUTH WITH CANDY AT A NEIGHBORHOOD FAIR.

YOU IMMEDIATELY BEGAN TO CRY, YOUR MOUTH STILL STICKY WITH SUGAR, SWINGING FROM...

...ANGER...
IF YOU FOUND THE THIEF YOU WOULD SMASH HIS FACE IN.

...TO DESPAIR...
WOULDN'T CASH WHUP YOU GOOD?

YOU WERE FINALLY TOLD TO GO SEE JOE MARTIN, A COP WHO WOULD SURELY TAKE DOWN YOUR COMPLAINT. HE WAS AT THE GYM, AS USUAL.

WHEN YOU ENTERED THE TRAINING ROOM, YOUR EYES FULL OF TEARS AND YOUR MOUTH DRIPPING WITH PINK SALIVA, YOU RUSHED TOWARD THE WHITE COP, SEEKING JUSTICE.

BUT AS YOU STARTED TALKING, YOUR HEART WASN'T IN IT ANYMORE.

YOUR TEARS DRIED UP AT THE SIGHT OF THE YOUNG BOXERS, THE SOUND OF THE PUNCHING BAGS, THE SMELL OF THE SWEAT, AND THE DUST FLYING IN THE AIR LIKE MILLIONS OF GLIMMERING DROPLETS.

YOU EVEN STOPPED TALKING...

...WHICH WAS RARE.

AND JOE MARTIN GAVE YOU THE REGISTRATION FORM. YOU WERE 12 YEARS OLD.

SOUTHERN TREES BEAR A STRANGE FRUIT.
BLOOD ON THE LEAVES AND BLOOD AT THE ROOT.
BLACK BODIES SWINGING IN THE SOUTHERN BREEZE,
STRANGE FRUIT HANGING FROM THE POPLAR TREES.

PASTORAL SCENE OF THE GALLANT SOUTH,
THE BULGING EYES AND THE TWISTED MOUTH.
SCENT OF MAGNOLIAS SWEET AND FRESH,
THEN THE SUDDEN SMELL OF BURNING FLESH.

HERE IS FRUIT FOR THE CROWS TO PLUCK
FOR THE RAIN TO GATHER,
    FOR THE WIND TO SUCK,
FOR THE SUN TO ROT, FOR THE TREES TO DROP,
HERE IS A STRANGE AND BITTER CROP.

"STRANGE FRUIT" (1939)
SUNG BY BILLIE HOLIDAY
LYRICS BY LEWIS ALLAN
© COMMODORE RECORDS APRIL 20, 1939

THE MURDER OF EMMETT TILL

IN 1955 IN MONEY, MISSISSIPPI, EMMETT TILL MET UP WITH A GROUP OF BLACK KIDS AT THE LOCAL CORNER SHOP WHERE THEY WOULD OFTEN GO AFTER WORKING IN THE FIELDS...

CAROLYN BRYANT, THE OWNER, STATED THAT EMMETT HAD FLIRTED WITH HER, AT THE RIPE AGE OF 14...

...AND THAT, AS HE WAS TRYING TO CATCH HER WAIST, THE STUTTERING TEENAGER HAD WHISPERED DIRTY WORDS IN HER EAR.

WHEN HER HUSBAND ROY CAME BACK FROM A TRIP, HE BECAME AWARE OF THE SITUATION, WHICH WAS ALREADY KNOWN ALL OVER TOWN. OBVIOUSLY, HE WAS EXTREMELY INSULTED AND DECIDED, WITH HIS HALF BROTHER J.W. MILAM, TO "WHIP HIM...AND SCARE SOME SENSE INTO HIM."

ON AUGUST 28, IN THE MIDDLE OF THE NIGHT, THE BOY WAS TAKEN FROM HIS UNCLE'S HOUSE, THEN SAVAGELY KILLED AND THROWN INTO THE TALLAHATCHIE RIVER.

ON THE DAY OF THE FUNERAL, MAMIE TILL TORE OUT THE NAILS FROM THE COFFIN HERSELF SO EVERYONE COULD SEE HER SON'S MUTILATED BODY.

THE WHOLE COUNTRY WAS CONFRONTED WITH EMMETT'S FACE, IRREVOCABLY SUCKED INTO THE TWO GAPING HOLES WHERE HIS EYES HAD ONCE BEEN.

IF YOU ASK PEOPLE ABOUT AMERICA IN THE FIFTIES, THEIR EYES WILL LIGHT UP. THEY'LL TELL YOU ABOUT THE AMAZING CARS, THE ELEGANT WOMEN, ELVIS PRESLEY, AND HOLLYWOOD.

ON OCCASION, THEY'LL TALK ABOUT THE COLD WAR BUT NEVER ABOUT SEGREGATION.

IT'S ALWAYS HARD TO KNOW IF THEY'VE FORGOTTEN BECAUSE OF SHAME OR CONTEMPT.

SLAVERY HAD BEEN ABOLISHED, BUT DESPITE THE VIBRANCY OF THE TECHNICOLOR FILMS, THE UNITED STATES REMAINED A BLACK AND WHITE COUNTRY.

NEIGHBORHOODS FOR BLACK PEOPLE.

SCHOOLS FOR BLACK PEOPLE.

JOBS FOR BLACK PEOPLE.

COLORED
SEATED IN REAR

RESTAURANT ROOMS FOR BLACK PEOPLE, WHO WEREN'T ALLOWED, UNDER ANY CIRCUMSTANCES, TO MINGLE WITH WHITES.

COLORED ONLY
No Whites Allowed

ACE SIGN CO

MARCH 1921

BLACKS WEREN'T ALLOWED TO BE INSOLENT TOWARD WHITES AND CERTAINLY COULD NOT APPROACH A WHITE WOMAN.

BEING A GOOD NIGGER WAS AN ART IN ITSELF: THE ART OF STAYING ALIVE.

LOUISVILLE

YOU CAME INTO THIS WORLD IN KENTUCKY ON JANUARY 17, 1942. YOUR PARENTS HAD BOUGHT A HOUSE FOR $4,500 IN ONE OF THE CITY'S THREE BLACK GHETTOS, WHERE THE MIDDLE CLASS LIVED.

Recounting the history of boxing is like recounting the history of the African American people, for they are intimately interlaced. Poverty, exclusion, injustice, and the resulting legitimate anger have not stopped feeding this sport dominated by great black boxers, many of whom learned to box in prison. Muhammad Ali is the product of the history of boxing. The historical conditions of the black people and the genius of Ali for the sport made for a perfect marriage that produced the man known as "The Greatest." Muhammad Ali arrived during a turning point, and his formidable personality allowed him to find his place in his time as if by magic. That wasn't the case for "The Galveston Giant," Jack Johnson, the first black heavyweight world champion (1908–1915). He was an exceptional boxer, a free thinker, and a scholar who was imprisoned for marrying a white woman and lived in exile in Europe.

An examination of Ali's boxing style throughout his career reveals that it perfectly matches both his biography and the progression of black rights in America. At the time of segregation, the young Cassius Clay, more clever than his opponents, avoided their blows by constantly moving in the ring, developing a unique style unmatched to this day, and dodging stones (he actually asked his brother Rudy to throw them to help him train), just like the black people in the ghettos knew how to avoid trouble with whites . . .

But the civil rights movement was on the march, and in the second part of his career, after having been so despised, Ali decided to roll with the punches and stand up for his rights–just like the black people were doing in the streets, because you needed to "have guts"–until his opponent tired out and he emerged victorious. Thus, his harmony with his people's history made of him a historical figure we, as the audience, are fascinated with. As Mike Tyson once said, Ali is so special, so wonderful, that words are too weak to capture him: one would have to invent a new word especially for him, and indeed, Muhammad Ali is one of the only people still on earth who can make us want to believe in God–or, at least, in superheroes.

—Sybille Titeux de la Croix

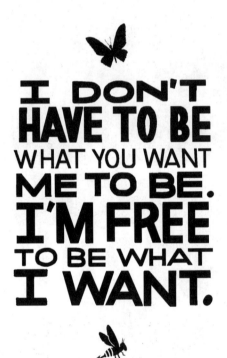

I DON'T HAVE TO BE WHAT YOU WANT ME TO BE. I'M FREE TO BE WHAT I WANT.

INTRODUCTION

Boxing has been around since ancient Rome. We know that as early as 900 BC, nobles loved to be entertained by gladiator fights: two men, face to face, punching each other with hands wrapped in leather straps adorned with metal spikes. Whoever died first was the loser, of course. Much later, American slave owners are known to have forced black men to fight while gambling on the outcome. They would chain them in iron shackles so that neither man would run away before it was over.

Boxing as we know it began informally in the eighteenth century in England and, although prohibited, it fascinated the crowds. The fights were recounted in early versions of comic strips sold by street hawkers. Later, newspapers published detailed accounts of the fights, and many writers became brilliant chroniclers of the sport.

Boxing is like Greek tragedy. To be a boxer is to repeatedly act out the miracle of birth and defeat through death in a short span of time. So when the boxer climbs up to the sacrificial scene that is the ring, he reaffirms his existence in the face of adversity, in this case against an opponent as determined as he is to remain standing in the face of hardship. He will have to endure pain in order to triumph, but he could lose, and if KO'd, he will be humiliated in front of thousands of people . . . (Remember Floyd Patterson, who said that after his fight against Sonny Liston he went out wearing a false beard so that the people he had disappointed didn't recognize him.) Worse still, the boxer could be killed, and it has happened many times. And certainly he puts his health at risk; at thirty-five, a boxer is considered old, and he'd do better to retire before it's too late.

Boxers are professional haters. Because they are allowed to defy the law, they act out their transgressions in the place of the audience that encourages them, thirsting for revenge against life, against the other. They express the unspoken violence in every human being who is watching . . . but always, they stay within the rules. Boxing, which is called a "noble art" or a "sweet science," is a primitive art always in danger of being condemned in this society where, to many, the clashing of two nearly naked bodies seems utterly barbaric. Our modern society prefers more hidden brawls, such as reality shows where violence is expressed symbolically and verbally, degrading those who participate as well as those who watch. Blood (almost) never flows, and the violence and oppression that are expressed through metaphorical cultural shackles seem to reassure our society of its high degree of civility.

MUHAMMAD ALI

Written by **SYBILLE TITEUX DE LA CROIX**
Illustrated by **AMAZING AMEZIANE**

Dark Horse Books

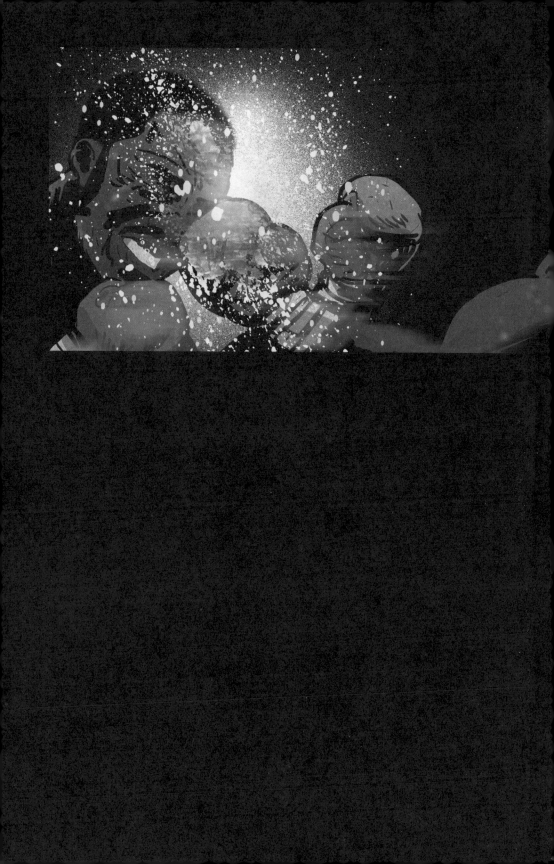

Malcolm X

1925–1965
Number two in the Nation of Islam before leaving it after discovering a scandal concerning Elijah, he fights for the rights of African Americans. Ali regrets turning his back on him, considering it the biggest mistake of his life.
Assassinated.

Martin Luther KING

1929–1968
Pastor, African American civil rights movement leader, and icon. Author of "I Have a Dream" speech. Advocate of nonviolence.
Assassinated.

John F. KENNEDY

1917–1963
Democrat, president of the United States from 1961 to 1963. Keeps close ties to show business and organized crime, but this doesn't prevent him from becoming the most popular president of the US.
Assassinated.

Robert KENNEDY

1925–1968
JFK's brother. Senator and U.S. Attorney General. He fights organized crime and helps advance the cause of the African American civil rights movement.
Assassinated.

J. Edgar HOOVER

1895–1972
FBI director for 48 years. Controls America with an iron fist. Has files on everyone. Famously denies the existence of organized crime.
Impossible to assassinate.

Sonny LISTON

Died 1970
Says he was born in 1932, but many people believe he was born in the 1920s. Heavyweight world champion from 1962 to 1964. His bad temper is what many remember about him. The only boxer Ali fears. Possibly assassinated.

Floyd PATTERSON

1935–2006
Heavyweight world champion from 1956 to 1959 and 1960 to 1962. He is one of the most admired men in America until he loses to Sonny Liston in the first round. Inventor of the Gazelle Punch. Like Joe Louis and Jerry Quarry, he suffers from dementia pugilistica at the end of his life.

"Smokin'" Joe FRAZIER

1944–2011
Heavyweight world champion from 1970 to 1973. His left hook is called the "Heaven Hook." He stays in Ali's shadow throughout his career.

George FOREMAN

Born 1949
Heavyweight world champion from 1973 to 1974. His style is characterized by his strong hooks that knock out his opponents. At 45, he will go after Angelo Dundee to make a successful comeback and regain his title, which he will hold from 1994 to 1995. Maturity brings to him a completely different but much more agreeable personality.

Larry HOLMES

Born 1949
Heavyweight world champion from 1978 to 1985. Third-longest reign, after Joe Louis and W. Klitschko. He is Ali's sparring partner but also the one who put an end to his career.